T0304804

ENGINEERS OF
HUMAN SOULS

ENGINEERS OF HUMAN SOULS

Four Writers Who Turned to Politics

SIMON INGS

The
Bridge
Street
Press

THE BRIDGE STREET PRESS

First published in Great Britain in 2024 by The Bridge Street Press

1 3 5 7 9 10 8 6 4 2

A CIP catalogue record for this book
is available from the British Library.

Hardback ISBN 978-0-349-12856-6
Trade paperback ISBN 978-0-349-12857-3

Typeset in Sabon by M Rules
Printed and bound in Great Britain by Clays Ltd, Elcograf S.p.A.

Papers used by The Bridge Street Press are from well-managed forests
and other responsible sources.

The Bridge Street Press
An imprint of
Little, Brown Book Group
Carmelite House
50 Victoria Embankment
London EC4Y 0DZ

An Hachette UK Company
www.hachette.co.uk

www.littlebrown.co.uk

For Ren
and for Cheryl –
You're my wife now

Mistaken ideas always end in bloodshed, but in every case it is someone else's blood. That is why some of our thinkers feel free to say just about anything.

Albert Camus

CONTENTS

INTRODUCTION

Governments do not listen to their people, and nowhere are the people free.

Very rarely, an old dispensation is overthrown, and new institutions come to power.

But they don't listen to the people either. They have no means of listening, and even in the attempt to listen, they bring their people once more into bondage.

A few visionaries have attempted, at one time or another, to reshape society so that the people's will might be heard. They are self-styled gods, or religious leaders, or political fanatics.

They all fail.

At the turn of the twentieth century, enthusiasm for democracy consumed the world: Russia in 1905, Iran in 1906, the Ottoman Empire in 1908, Portugal in 1910, Mexico in 1911, China in 1912. For the first time, and across the planet, a literate and educated mass imagined itself on the brink of power.

Some writers thought they understood these masses. They thought that, through their work, they could make these masses heard.

This book is about four of them: three men and a woman whose political visions shaped and misshaped their century.

*

Inevitably, this book falls into two halves, left and right.

At the heart of leftist politics is the idea that you can transform the oppressed masses into a cultured body of men and women of progressive taste. And this is handy for you since, given the right education, aren't people bound to prefer those who fight for truth and progress?

Leftist intellectuals imagine that an enlightened population will naturally choose them as leaders. So British academics at Oxford University in the 1860s proposed reforms to encourage an alliance of 'brains and numbers on the one side' to carry the day against 'wealth, rank, vested interest, possession in short, on the other.'

The 'numbers' will recognise the 'brains'' right to rule, and vote accordingly. It takes nothing away from the democratic idea to realise that it doubles as a bubble-bath for intellectuals.

The trouble begins when the masses (through some flaw in their upbringing) fail to vote the way they're supposed to. Then the educational impulse hits a much higher gear.

Modern socialist consciousness can only arise on the basis of profound scientific knowledge (says Marx), and you can't expect ordinary people to understand *that*. You need a vanguard party (says Lenin): a body of trained, educated, committed intellectuals to lead the working class to enlightenment.

Karl Marx's rival Mikhail Bakunin saw where this sort of thinking led: to a society where 'savants form a separate caste, in many respects analogous to the priesthood. Scientific abstraction is their God, living and real individuals are their victims, and they are the consecrated and licensed sacrificers ... Mr. Marx's People's State,' Bakunin wrote, would mean 'the reign of the scientific mind, the most aristocratic, despotic, arrogant and contemptuous of all regimes.'

*

The right is a slightly muddier proposition, because it is itself split between reactionaries, who never believed in the democratic impulse in the first place, and romantics, who believe that there has to be more to democracy than just a contest between rival intellectuals.

Friedrich Nietzsche, whose work provided essential reading for Russian Marxists before becoming a fascist bestseller, argued in *The Birth of Tragedy: Out of the Spirit of Music* (1872) that the pursuit of reason was sapping humanity's creativity, annihilating myth and driving poetry 'like a homeless being from her natural, ideal soil'.

If democracy is purely a rational mechanism, goes the argument, then God help democracies, for they will become engines of alienation. Deprived of happiness and hope, democracies will find themselves populated not by living men and women, but by the kinds of defeated, zombie masses that were so brilliantly depicted in Fritz Lang's *Metropolis*.

Metropolis was written by Thea von Harbou, who eventually joined the Nazi Party, the NSDAP. But the anxiety that underlies her story – that the *machinery of government* (savour that phrase) will rip the heart out of a people – proved universally resonant. When Charlie Chaplin, dressed in Adolf Hitler's motley, breaks the fourth wall at the end of his 1940 film *The Great Dictator*, he doesn't single out *Nazis*. He includes Nazis under a much wider and more terrible heading: the coming war, he says, must be fought against 'machine men with machine minds'.

And who better to lead the fight against our inner robot than that high priest of all things humane, *the writer*?

The Frenchman Maurice Barrès once sought spiritual solace at the bottom of 'certain Venetian ponds'. Gabriele

D'Annunzio's inept sailing once led to him being rescued by an Italian warship. Ding Ling's bid for movie stardom ended when she realised, to her horror, that the industry was full of transvestites. One night, on the banks of the Kazanka, Maxim Gorky fired a pistol point-blank into his heart, and missed.

All four, once they'd left their youthful funk behind them, conceived extravagant visions of the future, and came to believe that by wielding their creative weaponry, they could realise their dreams. They all, at one time or another, fancied themselves shapers of human destiny.

Maurice Barrès diagnosed his whole generation: we are sick, he said, from all the assurances of science, and all the false promises of politicians. He sought a cure in egoism – first personal, then national.

Gabriele D'Annunzio likened his verses to the blows with which the foundryman strikes out a plug to let liquefied metal flow into a mould. He declared the crowd an incandescent mass of molten bronze, ready to be shaped by his will.

Josef Stalin's notion of writers as technically trained believers, handling malleable human material, found its expression in the precise phrase 'engineers of human souls', a badge he bestowed personally on Maxim Gorky and which landed, at last, on China's Ding Ling, who feared that she was not worthy (the 'engineer' having become by then a badge of sainthood): 'When one's own soul is vile and ugly how can you talk about reforming and teaching other people?'

'Today, most great soul-conquerors no longer have altars,' wrote the popular psychologist Gustave Le Bon in his peculiar 1895 masterpiece *La Psychologie des Foules* (*The Crowd: A Study of the Popular Mind*), 'but they still have statues or images, and the cult surrounding them is not notably different from that accorded their predecessors. Any study of the philosophy of history should begin with this fundamental point, that for crowds one is either a god or one is nothing.'

MAURICE BARRÈS

1862—1923

CHAPTER ONE

Wednesday, 11 July 1900. For three long months the Exposition Universelle has been gumming up Paris. Maurice Barrès, novelist, politician and grouch, enters the exhibition through the chiselled and mosaic-clad Porte Binet, a dome resting on three arches, and topped by Paris's largest and most notorious tart.

Fifteen feet high, clad in a plaster gown designed by the couturier Jeanne Paquin and – is that a ship on her head?

Anyway: *La Parisienne.* All the jibes you could possibly poke at her must surely have been poked by now: what a shocking advertisement for France!

For the past five years Barrès – at thirty-seven, a bona fide literary lion – has been writing grumpy articles against the whole idea of holding yet another international exposition in Paris. Having hosted five of the blessed things in less than half a century, the city no longer feels like a national capital. More the fruiting body of an international capitalist mycelium. A toadstool! That's it: slick, temporary, dilapidated within days of its first display—

But the metaphor refuses to parse. He can't see how to resolve it. It comes apart in his head and, with a sigh, he dismisses it. Not that it matters. Who would publish such invective now? Even Barrès's usual outlet, the stalwart *Figaro,* has had its head turned, and is now fully behind the Expo.

Oh, France! There's nothing of the real France – vast, diverse, wounded, ancient – in this fantastic farrago. France hardly gets a look-in in this lathe-and-plaster funhouse.

He looks back at *La Parisienne* and, scowling, pictures her consorting with her foreign johns across the Seine: the English and German pavilions, hiding their imperialist intentions in plain sight. Here they are, the two most dangerous nations on Earth, and the German pavilion looks like it sprang out of a tale by Hoffmann while the English one is actually worse: gabled, timbered, pure *rosbif* – who are they trying to kid?

Barrès, emerging from between glasshouses dedicated to the world's horticulture and arboriculture, cannot face the next attraction, 'Old Paris', with its loose cobbles, itinerant hurdy-gurdy players and general froufrou. (This is illustrator and writer Albert Robida's bailiwick, and is as science fictional in its way as those novels and *bandes designées* of his – as though at any moment the gabled roofs of his faux medieval city may split apart under bombardment by missiles dropped by balloon-bicycles.) So Maurice Barrès crosses to the Left Bank by the Ponte de l'Alma.

A *grand écrivain* of a quite different stripe, Anatole France, will find in the exhibition spaces of the Champ de Mars 'contrasts and harmonies of all kinds of human habitation, the fever of work, the wonderful workings of industry, the enormous amusement of the genius of man, who has planted here the arts and crafts of the universe.' But Barrès is cut from different cloth, and it's enough to make him weep, these piled-up heaps of disconnected stuff: kiosks, tents, huts, cabins, water towers, kremlins, pagodas ... It's as though a small boy had gone round his mother's garden, yanking up every cherished bloom and piling them up by her bedside 'to cheer her up'.

And what is true of flowers is, alas, equally true of people, and peoples: *whatever you uproot, you kill.*

This is Barrès's great lesson for the world. It's been the dynamo powering all his books, at least since 1889's *Un Homme libre* (*A Free Man*). Later observers will take a dim view indeed of Barrès's 'national-socialist' politics (just look where they led!) but the way Barrès sees it, he just wants to recover the past: 'The qualities I love in the past are its sadness, its silence, and most especially its fixity. Every thing that moves disconcerts me.'

Barrès crosses back over the river again by the Pont d'Iéna. At the foot of the Trocadéro, thick walls rise, pierced and castellated: an orientalist power-fantasy that owes not a little to Gustave Flaubert's *Salammbô*. From inside the pyramidal Egyptian theatre, derboukas purr and reed-flutes whine, and cries, guttural and rhythmic, split the air with a queer, tortured joy. How anyone considers this 'entertainment' is beyond poor Barrès, but Oscar Wilde seems to be enjoying himself. (There, on the pavement outside the Café d'Égypte: a large Englishman in a slightly rumpled white suit. He's tapping his foot, all the while mopping his brow with a silk handkerchief, while a slim brown man, rather like a handsome bamboo walking stick, serves him tea.)

Barrès wonders whether he should introduce himself. The idea of taking tea with Wilde, a fellow 'decadent', is tempting. The banquet this afternoon promises to be a long one, and there will be endless speeches. But the smell of strange foods in this mocked-up corner of Araby puts him off. Success has hardened him against experience. He is too much invested in the narrowness of his tastes. Among the treasures he will miss at the Expo: Japanese lacquer-work and Russian ballet; the music of Ravel and Debussy and Stravinsky; the paintings of Van Gogh and Picasso.

His literary tastes are just as narrow. He won't even try the novels of Gide and Proust. He'd rather read the gun-slinging antisemite Marquis de Morès ('a heroic thinker,' he reckons, 'a man who gave his life to the highest form of speculations'. *Really?* Chief among those was: 'Gaul for the Gauls'.)

This sort of thing – Gaul for the Gauls, France for the French – speaks to Barrès's mystical regionalism, to his belief in the quasi-magical power of the land, and to the love he feels for his own bloodied homeland, Lorraine, now part-French, part-German, disarticulated by the war of 1870.

Why should loving one's own place mean that one has to feel contempt for every other place? This is something Barrès will spend his life trying to explain. A thirteenth-century French crusader's castle is far superior to the Parthenon, he writes; how can he, Barrès, be expected to appreciate the beauties of Athens, when 'the blood of the valleys of the Rhine' flows through his veins?

This being Barrès's well-publicised attitude, one may reasonably wonder why on earth Action Française – a league of rightists and monarchists – invited him today to the Restaurant International du Trocadéro. Located slap-bang in the middle of the Colonial Exhibition, it is hard to imagine a place less suited to Barrès's political tastes. Barrès is a blood-and-soil nationalist. Imperial speculations leave him cold. The Scramble for Africa is something he views with contempt. (Indeed, among the royalists, Boulangists and anti-Dreyfusards invited along to toast the publication of Barrès's new novel *L'Appel au soldat* (*A Soldier Summoned*), you'd be hard put to find a single colonial.)

At the head of the table sit Paul Bourget, a novelist and Academician, and Charles Costa de Beauregard, a historian. They've agreed to chair this 'intimate dinner' while Charles Maurras, Action Française's *éminence grise*, sits back a little, enjoying the scene: the occasion was his idea.

There are around thirty guests around the table. Henri

Vaugeois, Camille Jarre and other significant rightists. Some friendly press: Lucien Moreau (young to be a royalist, but there's idealism for you); Paul Copin-Albancélli, a former free-mason who now runs *A bas les tyrants*, exposing all manner of Masonic and Jewish conspiracies. Also Barrès's old child-hood friend and fellow Lorrainer, Maurice-Charles de Brem.

Adulatory as this audience is, Barrès needs to watch his step here. He's a convinced and passionate republican, and he will need to hold his ground, as politely as he can, against all these admiring royalists. Charles Maurras, for a start: the man's relentless. Twenty thousand articles of his survive, and hardly one that steers from the main point: restore the House of Orléans! They say years ago Maurras was travel-ling on board a ship and noticed something wrong with an Englishwoman's manners: he's been a convinced xenophobe ever since. The Pope says Maurras has a very fine brain, 'but alas, only a brain'.

Given their long association, Barrès the republican and Maurras the royalist can probably agree to disagree. But what about de Cléry? He's more than capable of causing a scene.

The meal passes without incident. The food is pleasant and not too heavy. And this is as well, since some of the after-dinner speeches will take some digesting.

'My dear Barrès,' Paul Bourget begins, 'it was decided, when you agreed to be our host, that this intimate dinner would not be saddened by any speech. Yet your friends at Action Française can't let you leave without thanking you for sitting at their table and without having raised – I was going to say a "toast", but what about that old and pretty French word, "health"? So I lift my glass – health to a great literary artist! So delicate and so strong! So a-quiver with sensibility! So courageous with civic energy!'

And so on and so on. Since *Les Déracinés* (*The Uprooted*)

was published – the first volume of his second trilogy, 'Le Roman de l'énergie nationale' – Barrès has been hailed as the voice of his nation. (This is no mere fad. Generations to come will hail Barrès's influence – even those who find his politics appalling: Paul Léautaud, Louis Aragon, even Albert Camus.)

Bourget breaks into a canter: 'In the days of agony that followed the war of 1870 Gustave Flaubert said, "We all suffer from France's malady." This was an eloquent way of putting things, one you yourself hit upon when, at the age of twenty, you went through those spiritual crises you recorded in *Sous l'œil des barbares* (*Under the Eyes of the Barbarians*) and in the early chapters of *Les Déracinés*. You understood that the malaise you felt was more than personal: that France was sick in you, as it is in all of us. And with extraordinary lucidity, you discerned, if not all causes, at least the most immediate and powerful one: *the wrong turn we took in 1789!*'

Barrès ought to have seen this one coming. He takes a steadying breath. The French Revolution was no 'wrong turn'! Though, heaven knows, its promise has been betrayed often enough.

Barrès has recently been stepping back from politics, following his failure at the 1898 General Election. He's been developing an educational programme: something roughly along the lines of Paul Déroulède's original far-right Ligue des Patriotes. He imagines a non-partisan programme of military and patriotic education, to repair the damage Captain Dreyfus's exoneration has done to the army and to the standing of the French state.

A couple of years ago he founded the literary-academical Ligue de la patrie française. It's not doing too badly: it boasts over twenty Academicians, several dozen members of the Institut, hundreds of university professors, writers, magistrates, doctors; Jules Verne once signed its petition.

Since the Dreyfus debacle, leagues of this sort have been popping up all over France like mushrooms after a spring rain. Action Français is the cream of a large and diverse crop. The trouble is, no one seems interested in doing the spade-work necessary to tie these groups together and build a true right-wing consensus. Royalists and nationalists, Catholics and national socialists would rather spat among themselves than tackle their common enemy.

One more year of this – and one more cross-purposed literary dinner in February 1901 – and Barrès will give up the effort in disgust. In a letter to his friend Paul Acker: 'I had been at the baptism of nationalism. Now I am at its burial . . . I know what nationalism is, but I do not know what the Nationalist Party is. I have never been shown anything but an anti-ministerial party.'

Back at the dinner, Paul Bourget – who has been laying into the very idea of republicanism – finally moves to less contentious territory.

'Once persuaded of this truth, my dear Barrès, you sought, following your own formula, to understand yourself as "a moment of an immortal whole". You rooted yourself in your past once more, in your land, in Lorraine, where your family comes from. And at the same time you dreamed the same for France: that it too might reconcile itself with its land, its past, and its illustrious dead – with generations so long, so criminally denied! You found them yourself, not in ruins, not in leavings, but in the very intuitions, the very instincts of the people. And it is their spirit which animates *L'Appel au soldat* through and through – the call to Race!'

Barrès stands to make his reply. This, though emollient, also speaks to the racial idea:

'Certain words – *France, Patrie* – evoke in certain men, you and I among them, so many anciently connected ideas that they rustle in the mind like leaves in the forest. They cannot be heard by people lacking these associations. Intelligence has nothing to do with it. However swiftly their minds work, they cannot feel as we do. A single instinct – I would venture to say a single *physiology* – defines us. How proud I am to receive the approbation of minds such as yours, for this idea of "rootedness", for this cult of the Earth and the Dead!'

Maurice Barrès's father Auguste studied engineering at the Ecole Centrale, married the daughter of the local mayor, and avoided steady work for over seventy years. His own father was an army officer who retired at the grand old age of forty-nine.

Maurice could have had an easy life: like grandfather like father like son. Men of his class, buoyed up by fixed incomes and falling prices, dabbled about in business, trade, the army or the professions, but by their forties they were like as not to be living off savings or an inheritance, supplemented by rents.

What made Barrès's journey unobvious, winding, full of incomprehensible literary twists and political turns, was an accident of youth.

At school, Barrès became great friends with Stanislas de Guaita, a remarkable boy who would grow up to be an influential occultist, founder of the Ordre kabbalistique de la Rose-Croix, and an admired esoteric poet, before a heady collision of occult rites and drugs finished him off a few days before Christmas 1897.

At first the pair obsessed over Baudelaire and Flaubert, as teenagers will. Soon they developed a taste for stranger fare: Gautier, Mme Ackerman, Leconte de Lisle, symbolists and decadents of every conceivable stripe. Until 1883 the two shared a house in Nancy (they argued all the time) and, literally, set the record for absenteeism at the university.

Then, aged twenty (as soon as he could, really), Barrès left for the capital.

In Paris, young Maurice Barrès embraced all the cosmopolitan trappings. Rarely gracing the halls of the Faculté de droit and the Ecole pratique des hautes études (where he was supposed to be studying law) he spent his time in brasseries, in literary dispute with Latin Quarter friends including Jean Moréas, Stéphane Mallarmé, Villiers de l'Isle-Adam, and Charles de Goffic. His hero was Disraeli, 'poet, dandy, ambitious, and leader of men'. Anatole France took him under his wing and introduced him to the salon of the Countess de Loynes (the original Lady of the Camellias). Pieces in the literary magazine *Jeune France* earned him a reputation as a symbolist.

He bit that hand that fed him, as all young Turks must. He wrote: 'Our malaise comes from the fact that we live in a social order imposed by the dead, not chosen for us. The dead poison us.' And he proposed, in place of all the tiresome talk of men older than he was, to establish a cult of the self, a *'Culte de Moi'*. 'Our morality, our religion, our feeling of nationality are all crumbled things,' he wrote in 1892, 'from which we cannot derive rules for living, and while waiting for our masters to reestablish certitudes for us, it is advisable that we hold on to the only remaining reality, the Self.'

One doesn't need to scratch too hard here to discover, below the glittering and spiky surface, an insecure young man making the best of things. Barrès the egotist lived in fear of drowning in egos larger than his own. 'Cultivation of the self' is a splendidly arrogant pose, but in the end it's the act of a hypochondriac: someone desperate to avoid moral contagion.

In November 1884, Barrès used his parents' allowance to establish a review of his own, *Les Taches d'encre (Ink Spots)*,

printed expensively on the priciest brochure paper he could
find. He experimented with advertising; the murder of a
journalist (called Morin) by the wife of a politician gave him
the perfect excuse to send men wandering around the city
wearing tasteless sandwich boards that read 'Morin no longer
reads *Les Taches d'encre*!'.

Still, there was something refreshing about this young
man's insolence. 'It seems to me,' he wrote, 'that, under our
current literary disposition, the study of superior spirits is
sacrificed a little too much to the study of ordinary people.'
(A dig at Zola here, and at realism in general.) 'I'm with those
who think there's nothing quite so dramatic than the play of
ideas in the head of a sage, artist or philosopher.'

The fleshier and more exotic the bloom, the quicker it rots,
and soon even Barrès's champion Anatole France began to fret
about the boy: 'His mind,' he wrote, 'was restless, unhealthy,
perverted, and spoiled.' *Les Taches d'encre* folded after four
irregular issues. Barrès had hoped to make some money from
it. Now he had to rely on writing reviews for the newspapers,
even as his old cohort turned their backs on symbolism, a
movement he'd made his own.

Enough with symbolism's incomprehensibility and obscurity, its gnarled diction and ridiculous syntax! *Le Figaro* of 8
September 1888 namechecked Barrès, but not in a good way,
as one of a group with 'the same objective: a refined and sickly
incoherence which causes one to fear for their reason if they
linger in their ways.'

Exhausted and depressed, Barrès withdrew from the fray
and went back home, to Lorraine.

Did the visit to his birthplace renew his spirit? In one epiphanic gush, did our hero recover his spiritual connection to his
Earth and his Dead?

No.

Soon he was packing for Venice, and it was here, in a place that had nothing to do with him, that young Maurice 'got a fairly accurate idea of the lucid delusions that the ancients experienced at the edge of certain ponds.'

Whatever this means precisely, the city did him good. We know this because we have some of his youthful notes, only lightly edited in his 1916 memoir 'The Death of Venice'. Barrès visited the place three times between 1887 and 1888, 'and this abstract city, built for my personal use, unfolded before my closed eyes, out of time and space.' Like all well-educated egotists, Barrès knew how storied surroundings can be used to reinforce the self: 'I was ready to love myself,' he wrote, 'to understand myself even in my darkness: to guide me, I relied on Venice.'

Never mind the real place ('a city of dead fish and decaying houses, inhabited by a race of waiters and touts' is how the poet Filippo Marinetti described it); it's the Venice of the mind that counts!

Is Barrès poking fun at himself here? He knew Huysmans's 1884 novel À rebours (Against Nature), and the way its aesthete hero Des Esseintes decides, at the very last minute, to abandon his ferry crossing to London, and sit instead with his eyes shut, conjuring a Dickensian city out of his imagination. In his second, he steals shamelessly from Huysmans, down to the way Philippe, his alter ego, rushes to his hotel on his arrival in Venice, the better to enjoy the Venice of his imagination.

Barrès isn't the sort of writer you would expect to be telling jokes at his own expense. But his self-awareness is sharp. Sous l'œil des barbares is his first book, and the first of his trilogy 'The Cult of the Self'. Here's where we first meet Philippe, our protagonist: a clueless, jaded dilettante.

A philosopher, 'Monsieur X', gives him a talking to: 'Your

masters, their books, and their long-winded speculations gave you an excellent outlook: a world entirely devoid of the idea of duty ... an orchard where, quite frankly, you have only to satisfy yourself ... I assume you have health and some *rentes*?'

Philippe, like Barrès, is never going to run out of money. His spiritual education (the subject of this and the next two volumes of Barrès's 'Cult of the Self' trilogy) will set him back 14,000 francs. That's about ten times a lecturer's salary. A fair bit of it goes on a remote country house and some comfortable armchairs because 'no thinker ever combined anything respectable outside an armchair'. The source of all this cash? *Rentes*.

How will Philippe escape the prison of his own ego?

This is the kind of question that obsessed writers of the *fin de siècle*. They were the first writers who could afford to ask it.

Barrès and his generation are, more than anything, bored out of their minds. They're hungry for action, for fame, for something to do, for a foothold in the real world. But they're rich. The necessities of life are all taken care of. So there's a hard limit on how serious their lives can actually get. No wonder they treasure feelings, even when they hurt! No wonder they obsess over abstractions, and champion decadence over progress, and see no point in anything! They don't *need* anything.

Barrès's whole project, literary and political, was about finding something to do. His search for a meaningful life doesn't just find its way into his novels: it's what his novels are about.

In *Sous l'œil des barbares*, the sickly Philippe, fresh out of school (where he's been mercilessly teased and humiliated) longs, in his egoistic loneliness, to be rescued by some master, some religion. Where is the spiritual principle that will end his loneliness and his suffering? Spiritual exercises on the island of Jersey prove unsatisfying so he moves back home to Lorraine. There, he feels the road forking before him. Will he seek meaning in public service, or in a life of solitude and contemplation?

Philippe chooses solitude, and holes up in the town library to study and emulate the spiritual exercises of Ignatius of Loyola.

After a while of this, however, Philippe is finally forced to admit that there is something wrong. He has plumped for a life of solitude – but is this not as likely to turn him into a monster as make him a saint? He knows what the monster would look like, because he's already met him: Old Monsieur X, the man who asked after Philippe's *rentes*, a monster of egotism for whom money is power ('*Ayez de l'argent et soyez considéré*', he observes, at which an outraged Philippe beats him with a stick).

The alternative, in his loneliness, is for Philippe to become a saint. And it is while he is contemplating his ill-suitedness for that role that he wakes up to his surroundings, the outdoors, the extraordinary beauty of sky and countryside, the simple, cardinal truth that he is, after all, *at home*. Lorraine fills him with an indescribable peace that dissolves his loneliness.

How is this even possible? Philippe investigates. Visiting local churchyards, he listens to the echoes of his footfalls on the flagstones, and for the first time he becomes aware of the lost voices of the dead. Communing with the ancient language and culture of Lorraine, Philippe feels his self vanish into the eternity of his race.

Philippe's ecstatic discovery of his homeland and its people is charming enough. Young men will have their epiphanies. And there is no shame in the way Barrès the novelist relocates his own experiences in Venice to his Lorraine birthplace. It is not a writer's job to be accurate. The writer's job is to be tidy.

The main point – and this was as true for Barrès as it is for the fictional Philippe – is that detachment from the world is an intellectual and emotional dead end. You can refine the self as much as you like – but you still have to feed it.

Wounded and alone in Venice, Barrès discovered that loneliness wasn't preserving his thought; it was starving it. And conversely: taking an interest in other people didn't erode his ego; it enriched it!

Which left just one question. which 'other people' was Barrès going to take an interest in? All of them?

Hardly! Like all egotists, Barrès drew energy from his own reflection. The land he cared about was *his* land; the dead, *his* dead.

From his notebook: 'What I have followed everywhere, in my enthusiasm for Lorraine and France together, in traveling, in seeking power, is an immense increase of my personality.'

CHAPTER TWO

France's Third Republic was born in defeat following Napoleon III's disastrous six-week war against Prussia in 1870. Following his abdication, a treaty had forced France to cede Alsace and much of Barrès's beloved Lorraine to Germany. An armistice was signed with the Germans at Versailles, but the rebellious Paris commune, with almost the whole National Guard at its back, refused to lay down its arms.

In the 'Bloody Week' of 21 to 28 May 1871, the centre of the city was set on fire and between 20,000 and 50,000 Parisians died at the hands of their own countrymen.

From then on, the constitutional government had lurched from one crisis to another. Conservatives found the whole edifice reeking of capitulation to German ideas, German efficiency, German management. France was becoming nothing more than a cadet Germany: not a power at all, but a genial host to a generation of rootless cosmopolitans. There were so many different factions in France's Chamber of Deputies, all governments ended up being coalitions. It was quite usual to find a new government boasting nearly all the same ministers as the previous one.

Extremist factions of wildly different stripes agreed on this at least: there had to be a more direct and visceral connection between the state and its people – some emotional bond.

Georges Boulanger was born at Rennes in 1837. His father, a solicitor, had relatives in the Anglo-Welsh aristocracy. He was also a bankrupt, and it made good sense for his son to turn his horsemanship – acquired on long vacations in England – into a military career. Georges graduated from the academy at Saint-Cyr in 1856, took part in four campaigns and acquitted himself with bravery and distinction.

West of Milan, during a rout of Austrian forces during the Italian War of Independence in 1859, Boulanger was seriously wounded. A knighthood in the Legion of Honour followed, and a life of almost constant pain. He served in the Franco Prussian war, then in the suppression of the Paris Commune. It was just as well a further injury plucked him from that fight early on, given his later politics.

In 1871 Boulanger, an officer of the Third Republic, married to the daughter of a career diplomat and father of two children, was made a full colonel. This was indeed a meteoric rise, and it did not go unnoticed. For his betters, his progress had been much too fast, and they promptly had him demoted to lieutenant-colonel.

Boulanger's disgust at this may be imagined. His talent and loyalty had been better rewarded under Napoleon III. It took the Minister of War himself to persuade him not to resign.

Garrisoned midway between Lyon and Geneva, Boulanger wore himself out on horses and on the wives of local politicians, lobbying all the while for promotion. The Duc d'Aumale was inspector general of the army at that time, and was the devoutest of Catholics. Boulanger became overnight an ardent Papist. He insisted that his staff attend mass every Sunday, and was regularly seen walking to church with a deluxe, gilt-edged prayer book tucked under his arm. In 1879 the anticlerical republicans gained power, and Boulanger's prayer book vanished, never to be seen again.

Léon Gambetta, president of the Chamber of Deputies, caved under Boulanger's flattery, and in April 1880, at the age of forty-three, Boulanger became a general.

He soon acquired a taste for the political high life. In 1881 he was added to a French delegation visiting the United States. Bands blaring the 'Marseillaise' greeted him at every stop. 'It was beautiful,' he wrote, 'it was grandiose, it was gripping.'

They had come to celebrate the centennial of the final battle of America's Revolutionary War. But the delegation travelled far beyond Yorktown, criss-crossing the continent and inspecting army garrisons as far west as Cheyenne. And they travelled in style; Boulanger arrived at Niagara Falls in a train fitted with two parlours, a dining room and a kitchen run by Delmonico's restaurant.

Boulanger was bowled over. This was how to run a country! What France needed, if it were ever to recover its standing, was an American-style president, and a direct relationship between the people and executive power.

On 30 January 1882, the French chamber appointed yet another new prime minister, Charles Louis de Freycinet. He appointed Boulanger inspector of infantry. In the two years Boulanger held that post, he saw four prime ministers and sixty-five ministers come and go. No wonder he began to feel he could do a better job.

Late in 1883, Boulanger received a visitor.

Paul Déroulède, a poet and dramatist, wanted permission to march members of his year-old Ligue des Patriotes through Paris bearing arms. This league, founded the year before, was fanatically dedicated to *revanche* – the restoration of Alsace and Lorraine to France. Boulanger was only too happy to sign off on that.

Meanwhile, Déroulède talked and talked. A former soldier, knight of the Legion of Honour (his brilliant career had been cut short in 1874 when he fell off his horse), Déroulède had been making a catalogue of patriotic books and songs. His findings were stark: German children were being taught to be proud of their nation. French children weren't. His committee had offered a programme to cure the French indifference to nation-building, but the new prime minister, Jules Ferry, was ignoring it. And what about these colonial adventures Ferry had embarked upon? Déroulède considered these especially pointless, while Alsace and so much of Lorraine still lay in German hands.

The less Boulanger said, the more convinced Déroulède became that he and Boulanger saw eye to eye on all the important issues of the day. When he returned to his League's meeting hall he told several friends, 'I have found our man. His name is Boulanger.'

The day after Boulanger's appointment as war minister, Paul Déroulède paid him another visit. This time he had no mere chit to sign.

The time had come, said Déroulède, to prepare for the reform of French government – and that could only happen under the war minister's leadership. Three hundred thousand members of Déroulède's Ligue des Patriotes were waiting on his call! Meanwhile Déroulède personally would travel throughout Europe, explaining the coming revolution: a coup to restore order, end all these sterile parliamentary agitations, root out corruption, and usher in a new era of social reform. Déroulède told Boulanger that the presidency could be his within the year – assuming he wanted it.

Boulanger nodded, and smiled, and if he said anything at all, it has not been recorded.

Déroulède took that smiling silence for a yes. He travelled the length and breadth of France preaching the good news. Alsace and Lorraine at last had their champion! 'Throughout the whole of my journey,' he told a large crowd that had gathered at the Gare du Nord to welcome him home, 'the name of a single man, the name of a brave soldier, has been my touchstone. It is the name of the supreme head of our army, the name of General Boulanger!'

As war minister, Boulanger shone. A whole series of minor-sounding reforms endeared him to the men of the army. You were drafted for three years, not five. You could grow a beard now, and at the end of the day, you could bed down on a sprung mattress rather than a straw pallet. Best of all, the old draft-dodging loopholes had been tightened: imagine finding yourself billeted beside the son of an aristocrat, or a priest!

And wasn't that the point? That you were there, all of you together, serving France? In 1886, when coal miners went on strike in the town of Decazeville, you weren't sent in to break heads. You broke bread, and shared your soup, and kept the peace. The military occupation of the town, Boulanger wrote, had no aims contrary to those of organised labour: 'At this very moment, perhaps every soldier is sharing his rations with a miner.'

At this, the administration experienced its first anxious *frisson*. Boulanger's 'minor reforms' suddenly didn't seem nearly so minor. When he revived the Bastille Day military review, no one so much as blinked. But at Longchamp, on that day in 1886, more than 100,000 spectators turned up to cheer Boulanger astride his magnificent, newly acquired, and phenomenally expensive black horse. White plumes fluttering, Boulanger cantered around the racetrack to shouts of '*Vive Boulanger! Vive l'armée!*' Somewhere in that cheering mob were ministers of the government. They were ignored; and when the soldiers marched by their president, they faced the other way, towards Boulanger.

*

As a youth, Barrès had been as besotted with German culture and German philosophy as everyone else. At this period, German culture *was* European culture, at least at its more rarefied latitudes. School taught Barrès to distinguish his Kantian categorical imperative from his Hegelian absolute spirit, Fichte's ego from Schelling's non-ego; and like every other man of his age and class he absolutely adored Wagner. In 1886 Barrès travelled to Bayreuth and found there 'a sentiment I would describe as made of envy and bonhomie'.

A year later, though, he found everything changed. 'I am assured ... that a Frenchman is still able to travel in Bavaria without vexations; I admit that, but according to the mood I saw, most of Germany has become impossible for us.'

The cause of the unpleasantness was a dispute on France's border with the German half of Lorraine. On 20 April 1887 German police seized Guillaume Schnaebelé, a French border official, at the line of demarcation. They accused him of espionage, beat him up, and threatened him with a court-martial.

Then, to Germany's intense embarrassment, it turned out that Schnaebelé had entered Lorraine at the invitation of his German counterpart.

Bismarck, with his usual lack of grace, allowed ten days to pass before the poor man was freed, by which time the French press had whipped themselves up nicely. Many column inches were spent praising the government's hawkish war minister, Georges Ernest Boulanger, whose draft ultimatum to Germany, had it passed cabinet (it failed, six votes to five) would surely have triggered a war.

Returning from Italy through Nancy, Barrès caught the mood. He wrote: 'The sentiment rises daily in everyone that France is sworn to master her fate.' The good student of Kant and Hegel, the Wagner obsessive, has all of a sudden acquired a national identity.

Barrès found himself thinking more and more about Boulanger. His article for the symbolist journal *La Revue indépendante* – 'M. *le général Boulanger et la nouvelle génération*' – is his first public political statement. Appealing to the new generation, he calls to his side 'those who will be at one with ... a France which impatiently endures the parliamentary tumult, and aspires to find the man of vigour who will open the windows, throw the babblers out of them, and air out the place.'

Talk about seizing the bull by the horns! No sooner does Barrès take an interest in his surroundings, than he's calling for the regime's overthrow – though it would have been hard, at this period, to find a member of the chattering classes who wasn't expecting, if not actively advocating, the Third Republic's demise.

For parliamentarians convinced of Boulanger's dangerousness, the Schnaebelé incident confirmed their worst fears. Songs in praise of 'General Revenge' were echoing through the streets of Paris! So, in May 1887, parliament conspired to get rid of him. They brought down the prime minister, the blameless René Goblet; this made way for a new cabinet, from which Boulanger could be excluded.

Three times within the next month, crowds assembled on the streets of Paris to protest the general's forced resignation. Fearing a coup d'état, a new role was found for the general, as far away from Paris as possible: he was made commander of the 13th Army Corps at Clermont-Ferrand, in south-central France.

That this amounted to internal exile was obvious to everyone. On the day Boulanger was due to leave, more than 20,000 devotees turned up at the Gare de Lyon. They seized hold of his carriage and gave the police hell, while Boulanger, in civilian dress, worked his way through the mob, waving his top hat for everyone to see.

Maurice Barrès, the loner who confessed to his journal that he 'relished the instinctual pleasure of being in a herd', wrote of Boulanger's departure from the Gare de Lyon in his novel *L'Appel au soldat*:

'It is an extraordinary impression to see a man carried through a human throng ... the centre of such a hurricane! The immense wave, the powerful animal which is the crowd throws itself with its frail hero from side to side in formidable undulations which betray the thrust of its desires and fears, its weaknesses and strengths ...'

Inside the station: chaos. Protesters filled the great hall, barricaded platforms, stood four deep on coaches, on girders, on canopies. Scrawled across a locomotive: 'He will return!' Boulanger was hustled to his private coach. Another delay while the police removed protesters lying across the tracks – and then, at last, General Revenge began his progress south.

Parliament's sigh of collective relief came too soon. On 7 October 1887 news broke that Daniel Wilson, son-in-law to the French president, Jules Grévy, had been selling memberships in the Legion of Honour to help shore up his newspaper business. Grévy, blameless in the affair, and knowing the Republic hung in the balance, tried to cling on. He was, after all, the first real republican president France had ever had; all his predecessors were royalists who had tried without success to restore the monarchy.

But the scandal only grew – the story now involved two brothels and a general – and crowds and demonstrations flooded the capital. On 30 November, Déroulède's Ligue des Patriotes (an equal mix of top hats and workingmen's caps, according to the police) choked the Quai d'Orsay, chanting insults and throwing stones. Grévy resigned.

It's hard to tell just how closely Georges Boulanger followed these events. His wife had left him and exile was affording him a delicious distraction in the form of Marguerite Brouzet, the Vicomtesse de Bonnemains, a woman much younger than himself. They used to arrange clandestine meetings in a spa hotel just outside Clermont-Ferrand.

But some have greatness thrust upon 'em, and Boulanger was certainly one of those. Royalists Baron de Mackau and the Comte de Martimprey left their secret midnight meeting convinced of Boulanger's devotion to the royal house of Orléans. Five days later, Boulanger slipped across the Swiss border to pledge his loyalty to Jérôme Bonaparte, Napoleon Bonaparte's nephew and an outspoken liberal. In Paris, meanwhile, a dizzying array of political interests decided for reasons all their own that Boulanger was their natural champion. The Church expected Boulanger to reverse the Republic's anti-clerical legal campaign. Radical republicans proposed to make him minister of war in a future cabinet. Aristocrats wore his emblem, the carnation, at parties in the Faubourg Saint-Germain. Anne de Rochechouart de Mortemart, the Duchesse d'Uzès (who had inherited an immense fortune from her great-grandmother, the founder of Veuve Clicquot champagne) opened her coffers to fund Boulanger's political campaign.

Then there was this chap called Maurice Barrès, springing out of nowhere to pledge his tireless service to 'the cause'. A friend of Barrès offered to explain to the former war minister what his literary champion had said about him, but Boulanger demurred: 'No, it is enough that M. Barrès admires me. I will dispense with his reasons for it.'

Success piled on success. Legitimists, Orléanists, Bonapartists, socialists, assorted neo-Jacobins – in short, all the malcontents nibbling at the edges of the Third Republic – declared their 'Boulangism'. When Boulanger entered his name in by-elections across France, he won virtually every seat, regardless of who or what he was actually standing for. Frankly, no one really cared. Royalists and radicals ensured Boulanger's success as Bonapartist candidate in seven departments.

The less Boulanger said, the better he did. The vaguer his promises, the wider his appeal grew. In mid-March a daily appeared called *La Cocarde: Organe Boulangiste*. The first issue sold 400,000 copies, presumably because so many were curious to know what Boulangism actually was. *'Dissolution,' La Cocarde* thundered, *'Révision, Constituante!'* Dissolve parliament! Revise the constitution! Elect a new assembly! This is the political equivalent of saying you can play the flute by blowing down one end.

'All visitors, after meeting him, were stunned by the hollow sound the idol made when they tapped him,' remarked the diplomat Eugène-Melchior de Vogüé. Foreign observers, too, surveyed the French scene with mounting apprehension. Emperor William of Germany neatly skewered him, dubbing him 'His Majesty Ernest I'. An editorial in the *New York Times* ponderously observed that 'a government that takes its tone from a popular hero partakes of his personal character. When he is a soldier who looks upon the politics of civilians only as affording him an opportunity to run a professional career, when he is "the man on horseback" as the phrase goes, his ascendency distinctly threatens the peace.'

Eventually Boulanger, who was supposed all this while to be sitting on his hands in Clermont-Ferrand, was hauled up for questioning by his superiors.

He flustered and fudged. 'I had and still have no knowledge of anything connected with the legislative elections of February 26,' he assured General Logerot, minister of war. But he was badly caught out: Logerot knew damned well he had made three unauthorised trips to Paris – in disguise, at that – and did not hesitate to suspend him.

On 26 March, Boulanger, the career soldier, was discharged. In April he was elected to parliament in the Dordogne, having not even campaigned.

A week later he won a seat in the industrial north-east, a place he could scarcely point to on a map.

What was this inexplicable vertigo that had gripped the masses and left no room for rational thought?

Georges Boulanger was something new: a man who was also a brand. A commodity. 'General Revanche' didn't just turn up in song. He turned up in soap and on souvenirs. Boulanger's image graced dinner plates and pottery, pipe bowls and shoe horns, handkerchiefs and quill pens. His rise coincided with advances in photographic printing that saw nearly a million full-length portraits distributed throughout France, so that you could hardly move for the man.

Move? You couldn't *eat*: 'Everyone owes their bread to Boulanger. You can't do without a baker!' ran one slogan, promoting foodstuffs guaranteed free of German imports.

The phenomenon of celebrity was not new. But Boulanger and his managers Georges Thiébaud and Arthur Dillon were the first to exploit its political potential. Very soon, they found themselves riding the tiger: what strange energies had they unleashed?

'Those who in recent years have studied the popular movement known as Boulangism,' wrote the social psychologist Gustave Le Bon, 'have seen with what ease the religious instinct of crowds can spring to life again ... He was credited with the power of remedying all injustices and all evils, and thousands of men would have immolated themselves for him.'

The manufacture of political celebrity. The advent of mass politics. The rise of public opinion. These are all chewy subjects. But what lies at the heart of Boulanger's appeal was – let's cut to the chase here – *nothing*. Boulanger's sheer vacuity suckered everyone, and especially Maurice Barrès.

Till now Barrès had been a dilettante. He had had no concrete ends in mind, no ideals, even; only a desperate need to break the boredom of an existence drained of necessity. We know this because Barrès is his own fiercest critic. He writes of entering politics – a 'glorious adventure frivolously engaged' – to 'participate in the passions of my epoch.'

Is it any wonder, then, that Boulangism struck him like 'a tumult and a fever'? It was mystical, obscure, irrational, and it ran completely against convention! Royalists thought Boulanger was a royalist. Socialists thought Boulanger was a socialist. Barrès had him down for a *symbolist*: a lightning conductor for the popular unconscious.

Barrès's infatuation with Boulanger was commonplace enough. What no one expected was that, come the general election in 1889, Barrès would become at twenty-seven the youngest deputy in the Chamber of Deputies. He did it by understanding better than most Boulangists – and better than Boulanger himself – what it would take to turn this sentimental grouping of malcontents into a political movement.

'I do not want to fight for a party,' Barrès declared, once he entered the Chamber of Deputies. 'I do not want to fight for parties.' Barrès understood that Boulangism was not a parliamentary movement. It was a psychological one.

Boulanger's great strength lay in saying as little as possible. Asked by a *New York Times* reporter what the 'revision' in his mantra '*Dissolution, Révision, Constituante*' actually meant, Boulanger replied: 'That is my secret which I shall keep to myself.'

Barrès's strength was his willingness to make and keep clear promises on simple issues. A crowd thinks simply, sentimentally and morally. It thinks not in facts but in values. So, Barrès reasoned: do something everyone will understand, immediately and instinctively. Help the poor.

Listening and learning from his campaign manager, the leftist Alfred Gabriel, he put forward a programme of old-age pension support, an upper limit on working hours (and suppression of night work) for women and children, credits for striking miners, amnesties for socialist and syndicalist militants – a whole raft of social reforms.

Barrès's close and happy relationship with Gabriel exemplifies just how broad a church Boulangism was, and just how protean were Barrès's politics. Barrès, arriving to contest the seat in Nancy, cared most for national revival. Gabriel, who knew Nancy backwards, had a fully developed social reform programme in his back pocket. They were both convinced Boulangists because to both of them, a strong leader seemed essential.

As Gabriel's ideas rubbed off on Barrès, so Barrès's ideas of strong leadership began to evolve. 'Liberty of commerce, all this pretended liberalism is only a fiction,' he declared. 'The contest is not equal between the workers and their exploiters. It is necessary that a force intervene in favour of the first to re-establish equality.'

Can this really be Maurice Barrès, arguing that a strong president, there to represent the workers, will bring about the triumph of socialism?

Indeed it can. 'It is impossible to live for several weeks in the milieu of the disinherited without receiving from them an emotion, a sincere impulse of love,' Barrès gushed (relishing, one presumes, that 'instinctual pleasure of being in a herd'). Nor need we sneer at the lonely egotist's profound surprise and relief to find himself, even if only for a moment, among 'dear workers' in their 'sad working-class sections' as they 'fraternally smoked their cigars'.

Barrès was not a natural campaigner. 'He did a great many minute services and shook hands with everyone, but with the air of a king of France touching his subjects in order to cure their scrofula.' Barrès's speeches were underwhelming, his manner stand-offish. But his collaboration with Gabriel was sincere, and their tactics were spot-on. They spent over six months campaigning in Nancy, all of it without outside Boulangist help, and Barrès won the seat.

As a deputy, Barrès advocated the abolition of parliamentary government in favour of a presidential system that would bring government closer to the people. He championed the French working classes against fat cats (*'les gros'*), against a corrupt political elite, and against foreign competition. He fought hard to deliver on his election promises to the poor.

But Georges Boulanger, his hero, in whose name he had entered politics, had fled the field.

Boulanger stepped into the Chamber of Deputies in 1888 and at the end of the year he contested a further seat in Paris. Here, left-wing Boulangists operated an impressive electoral machine, financed – such was the 'broad church' Boulanger inspired – by half a million francs from the Duchesse d'Uzès, a constitutional royalist. The result was hardly ever in doubt, but Boulanger won by more than 80,000 votes. A figure like that wasn't just a victory: it was a mandate.

On election night, 27 January 1889, an enormous mob surged around the café where Boulanger and his party machine were celebrating. '*À l'Elysée!*' they shouted, '*À l'Elysée!*' and Boulanger's colleagues – Maurice Barrès among them – urged him to follow the crowd.

Boulanger was scandalised; or affected to be so: 'Why do you want me to take power illegally,' he demanded, 'when I'm sure of being carried to power in six months by the whole of France?'

It was a missed opportunity, though calmer heads reckoned Boulanger's hesitancy made a kind of sense. It would not have been sensible to antagonise the gendarmes, the Republican Guards, or the regiments then garrisoned in Paris.

Better, Paul Déroulède agreed, to wait till morning, then go to the chamber and demand a dissolution of parliament. The success of their coup was a foregone conclusion; there was no need to break heads over it.

Come the morning, though, Boulanger still wouldn't act. Regimes born of coups d'état died of original sin, Boulanger complained. Why not wait for the general election?

Déroulède was beside himself. The entire point of Boulangism had been to revise the workings of the state, to create a plebiscite and a new kind of presidential government! And here was Boulanger queueing up to be a mere *prime minister*?

A few days later Boulanger, concerned as usual with his reputation, asked Déroulède what people were saying about him.

Déroulède replied bluntly, 'They say to themselves, "what sort of a broom is it that does not sweep?"'

Boulanger came unstuck very quickly. Had he stayed in the chamber doing his job, he might have survived, but he was by now addicted to the exchange of formless promises. Rather than take his seat on 1 February 1890, he took a train for Clermont-Ferrand; with him went his mistress, Marguerite. Five days later he emerged, but only so he could attend countless dinners and salons, hobnobbing with supporters who had begun to wonder exactly when he planned on delivering on his promises (and what were they again?)

At a banquet on 17 March in the city of Tours, Boulanger finally ran out of rope. At a dinner hosted by a Catholic deputy, Boulanger told the clerics what they wanted to hear: that 'a royal or imperial restoration, if such a thing were possible, would leave the nation as divided, more so perhaps, than it is at the present time,' and, equally, that 'the Republic must repudiate the Jacobin inheritance of our Republicans in power.' No to absolutism, then, and no to the Republic's legislative attacks on the clergy. The Church, in other words, should once again be allowed to lay its hand on the reins of political power!

This went down well enough as an after-dinner speech, but how, now, could Boulanger possibly say one thing to one group, without all the other groups getting to hear of it? No fewer than seven police brigades had been needed to handle the crowds that had turned up to greet him in Tours, and it took no time at all for the contents of his speech to reach the ears of the press. Overnight, Boulanger had become 'the Boulanger of curates' and 'the Jesuits' revenge'. Boulanger's royalist backers were appalled.

Boulanger left it to his party to sort out the muddle he had stirred. Barrès, campaigning in Nancy, did his best to paper over the cracks, painting his leader as another Bonaparte:

It is not at the side of monarchy that this country wants to go; it is attached to the republican form. The enormous effort of a right-thinking portion of republicans goes to give us a purified republic: a republic where all honest men can live, where the scoundrels will be unveiled, where the interests of the workers finally will be taken to heart. At the present time only General Boulanger is able, without reversing the Republic, so justly dear to the masses, to give France an honest government, as only he has known how to cry to all: Down with the thieves!

Once inside the chamber, however, such blandishments wouldn't play, and Deputy Barrès's modest rhetorical gifts showed up very badly. He did his work, but as a spokesman – and for a virtually leaderless party, at that – he fell short.

> M. MAURICE BARRÈS: Gentlemen, I come before you to plead the sacred cause of the worker, the proletarian. It is our role to grasp the ingenuous victory of suppressing the shadows. Thus, the worker is in the shadow of the dominant personality.
> *(Murmurs from the Centre: Explain yourself. We do not understand.)*
> THE PRESIDENT: I invite the speaker to clarify his thought.
> M. BARRÈS: Poor worker. Better his lot. *(Agreement from the Left: We have understood.)* Let him come to us, in our arms *(Protests from several benches)* and in our arms smile dreams ...
> M. CONSTANS: *(To his bench)* It will be difficult to reply to the previous speaker.
> M. DÉROULÈDE: I understand him. That is enough.

Albert Millaud wrote this magnificent parody of Barrès's parliamentary style for *Le Figaro*. The poor put-upon M. Constans is Ernest Constans, minister of the interior, and it is Constans who, in the cut and thrust of real events, had the last laugh. A fierce defender of the Third Republic, Constans used the six months' breathing space afforded by a hesitant

Boulanger to demolish everything he could of Boulanger's already gimcrack electoral machine. In March 1889, he proscribed Déroulède's Ligue des Patriots, and spread rumours that Boulanger would soon be charged with conspiracy to subvert the government.

His idea was to scare Boulanger out of the country, and sure enough, on 1 April 1889, Boulanger and Marguerite de Bonnemains, trailed by police, headed for the Gare du Nord. There, they boarded a train for Belgium. A nervous Belgian government asked them to leave, so they settled instead in London, where Boulanger was treated like an exiled head of state.

Return to Paris, his backers urged him. If you fight the next election from within a French prison, this short-lived martyrdom of yours will assure your victory!

But Boulanger did not want to leave Portland Place, and Boulangism was quickly wiped off the political map. The party's royalist backers finally saw sense, and Boulanger's funds began to dwindle.

'General Boulanger didn't deceive us,' wrote Arthur Meyer, the royalist press baron. 'It was we who deceived ourselves. Boulangism is failed Bonapartism. To succeed it needs a Bonaparte, and Boulanger as Bonaparte was a figment of the popular imagination.'

Boulangism evaporated like the morning mist. The playwright Jules Lemaître predicted that the moment the new chamber sat, the surviving Boulangists would all rebadge themselves as radicals, leaving 'no more than a single Boulangist deputy: M. Maurice Barrès. Yet, he is one for exclusively literary reasons understood by him alone.' He added that by spring 1890, Boulanger would have been offered a job as an agent for a London life insurance company.

In fact, Boulanger met a sadder end.

Now that Anne, Duchess d'Uzès's funds had dried up, the self-exiled couple could no longer afford their London life, with its servants, stables and Georgian townhouse. In October they moved to Saint-Hélier on the island of Jersey. Their new address: the Hôtel de la Pomme d'Or.

Maurice Barrès was by now working hard (and making a bit of a public fool of himself) in the new Chamber of Deputies. In November 1889 he led the effort to persuade Boulanger to return and lead. Bringing a delegation of twenty-one to Jersey – virtually all that was left of the party – he put a programme of social reform into Boulanger's hands. The left were sure to support such a programme, and the left could win them Paris in the 1890 elections!

But France's increasingly out-of-touch Bonaparte-in-waiting remained in Jersey. Come the Paris municipal elections, the party died a fairly ignominious death. A great many resignations followed. (Boulanger was outraged: 'I didn't believe that I would ever in my life witness such a shameful flight,' he declared.)

How had Boulanger managed to comprehensively bottle every political opportunity that a desperate nation had afforded him? In his epitaph for Boulanger, Arthur Meyer suggested that 'the horseman fell from his mount because love was riding pillion with him'.

Marguerite's health had never been strong, and in January 1891, she entered her final crisis. Pursuing treatments for TB and possible stomach cancer, the couple ended up in a rented flat in Brussels. There, Marguerite wasted away; she died on 16 July.

Boulanger toyed with suicide. He put a brave face on things

at first – brave and rather conceited: 'It would be a cowardly act to shirk what I consider my duty and to bankrupt the hopes of so many good people,' he told a friend. But he couldn't kid himself for long: 'I'm weeping like a child,' he wrote. 'I can't do anything, I can't work, I can't think. I would never have believed that one could live this way, with one's heart torn apart. Ah! If only there were a battle to be fought somewhere, a war, how willingly I would volunteer! What frightens and terrifies me is that my pain grows worse, more bitter, more difficult to overcome, with each passing day. Can I bear this grief? I begin to doubt it.'

He spent the last days of September 1891 sorting his affairs. On the thirtieth he took a coach to the Ixelles Cemetery in Brussels, sat up against Marguerite's tombstone, and shot himself in the head.

CHAPTER THREE

In 1897, some years after Boulanger's death, Maurice Barrès finally hit on a way to articulate the feelings of lingering hurt and betrayal that now consumed so many of his countrymen.

The novel *Les Déracinés* was an instant hit, though it wasn't at all what readers of his 'Cult of the Self' novels might have expected.

Barrès has packed away the knotted syntax and obscure image-making of his symbolist period, in favour of something dense, dry and sociological. After so many youthful essays spent burying Balzac, there is something oddly Balzacian – or at any rate old-fashioned – in this tale of seven friends, up from the province of Lorraine to take Paris by storm.

They've arrived in the city at the invitation of Paul Bouteiller, their old philosophy teacher, a charismatic radical with a head full of German ideas and ideals. Under Bouteiller's cosmopolitan influence, the friends try, each in their own way, to conquer Paris.

But Paris is savage: it chews them up and spits them out. The wisest of the seven head home. The best of those that remain – and that includes Barrès's mouthpiece here, Francois Sturel – take responsibility for their own failures. Others drift into anarchy. The poorest do worst (Barrès was always clear-eyed about poverty and its moral toll). Mouchefrin and Racadot, both scholarship boys, end up murdering a rich woman for her jewels, so as to get Racadot's political paper out of debt. The scaffold looms.

The trouble is, Bouteiller, himself a scholarship boy, has led his students up the garden path. Rather than imbue them with the traditions and virtues of their native Lorraine, he has instead stuffed their heads with Kant and other Germanic pretensions, as if 'they might some day be called upon to do without a mother-country.'

Professor Bouteiller is Barrès's thinly fictionalised portrait of Auguste Burdeau, who taught him philosophy at school between 1879 and 1880. Burdeau was indeed a scholarship boy, and later rose to become a government minister. Barrès never forgave him this impudence.

Bouteiller, the cosmopolitan teacher whose teachings have uprooted his pupils' minds, is a literary type. The 'pernicious professor', you can find him in Paul Bourget's *Le Disciple* (*The Disciple*) and *L'Etape* (*The Stage*), and in Miguel de Unamuno's *Amor y pedagogía* (*Love and Pedagogy*).

By 1902, Barrès has become even more explicit. In his book *Scènes et doctrines du nationalisme* (*Scenes and Doctrines of Nationalism*) he says that men like Bouteiller 'decerebrate' the nation. Ignoring the instinctive faith of the masses, they teach an 'absolute truth' instead of the 'French truth'.

This line of thinking will lead nowhere good.

Barrès's seven friends, chewed up and spat out by a city in which they cannot set down roots, are victims of *over-education*.

The idea may raise one's hackles, but look at the figures. There's a paragraph in *Les Déracinés* that refers to the plight of graduates looking for teaching posts. At the time referred to, 730 graduates in Sciences and Letters were competing for six teaching posts each year. 'Have you calculated how many graduates, each one remarkable and full of appetites, come to Paris every day?' asks the real-life banker Jacques de Reinach, springing up in Barrès's fiction: 'There's your danger: the overproduction of merit.'

Gustave Le Bon could not have put this more eloquently. Two years before the publication of *Les Déracinés*, in *La Psychologie des foules*, Le Bon looked out at a massively disrupted social world and wondered what would happen if you just kept applying more and more education to it. 'The acquisition of knowledge for which no use can be found,' he wrote, 'is a sure method of driving a man to revolt.'

'The mass of the indifferent and the neutral has become progressively an army of the discontented ready to obey all the suggestions of Utopians and rhetoricians. It is in the schoolroom that socialists and anarchists are found nowadays ...'

Barrès was not so apocalyptic. He believed that the right leader – an authoritarian, above ugly party politics and vested interests, and motivated by what was good for the national soul – could organise and redeem the forces of popular dissatisfaction.

In *L'Appel au soldat*, a sequel to *Les Déracinés*, Sturel and his surviving friends learn of General Boulanger's defeat. It is a devastating moment, but Sturel refuses to be downhearted: 'Boulanger is but an incident,' he cries; 'we'll find other "Boulangisms"!'

Meanwhile Le Bon's bleakest predictions of anarchist Armageddon edged ever closer to fruition.

The first anarchist attack on French soil was innocuous enough: in June 1881 some wag attempted to blow up the statue of Adolphe Thiers, first president of the Third Republic. But then an unemployed weaver got it into his head to shoot a doctor. Anarchist intellectuals decided that this was 'retribution for capitalism', and spent their days dreaming up paper atrocities: in Lyon in 1883 one journal was encouraging the dynamiting of bourgeois restaurants, churches and religious schools.

Finally, blood began to flow. Two waves of dynamiting and assassination swept across France. In March 1892, a gravedigger and accordionist styling himself 'Ravachol' set off bombs in the Boulevard Saint-Germain, the Caserne Lobau, and the Rue de Clichy. He met the guillotine promptly enough, but then someone targeted the restaurant where he was apprehended.

Six months later police removed a bomb from the offices of the Carmaux Mining Company, only to have it blow up in their faces; five gendarmes died. On 9 December 1893, a working man on his uppers called Auguste Vaillant threw a bomb into the Chamber of Deputies – incredibly, no one died – and after his execution a graduate student, Émile Henri, 'took revenge' by tossing a bomb into the Café Terminus at the Gare Saint-Lazare. And on it went. 20 February, the Faubourg Saint-Jacques; 15 March, the Madeleine; 4 April, the restaurant Foyot. On 24 April, the carnage moved to Lyon; and in June an Italian anarchist murdered the president, Sadi Carnot.

In the absence of another Napoleon, France desperately needed a standard to gather round.

A simple unifying idea.

Having spent his youth and young manhood defending his precious ego from 'barbarians', Barrès believes national identity can best be encouraged 'by means of hatred of our neighbours'.

The point here is not so much sabre-rattling (though that will come) as protection for the French working class. Barrès has campaigned in favour of protectionism, hoping to put 'some patriotism into political economy' and protect French labour from the competition of foreign workers and the innovations of German industry.

Why is Barrès's anti-German jingoism not enough for him? Why must he embrace antisemitism into the bargain? The thing about Barrès's hatreds is that he thinks he's in control of them. He thinks they're *tactics*.

'The crowd has always needed a battle cry to be rallied; it wants some cry of passion which will make abstract ideas tangible ... Hatred ... is one of the more vigorous sentiments which produced our civilisation.'

When the crowd howls against the Jews, Barrès explains in 1890, 'it is "Down with social inequalities!" they really mean. What do they care about the 80,000 Jews of France?'

The Jews are just the lightning rod for legitimate social resentment. Harness antisemitism properly, and you can mobilise against social inequalities!

That's the wonderful thing about antisemitism: it's simple. Everybody understands it. Who doesn't understand hate? It has appeal across all levels of society, and speaks to every (well, nearly every) vested interest. 'Boulangism must be antisemitic precisely in order to be a party of national reconciliation,' Barrès explains in *L'Appel au soldat*.

The other thing about antisemitism, of course – the downside – is that it comes in only one strength. You may pretend you're only a *mild* antisemite, a *tactical* antisemite, and the next morning you wake up – as Barrès did in 1898 – inveighing against internationalism, cosmopolitanism, progress, global commerce, and all the other 'unverifiable fictions which have issued from the imagination of a few messianic Jews'. (He could as easily have said 'the imagination of a few German industrialists'. But he didn't.)

The whole Dreyfus mess began in 1894, when the French Army discovered that secret military information had been received by the German embassy in Paris. A short investigation pointed the finger at a serving artillery officer, Alfred Dreyfus. A dossier of incriminating documents was waved around at his court martial, though in the end just one document was used to convict him, and Dreyfus was duly sent to 'Devil's Island', the French penal colony of Cayenne.

There the affair might have rested, only then came a new head of counter-intelligence, Colonel Picquart, and he discovered that the real traitor was another officer entirely, Major Ferdinand Esterhazy, and that most of the evidence against Dreyfus had been forged.

The case was far from clear-cut – Esterhazy had just been court-martialled and acquitted – and in the confusion Dreyfus's few supporters were taking the case to the public. Zola wrote an open letter. Anatole France signed it, and Charles Péguy, and Guillaume Apollinaire, and Marcel Proust, and Georges Sorel, and Claude Monet, and soon Zola's campaign had acquired more than 3,000 signatures, all from the great and the good.

Barrès refused to sign.

How did he contrive to place himself on the wrong side of this affair? Perhaps he didn't understand the stakes. At the time it was still possible to write off the Dreyfus business as a squabble over legal irregularities. And Barrès certainly had no reason to side with Zola's new socialist friends, who were making such a public fuss about the business. These were the very men who had let him down so badly at the Neuilly-Boulogne elections of 1896. By backing a second candidate (who just happened to have very deep pockets), they had lost Barrès his seat.

But Zola's letter wasn't just impassioned; it was researched. And there were so many charges fabricated against Dreyfus that for him to be cleared would discredit the entire army. The moment the letter was published, on 13 January 1898, Barrès had a stark choice: back Dreyfus, an innocent man; or back the state.

The matter really was that clear-cut.

In the last months of 1897, before Zola's letter was even published, antisemitic crowds had been rallying in every major French city against the Dreyfusard campaign. In the widespread violence, Jewish property had been destroyed and Jews attacked.

In the three weeks following the letter's publication, seventy antisemitic riots broke out across France. In Paris, university students poured into the Latin Quarter to protest *against* Émile Zola. On the Place de la Sorbonne, hundreds of law students chanted 'Out with Zola! Down with the Jews! Death to the kikes!' and set a bonfire going.

In Algiers, where every municipal council was controlled by antisemites, and newspapers were rife with xenophobic attacks, the violence was worse. Around 160 Jewish-owned shops were looted and burned and two Jews were killed, while the army stood by.

The man who gained most from the violence in Algiers was Édouard Drumont, cofounder in 1889 of the Antisemitic National League of France and author of *La France juive* (1886), an extraordinarily long (1,000-page) forerunner to *The Protocols of the Elders of Zion*. Drumont's reputation had received a tremendous boost when the paper he edited, the violently antisemitic *La Libre parole*, broke the story of the Panama scandal (in which a great many Catholic patricians had lost their shirts). A convinced Catholic antisemite since his conversion in the late 1870s, Drumont was elected deputy in Algeria after a campaign that featured an illuminated sign, '*Mort aux Juifs*', hung outside his campaign offices.

Drumont's antisemitism was too strong for Barrès, and to his proposals of exile or confiscation for Jews in France, Barrès replied: 'We repudiate, detest these savage words ... the Jew is what you Christians have made him; what astonishes me is that he does not hate you more.' But he forgave his old friend soon enough, and dedicated his next novel to him.

Drumont and Barrès had met as young men on Paris's literary circuit. They used to go together to attend lectures by Jules Soury, professor of physiological psychology at the Collège de France. Soury hated Jews almost as much as he hated women – the one exception being his mother, whom he entertained nightly with a magic lantern and a barrel organ, playing 'Ave Maria', 'The Blue Danube Waltz' and the 'Mignon Song' on perforated cards.

Political antisemitism (Barrès), religious antisemitism (Drumont) and pseudo-scientific antisemitism (Soury) rubbed shoulders on those nights, and by 1898 their colours were muddled and inseparable. In May 1898 Barrès stood for the Chamber of Deputies on a ticket that was not so much pro-tectionist as plainly anti-Jew.

'For twenty years the [party political] system has favoured the Jew, the foreigner, and the cosmopolite,' Barrès declared, and argued that 'Jewish influence' should be reduced in proportion to their numbers. There were, after all, only 80,000 of them.

Barrès lost the election, but not because of his antisemitic turn. Indeed, for the people of Nancy, he proved not nearly xenophobic enough. At the village of Champenoux on 2 May 1898, his audience, egged on by the chairman, hurled all kinds of bizarre accusations at him. 'Had he not sought to run in Constantine, Algeria, and marry the daughter of the Bey of Tunis?' On cue, the lights went out and the audience

set upon Barrès and his campaign director Gaston Save. They
fled through a back door but they still had to reach their carriage, a street away. The mob beat them as they ran, knocking
Barrès to the ground several times.

Barrès's beating was florid evidence that the right was in
disarray. This wasn't a crowd (defined as 'a single physiology',
connected by 'ancient ideas that rustle in the mind like leaves
in the forest'). This was a rabble.

Wednesday, 11 July 1900. The sun is setting over the Colonial
Exhibition and in the Restaurant International du Trocadéro
the banquet is cleared away and extra candles are lit. Barrès
has eaten and drunk more than is good for him, and Henri
Vaugeois, co-founder of Action Française, stands to deliver
the final speech of the afternoon.

Vaugeois's group split very early from Barrès's Ligue de
la patrie française, which had proved a bit literary for them,
insufficiently focused, not 'antisemitic, anti-Masonic, anti-
parliamentary and anti-democratic' enough.

Like all liberal converts, Vaugeois has quickly acquired a
taste for blood: 'All of us here agree, I hope, on the morality,
the legitimacy of iron?'

Barrès clenches his fists under the table. Here we go.

'We have no hypocritically puritanical objections to it, do
we? It seems to us that one has the right to save one's country despite itself. It seems to us that there have always been
instances of virtuous violence in history, and that beating a
sick man bloody is better than letting him rot.'

Barrès is an old hand at this game. He smiles and nods. But
he's not a fool. '*Save one's country despite itself*'? Where, in
that horrid and chillingly arrogant formula, is there room for
any genuine love of one's *patrie*?

Barrès runs the gamut of his friends and extricates himself as politely as he can. He needs space to think.

Maurras accompanies him as far as the Pont d'Iéna. Everyone else is heading through Robida's Old Paris to the gate; the grounds of the Expo are due to close in less than an hour. With a concerned eye, Maurras watches the old, irreconcilable republican's stiff progress against the looming and dismal mass of Eiffel's tower.

Eiffel's site was consecrated the day before Boulanger fled France, which makes it a fitting symbol of Barrès's political odyssey.

Barrès looks up at the tower, the tallest and most tasteless man-made structure in the world. It could be worse. They could have decided to make the bloody thing permanent. And there was that plan, at one time, to wrap *la dame de fer* in a sailcloth dress. Just imagine: a fashionably dressed three-hundred-metre-high giantess with a revolving electric arc lamp for a head!

Barrès stuffs his hands in his pockets. He fears the Exposition's empire of unreality has crept far beyond the Porte Binet. This is the world the Exposition promotes and anticipates: a world ruled by intelligence, by finance and commerce, a reasonable world for intelligent men and, in the triumph of all this intelligence, all the more mad.

He takes out his notebook. In the shadow of massive buildings devoted to the army and the navy, he writes: 'The individual! His intelligence, his ability to grasp the laws of the universe – it's time to quell these pretensions. We are not the masters of our thoughts. They do not spring from our intelligence ...'

He has never, truth be told, been very interested in saving society, or in improving people's conduct. What matters to him – he is a novelist, after all – is how men understand and feel the world. What is useful for the life of the individual is to increase the number of his dreams. He longs for a politics in which it is 'only those truths that make us weep that lead us.'

Within the Pavillon de la marine, there's a complete collection of Prussian uniforms sent by the Kaiser. Everywhere: German optics, German chemistry, German fabrics, German shipbuilding. The German pavilion looks as though it's been made out of marzipan, but at the Galerie des machines, the *Volkish* homespun is put away and the gloves come off: German dynamos and German cranes dwarf everything and everyone.

Barrès's guts twist as he recalls Lorraine, and his father and his grandfather, and the German invasion, and how German troops, entering the town of Charmes in Lorraine in 1862, took both men hostage to prevent civilians from firing on their troop trains. How old was Maurice then? Eight? His breath comes not so easily, as he plumbs the depth of the wound he suffered that day.

A man scarred for life by memories of being herded into a local school by Bavarian hussars. That's who he is now, that's how he describes himself, and we have no reason to disbelieve him.

But memory is a strange business. He may be traumatised now, as he nears his forties. But he seemed remarkably untraumatised in his youth: the decadent dandy, chasing performances of Wagner's *Lohengrin* around Europe. The war that so traumatised his childhood receives not a single mention from him until 1902.

Is it possible that his wartime trauma was sustained after the fact? Might it, after all, be a bad dream he has given himself? An artefact of his politics, rather than its mainspring? A consequence, rather than a cause?

Especially here, among all this electrically illuminated

plaster futurism, Barrès feels as though he has come unstuck from time.

From this Parnassian perspective, three truths come clear.

That his hero Georges Boulanger was an obedient child of a bygone century, who believed that social and political problems were real, and could be solved by political action. That's why his scruples stopped him from marching on the Elysée on the night of 27 January 1889; they later made him a staunch opponent of antisemitism.

Next: that Barrès, who followed Boulanger, and believed in him, is fundamentally different from his hero. Barrès is a modern. Barrès and his fellows have understood that, in this dawning age of mass politics, the crowd is what matters, and how the crowd thinks, dreaming its way out of problems until they are made to vanish altogether. All it needs, for this to work, is someone to blame.

Third and finally, that the Dreyfus affair perhaps only brought to the surface what was already in Barrès's mind, and under Barrès's pen. There is, after all, that sequence in 1897's *Les Déracinés*, cruel and painful and, with hindsight, so dreadfully provocative, in which Francois Sturel, our hero, is confronted with a horrible crime.

A dear friend, a beautiful Armenian woman called Astine Arivan, has been strangled, bludgeoned with a hammer, stripped and decapitated.

Sturel discovers the killers. They are vile, they are savage – and they hail from Lorraine.

Sturel examines his conscience, attends a public ceremony that reminds him of his precious *terre*, his dear *mortes* – and he lets the pair go.

No doubt the exotic Astine was a victim. But what's one foreigner's life, against the good name of one's home?

GABRIELE D'ANNUNZIO

1863–1938

CHAPTER FOUR

i

He's at the top of his game. He's introduced a slew of headline-making artists to Paris (Enrico Caruso; Strauss with his *Salome*; Toscanini and the Met), not to mention he's been Mata Hari's booking agent for over ten years. But Gabriel Astruc is also a Jew, and he writes to the celebrated Italian Gabriele D'Annunzio (poet, novelist, dramatist) 'I am rather worried because a group of ladies representing the French aristocracy has written to me to voice the fear that Saint-Sebastien, religiously speaking, may give the impression of a profanation. And I do not want to be accused of having crucified the Saviour for the second time.'

Even for a seasoned hand like Astruc, D'Annunzio's *Le Martyre de saint Sébastien* is a colossal undertaking: a five-act, five-hour spectacle with sets by Léon Bakst, music by Claude Debussy, and a rare speaking part for the largely self-taught Russian dancer Ida Rubinstein, who, it is said (and with reason), has the best legs in Europe.

'My work is a work essentially mystic,' comes the reply, as D'Annunzio seeks to reassure the impresario, 'and it is unassailable from a religious standpoint. Furthermore, my dear Astruc, when Ida Rubinstein makes her appearance almost naked at the moment of the supplication, it will be too late to protest. The public will have been conquered by that time.'

D'Annunzio came to Paris to escape creditors back home in Italy, and by god he needs a hit. A number of likely projects have fallen by the wayside. With Richard Strauss he roughed out an opera about a day in the life of a Montmartre prostitute, but the German press got hold of it and whipped up a scandal. Then there was the one about the Children's Crusade, which will drag on until 1913, to no avail. The Wagnerian D'Annunzio and the dapper Puccini are miles apart, temperamentally.

The *Martyre* is holding up, and this is good, since it's a project much dearer to D'Annunzio's heart: a medieval religious mystery in which, according to D'Annunzio's secretary and biographer Tommaso Antongini, 'the most violent and unspeakable passions of the turbid and sinister epoch of the dying empire clash and coalesce with the invincible and victorious splendour of the dawning of Christianity.'

Sebastian is the third-century saint who Mauretanian archers, on orders from Roman emperor Diocletian, shot with many arrows, making him a prickly subject ideally suited to D'Annunzio's theatre of blood. D'Annunzio's musical collaborator Claude Debussy (who desperately needs the work to feed his new wife and child) explains to his friend Robert Godet, 'I needn't tell you that the worship of Adonis is mingled in this piece with the worship of Christ.'

Or one could just admit that the *Martyre* is all about the saint's legs: so long, so smooth, so athletic, so ephebic. D'Annunzio has been to see *La* Rubinstein's portrayal of the sadistic title character in Diaghilev's production of *Cléopâtre*. Afterwards he nipped backstage and declared himself to her, kneeling to kiss her feet and running his hands up to her knees. During the Ballets Russes's run of *Scheherazade*, he used to sit in the third row of the stalls to get the best possible view of her lower half.

The thing is – and this is going to cause some difficulty – the saint's androgynous pins weren't always Ida Rubinstein's.

Sebastian's legs originally belonged to D'Annunzio's lover, the French-Russian soprano Nathalie de Goloubeff. Years ago he took Goloubeff, whom he had met in Rome, to San Gimignano to see Benozzo Gozzoli's painting of Saint Sebastian. He wrote letters to her with lines like 'My suffering is like carnal magic, oh St Sebastian!' and she replied with 'calls to the archer who loved him – come to St Sebastian stretched on his burning couch.'

Since coming to Paris, D'Annunzio has conveniently forgotten that he promised Goloubeff that she could play Saint Sebastian. He's been trying to shake her off altogether, but she keeps turning up like a bad penny. At dinners near the airfield, where D'Annunzio hangs out with Paris's pioneer pilots, she starts the most appalling scenes. Pursuing her lover to Arcachon, where D'Annunzio is a guest of Romaine Brooks, she gets the wrong address and bursts, fuming, into a neighbour's house. Then she gets the right address and is caught scaling the garden gate.

Goloubeff excites people's pity, more than anything. Her lover's sexual appetites, and his successes, and his cold-bloodedness, are the stuff of legend. 'He sees no reason to be compassionate,' Antongini explains in his memoir of his old employer, 'and is capable of witnessing the most poignant manifestation of feminine sorrow with as little compunction as a dentist feels for a nervous patient.'

Brooks may be the only woman in Paris who isn't that interested in him. He amuses her more than anything. 'In heaven, dear poet,' she writes, 'there will be reserved for you an enormous octopus with a thousand women's legs (and no head).' Anyway, D'Annunzio needs to get some work done, so he's moved out of Brooks's chalet into his own much more modest accommodation (money really is very tight), a damp little house lost in the Moulleau forest. A few rooms remain occupied by two elderly gentlewomen and their lame niece who look as though they fell out of a Balzac novel.

D'Annunzio spends a great amount of his time playing the cad, but an even greater amount locked in his room working like a dervish. For as long as it takes to write the *Martyre* he wants no visitors and *no news* (unless it has to do with his mother, who's not getting any younger).

D'Annunzio writes, freely adapting the story of Sebastian from *The Golden Legend*, a collection of saints' lives written in the thirteenth century. Antongini's job is to tear up and throw away all distractions (bills, hate mail, solicitors' letters . . .)

Halfway through, they run out of money, and Antongini ('adopting the most sprawling handwriting of which I was capable') writes out what little yet exists of the *Martyre*. He uses the bulked-out manuscript to blag a thousand-franc advance from the long-suffering Astruc.

At long last, Ida Rubinstein receives a telegram: 'Play finished. I kiss your bleeding legs.'

The *Martyre* has a prologue and five very long scenes. The climax takes place in paradise. The episodes are disconnected; it's Debussy's job to tie them together with his music. He has only two months, and is suffering the first symptoms of cancer. With the help of the conductor André Caplet he brings it in under the wire: the hastily corrected score for Act V arrives page by page after rehearsals have begun.

Debussy frets that the music and the action lack coordination, and tells Caplet 'Please persuade Léon Bakst that paradise is a place known to one and all as being "dazzling"' – though what a conductor is supposed to do about the set design is anyone's guess.

Otherwise the rehearsals run smoothly – so smoothly, indeed, that the press has to make up its own stories: for example, how, after rehearsals, D'Annunzio and Ida Rubinstein recline in state like the figures on an Etruscan tomb while the chorus files past, smothering them with red roses.

For D'Annunzio, who has been accused in the past of polygamy, adultery, theft, incest, murder and cannibalism, this is small beer. If anything, this sort of rumour mongering reassures him. His age is beginning to tell. Worse, far worse, it is beginning to *show*. The other day, during rehearsals, an American woman came up and, having studied him through her lorgnettes, announced: 'You look, *maître*, as though you were carved out of old ivory.' He's barely fifty!

The *Martyre* is calculated to set tongues wagging. The epilogue, in particular, is wildly sadomasochistic. Saint Sebastian will not renounce his faith, and so, according to *The Golden Legend*, 'the archers shot at him till he was as full of arrows as an hedgehog is full of pricks, and thus left him there for dead'.

'Oh archers, if ever you loved, let your love be known through your steel,' exclaims Ida Rubinstein, practically naked and tied to a tree. 'I pray you, I beg of you – he who wounds me most deeply, that man loves me most deeply!'

And so they do. (A clever bit of stagecraft here.) 'More!' she cries, in her heavy Russian accent (they're working on that); 'More!'

It does no good: Sebastian's body absolutely refuses to die. 'Your love! Your love! Again! Again! Again! Again!'

The archers are becoming frantic (so is the audience) until, at last, one arrow goes shooting wildly off into the sky, rising and rising into the empyrean – and it pierces God.

The play, opera, spectacle, whatever it is, premieres at the Theatre du Chatelet on 22 May 1911. There are more than two hundred performers on stage, a hundred musicians in the pit, and an audience bored out of their minds. They're stuck there till after one in the morning. Marcel Proust prised himself out of his cork-lined room for *this*?

There are so many entrances and exits, no one has a clue what's going on. The choristers keep missing their cues, because they can't see the conductor. (Bakst has rearranged the blocking at the last moment to balance the colours of their outfits.) Rubinstein's mime is superb as always, but her accent is still too thick, and after four hours of D'Annunzio's poetry no one has the energy to even try and make out what she is saying.

It's not even bad; just overlong, over-complicated, overdone in every department. 'Very boring,' Proust sighs, and does not seek out its author, and this is as well, as D'Annunzio is already fast asleep in a neighbouring café.

You win some and you lose some in this business, but D'Annunzio can't afford the show to just die. Column inches equal advances. He does not *want* money – he is in no sense avaricious – but he certainly *needs* money, partly to satisfy his appetite for beautiful things and beautiful women and beautiful gestures, but mostly so he can settle his affairs and go home.

You can't manufacture a hit, of course, but D'Annunzio has been in this business long enough to know how to manufacture a scandal, which is the next best thing.

The Vatican has played along, placing D'Annunzio's works on the Papal Index of prohibited books a fortnight before the premiere. Cardinal Amette, Archbishop of Paris, has weighed in, reminding Catholics to avoid a show 'offensive to Christian consciences'. D'Annunzio stoked this one nicely, telling the archbishop: 'I have exalted the most ardent defender of the Faith. And the interpreter I selected for him is pure in her manners and gestures – as pure as a Perugino painting of Saint Sebastian ... Madame Rubinstein is, in a certain sense here, asexual. She is Androgyne. The shape of her body awakens no sense of the voluptuousness of love ...'

The bishop knows he's being needled, but keeps his nerve and the moral high ground: there is more sorrow than anger in his observation that 'Today, a sacred drama no longer has a mystic or religious meaning; it is given simply to divert and delight the spectators. The ancient notion is profaned.'

Syphilitic and debt-ridden, if D'Annunzio can't make people hate him (and he does so love his hate mail: his 'diet of frogs', he calls it) then he's just going to have to make people love him. So D'Annunzio, in a frankly desperate move, dedicates the libretto of the *Martyre* to Maurice Barrès.

Barrès hides his embarrassment but naturally, he's appalled. What a poisoned chalice to hand to a new and vocal member of the Ligue des Patriotes!

For some years, Barrès has been identifying ever more closely with the cause of the Catholic church. He's not much of a believer and never will be, but he is increasingly taken with the way the Church conjures a social world beyond party politics. Barrès is wedded more and more to this world: wordless, intuitive, unrational. 'One must not dream of setting up men in a rule which imposes happiness,' he writes, 'but of suggesting to them a state of mind which allows happiness.'

And now this visiting Italian wants him to publicly endorse a play he has not seen and has no intention of seeing, in which a revered saint is played by a woman (and a Jew at that); in which a representation of Christ's sacred shroud is waved about; and which ends in an irreverent depiction of paradise!

Refusal would only make things worse, but Barrès is not pleased to be shackled to this 'hymn to pleasure'. In his notebook, he writes to D'Annunzio a letter he feels no obligation to send:

> *You do not like to mingle with pure beings ... I do not wish to go where there are fevers. You offer me an excommunicated book, a fruit of your sad shores. I would have been like you had I not belonged to a country that has duties. You do not have a duty.*

The note of envy is clear. Barrès will never lose control of a yacht, or make love to a woman in a punt, or touch Ida Rubinstein's knees. Barrès is walled up in his public persona now: the deputy of the Seine, a safe seat more or less handed to him in 1906, which he will retain until his death in 1923.

There's much about D'Annunzio's life to envy, if not admire. The salons fight for him. People point him out in the street. Theatrical managers and restaurant proprietors tremble in his presence. Up close, though, you'd have to be blind or besotted not to notice the price D'Annunzio has paid for such a storied existence.

André Gide meets D'Annunzio at a luncheon organised by Jacques Rouché, and writes: 'The eyes are without goodness, without tenderness; the voice cajoling rather than caressing, the mouth cruel rather than greedy; the forehead handsome enough. Nothing in him suggests genius rather than talent. Less will than calculation; little passion, or only of a cold kind.'

*

In the spring of 1910, Maurice Barrès is invited to a dinner given in D'Annunzio's honour at the Pré Catelan, in the Bois de Boulogne. Here, the two celebrated writers are to be formally introduced.

Barrès tries to get out of it. 'At first glance, I can't say that I like this Italian,' he tells Count Robert de Montesquiou, a friend of the hostess, Cécile Sorel.

He has reasons. For a start, D'Annunzio's a degenerate. Just a few months into his visit, and he has already bedded half of Paris. At the Hotel Meurice he has decided the Pompadour-style lift is some sort of public bedroom, and has outraged the barely-teenage Princess Bibesco there, not once but several times.

Then there are the borrowings, though it's possible Barrès is flattered by those. Andrea Sperelli, hero of D'Annunzio's novel *Il Piacere* (*Pleasure*), might have sprung wholesale from one of Barrès's 'Cult of the Self' novels, being 'completely saturated with Art, to the extent of being corrupted by it, demanding only experience and more experience of the sharpest kind to feed it.'

Montesquiou's blandishments win Barrès over in the end; consequently he has to sit through an entire evening of D'Annunzio being D'Annunzio. In a setting that might have been chosen for him (as indeed it has: all crystal and damask and swagged silk and silver) D'Annunzio sets about his charm offensive – and never did those two words marry so well.

He assumes at first a sort of brotherly familiarity with Barrès, because they both work in front of reproductions of the Sistine Chapel. Then, all of a sudden, he's turned and set about seducing his poor hostess, Cécile.

She's amused at first – she's a comic actress, so is forearmed against this sort of thing. Eventually she grows uncomfortable, and from out the rubble of her composure gasps something inane about the tenderness of the meat.

D'Annunzio stares at his plate. 'You know,' he says, with an embarrassed little smile, 'the flesh of newborn babies very much resembles lamb.'

The women rise to it, of course. 'You frighten us!'

'It can't be true!'

'Where did such frightful things take place?'

'In Africa,' says D'Annunzio, dead-pan as a gambler, 'a very long time ago.'

The actress Mme de Bartet tries to seize back the initiative, declaiming passages from his novel *Il Fuoco* (*The Flame*), but the author's in his element now. Barrès misses exactly what he says to Cécile – something atrocious about sex and lions – but it's enough that D'Annunzio's 'official' mistress, poor Nathalie de Goloubeff, sitting at the other end of the table, bursts into tears.

Cécile is aghast, but D'Annunzio's control of the table is ruthless: he tells the company not to worry themselves, since his lover 'is beautiful only when she cries.'

Barrès isn't so much scandalised by this carry-on as annoyed. Also, bored. He knows this playbook backwards: it's the studied insolence of the decadents of twenty years ago; of Wilde and Péladan, but without their tragic sense. 'He is a little Italian with a hard face,' is his judgement of D'Annunzio: 'a businessman looking for providers of funds.'

ii

By 17 March 1861, the warring factions of the Italian peninsula had finally managed to fashion themselves into a modern-looking state. But then, of course, they had to manufacture a sense of nationhood. The name of Massimo d'Azeglio, made prime minister of Sardinia in 1849, is immortalised daily in student essays, his having written in his memoirs that 'we have made Italy. Now we must make Italians.'

This was no simple task: the history of the peninsula was one of rivalry between city states and dynastic wars involving Austria and Spain, all conducted under the shadow of the down-but-far-from-out Holy Roman Empire.

The Italian peninsula had been battling Austria since long before the creation of Italy. This, in an era before decent roads, was driven largely by Austria's need for access to the sea.

Venice enjoyed a hegemony over the Adriatic stretching back to the ninth century. In Dalmatia's northern reaches, however, sat the sea port of Trieste, and Trieste was proudly (and profitably) Austrian. It had flourished under the Hapsburgs for centuries, and had several times thrown off attempts at occupation by Venice, its powerful southern rival.

The Austro-Hungarian Empire was absolutely reliant on Trieste's trade connections, and this made Trieste an obvious target for empire builders who wanted to clip the Austro-Hungarian Empire's wings. In 1796, under Napoleon's brief but foundational rule over the Italian peninsula, Trieste became Italian.

Napoleon's downfall gave Austria the opportunity to take back Trieste and secure Dalmatia once and for all. Austria seized territory at the expense of Italy and though in time the emerging Italian state would take back Veneto and Friuli, Austria held on to Dalmatia.

Italy's special sense of grievance over the loss of Dalmatian territories is more easily understood when looked at through the youthful eyes of Gabriele D'Annunzio.

He was born in Abruzzo, the son of the mayor of Pescara, on 12 March 1863. (This made him just a couple of years younger

than his country.) The region in which Gabriele grew up had
little knowledge of Italy's interior. Cut off from Rome by the
Apennine Mountains, Abruzzo was as remote as any region
further to the south. (In Pescara, fishermen and sailors were
considered racy and cosmopolitan.)

Abruzzo was a coastal country that had Venice for its political centre. Commercially and culturally it faced east, across
the Adriatic, to Albania, to Greece – and most especially,
to Dalmatia.

The newly unified Italy of 1861 felt far from complete to
the people of Abruzzo. And the campaign to recover lost
territories in Dalmatia lay at the heart of Italy's burgeoning
irredentist movement, which gathered pace even as Italy was
brought to birth.

Venice had been a major maritime power for over a mil-
lennium, and Rome for the thousand years before that. If you
were a proud Italian, particularly taken with the task of nation-
building, you could find traces of 'Italian' trade, culture and even
administration pretty much anywhere in the Mediterranean
that kept historical records. The irredentist movement, which
had once wanted to recover places like Trentino, eventually
ended up demanding the 'return' of the southern Tyrol, Trieste,
Corsica, the island of Malta, Nice – even Switzerland.

There was never the remotest possibility that Italy would
go to war with Europe over such wild claims. What enraged
the irredentists was not so much the futility of their inflated
cause, as the way successive governments, rather than attempt
to recover lost corners of actual Italian homeland, preferred to
cut a figure in elite European circles by attempting to turn Italy
into a colonial power.

They couldn't even conduct these adventures successfully.
In 1881, Italy fumbled away its influence in Tunisia, effectively
handing that territory to the French. The crisis in relations with

France that followed led the government into a pact with, of all people, Austria and Germany; that unlikeliest of alliances, the Triple Alliance signed in 1882, had stuck in Italy's craw ever since.

To outsiders, Italy's democratic experiment seemed to be going well. The civil service did its work quietly, and graft was minimal. William Gladstone, who could remember a peninsula rife with informers and overrun with police, was fulsome in his praise: 'The keen intellect and quick mind of this ancient people has at last made it possible for them to adopt methods elaborated by others, and to use them naturally, without effort.'

English visitors remarked that Rome was becoming just like London. Invited to the countryside, they found themselves hunting foxes with Milanese cotton-mill-owners. French statesmen noticed their Italian hosts dressing just like they did. German bankers gladly advised bankers in Milan. An Austrian cavalry instructor was paid to improve Italian horsemanship.

All might have come right in time, and the state grown ever more stable, had Prime Minister Francesco Crispi not insisted on ignoring public opinion, and pressing Italian hegemony, first on Eritrea, and then on Somalia on the south side of the Horn of Africa. In 1896 Crispi – by now exhibiting all the signs of mania – persuaded his generals to extend their occupation into Abyssinia. Their 15,000-strong expeditionary force was promptly annihilated at Adwa – the first time ever a European colonial power had been defeated by the locals.

That catastrophe could only further alienate the Italian people from their political class.

D'Annunzio was not an intellectual; he was a provincial writer who left Abruzzo for Rome in 1888 to write for the gossip columns.

That D'Annunzio chose Rome for his first literary adventures is itself significant. Had he been a natural politician he would have headed to Milan or Naples, where the important papers were. Instead, he headed to Italy's café capital. In Rome, you went to the opera not to watch the productions (which were rubbish) but to spy on the audience.

Though his early decadent poetry earned him a literary reputation, if you really want to understand D'Annunzio's foundational influence over the Italian mind, you're better off looking at the fashion and society columns he wrote for the Roman newspapers, and especially for the *Cronaca Bizantina*, whose bizarre mix of aspirational lifestyle pieces, pretentious codswallop and low scandal D'Annunzio would make his own.

D'Annunzio learned to articulate and feed the aspirations of a comfortably off, largely female audience. By following D'Annunzio's journalism you learned what to wear, and where and when to wear it; what to look at, and what to say about it; what to read.

With a hardly detectable change of pace or style, D'Annunzio's society-column writing found its way into his books. Novels like *Il Piacere*, for example, are a sort of shop window for fashionable ideas, and even then ideas are hardly the point. They play second fiddle to things. The most memorable scene in *Il Piacere* is a long, sumptuous, enraptured description of a house auction.

It was through his popular novels that D'Annunzio arrived at his unique and powerful rhetorical style: disentangled from mere opinion, full of symbols and sentiment.

The would-be aristocrat, gossip and coffee-house fashion maven believed that the Italian genius would reach its acme not in collective action, but through a process of 'natural selection', by which a select group of artists, poets and intellectuals would emerge to perpetuate and improve upon Italy's ancient heritage.

That D'Annunzio counted himself first among this self-selected elect goes without saying. More interesting is his social Darwinism. Gone is the idea that Italy falls 'naturally' under the rule of one component: the Piedmontese, say, or the Vatican.

No, the best Italians, according to D'Annunzio, emerge from strife and struggle. They are a mixed people – proletarians from Milan, serfs from the colonised south – all sharing an arena, all vying for domination. This is why they are so strong: they are mutts.

The rough lineaments of this argument are apparent in the 'Hedge Speech' D'Annunzio the parliamentary candidate delivered in the summer of 1897 to the rural workers and small landowners of his native Abruzzo. And he would deliver this same speech, in different circumstances, and with different stresses, for the rest of his life.

Here was a speech that at last gave Italians permission to feel proud of themselves – a speech that made Italians.

Like Barrès, a young D'Annunzio was drawn to party politics. He hated electioneering with a passion. Returning from campaigning in 1897 he wrote: 'My nostrils are still full of a sour human stench.' But he went on, in a letter to his publisher, Fratelli Treves, 'This may seem to you a strange undertaking, at odds with my art and principles ... But, my friend, the world must see that *I am capable of everything.*'

He stood for his home district of Abruzzi, and won the seat, as an independent: 'The Candidate for Beauty'. What exactly did he stand for? The 'politics of poetry', he explained. No one was entirely sure what he meant. He clarified: 'I am beyond right and left, as I am beyond good and evil.' (He was quoting Nietzsche, though he had yet to read him.)

What D'Annunzio actually offered the electorate was what he always offered, in the course of a long, prolific, chaotic life – extra helpings of D'Annunzio. The halls in which he campaigned were hung with posters advertising his novels and poems, as he converted literary fame into political influence, turned influence into increased sales, and sales back into political power.

By the lights of party politics, D'Annunzio was a dilettante, a joker. His domestic parliamentary career was short. His biographer Anthony Rhodes sums it up as 'two speeches and a duel'. But a dangerously large contingent (everyone from the starving Milanese to Sicilian smallholders to the queen herself) considered that party politics was the real joke, when election days resembled carnivals, and every borough was rotten with corruption.

Dysfunctional parliaments were a growing problem across Europe, and while liberals sought solutions in programmes of rational reform, an increasing number of radicals were looking for ways to jettison the problem altogether.

The idea of liberal democracy promises benign oligarchical rule. You vote for the candidate who, through birth, education and natural ability, knows more about the world than you do, and this candidate will then selflessly represent your interests in debate among all the other elected *cognoscenti* in parliament.

This reality fell short of the ideal in Italy, as it fell short everywhere else. The sketches D'Annunzio made of the failings of his own chamber may stand for all: 'Every time I entered the hall I would see fifteen of my colleagues drowsing on the benches. Occasionally, one of them would bestir himself and deliver a funeral monody which lost itself in vacuity.

The Marquis Visconti-Venosta, coming momentarily out of his twenty-year-old sleep, spoke of a certain country called Italy, in the tones of a dying man commemorating someone long dead.'

Meanwhile – and though the idea of colonies in Africa filled most people with either bemusement or contempt – ministers continued to agitate for an overseas colonial empire.

In 1911 Libya was a poorly defended, undeveloped zone into which, colonials argued, southern Italy's fast-expanding population might emigrate – and they sold this idea to irredentists by reminding them that Libya was a former territory of the Roman Empire.

Newspapers used this argument to whip up a storm around the prime minister, Giovanni Giolitti, and when French and German forces came close to clashing in Agadir, a Moroccan Atlantic port, Giolitti took advantage of the diplomatic distraction to start a squabble with the moribund Ottoman Empire. On 29 September 1911, Italy declared war, and its forces quickly occupied the towns of Tripoli, Derna and Benghazi.

The conflict with Turkey, which lasted a year, was extraordinarily ugly: Arabs killed more than 500 Italians in one engagement, and nailed their mutilated corpses to palm trees. The Italians retaliated by massacring thousands.

Read the Italian newspapers, though, and you would think a second Rome had arisen. The journalism of Enrico Corradini (later an ardent follower of D'Annunzio) was especially bellicose, and turned unopposed landings on rocks in the Aegean into major headlines and occasions for national celebration. The philosopher Benedetto Croce despaired of the press's 'Dionysiac delirium, investing the slightest incidents of the war and the most trivial manoeuvres with dazzling images and monstrous hyperboles.'

In Paris, caught up on a wave of Italian nationalism, D'Annunzio began composing his own contributions to the war effort, the *Canzoni della gesta d'oltremare* – verses in praise of Italy's adventures overseas.

'My first mission,' he wrote, blindsiding his liberal Parisian friends, 'is to teach my people to love their own country; the second is to hate unto death Italy's enemies, and always to fight them.'

In Italy the *Corriere della Sera* ran D'Annunzio's verses in bold type over an entire page. Better yet, it paid for the privilege.

The *Canzoni*, rich with visions of national grandeur, full of heroic exaltations, elicited packet after packet of admiring letters, some signed (often with a heartfelt, illiterate 'X') by whole companies of soldiers. They became for the army a sort of sacred text. One colonel, obtaining the manuscript of one of them, kept it in an improvised shrine next to his regiment's colours.

They came for D'Annunzio's bellicose patriotism, and stayed for his prose style. Count Sforza complained that his officers, 'honest, simple and modest men', had begun substituting D'Annunzian prose for their normal short, sober and caustic field reports: 'If they had to draw up an order-of-the-day after a battle, they suddenly felt they must produce an ornate, swelling prose, imagining it an appropriate style for the occasion.'

The *Canzoni* were ostensibly verses celebrating Italy's brave actions against the Turks, but inevitably, their focus widened to embrace (if that is quite the word) all Italy's perceived enemies.

Chief among these was the power to which Italy was bound by alliance – not that the Triple Alliance of 1882 between Italy, Germany and Austria had ever been a love match.

D'Annunzio's *Canzoni* were more blunderbuss than rifle, casting threats, aspersions and vitriolic insults at whole nations. (D'Annunzio always knew how to play to the cheap seats.) He achieved his personal best with 'The Song of the Dardanelles', a poem so insulting to Emperor Franz Joseph and so provoking to the Austrian people that the Italian government stepped in to prevent its publication. (It does not do to describe an ally's head of state as a hangman and an angel of death and his nation as 'the two-headed eagle which vomits back up, like a vulture, the undigested flesh of corpses.')

The *Corriere della Sera* turned down D'Annunzio's masterpiece. Treves, who was editing the *Canzoni* into a book, *Merope*, begged him to cut the vilest lines. And D'Annunzio, seeing an opportunity to turn scurrilous folderol into a political *cause célèbre*, agreed to the cut – just so long as it was accompanied by the notice: 'This song of the deluded fatherland was mutilated by order of Cavaliere Giolitti, head of the Italian government.'

Parisians had had D'Annunzio down for a decadent; a superannuated literary celebrity, a leftover of symbolism. When they discovered D'Annunzio's political side – his mystic nationalism, his sense of Italy's manifest destiny, his invention of the doctrine of *mare nostrum* (the idea that the Mediterranean was historically and culturally Italy's backyard) – they were disconcerted. Some even took it upon themselves to get angry, as though D'Annunzio had been flying under false colours. Hugo von Hofmannsthal was one of these: he had been a great admirer of D'Annunzio until the poet started writing fulsome verses about Italians at arms. 'You were a poet, an admirable poet,' he complained in an open letter. 'Now I do not see a poet, or an Italian patriot. I see Casanova whose luck has run out, Casanova at fifty, Casanova tricked up as a warrior, in a badly fastened dressing gown.'

The image Hofmannsthal conjures here is irradicable, but quite frankly the laugh's on him. He hasn't been paying attention. D'Annunzio's international celebrity may rest on French translations and French critics – it's why he used Paris as his bolthole in the first place – but his reputation in Italy is a quite different beast, shaped as much by his political work as by his poetry.

In Italy, D'Annunzio the columnist and politician had developed ways of speaking to the crowd without *speaking down* to the crowd. With the *Canzoni*, he was playing to his huge Italian audience, not his narrow Parisian one.

He impressed at least one Frenchman, though. Reading the *Canzoni*, Barrès convinced himself that D'Annunzio was a man of duty after all. The pair met more often. They became friends. Then they became close friends – ever closer as the prospect loomed of a war in Europe.

iii

Every generation imagines that the wars it wages will end all wars; meanwhile it struggles to comprehend why the wars of fifty years ago were fought at all.

Decimated by two hundred years of ostensibly religious conflict, Europe had by the late eighteenth century evolved a rational and contained style of warfare, involving semi-professional armies, pitched battles, complex strategic manoeuvres, the preservation of production and the avoidance of collateral damage. Next to the bloodbath of the Thirty Years War in Germany (which, incidentally, carried a death toll twice that of the First World War) the wars of the Napoleonic era had been positively gallant – and about as lethal as big game hunting.

The system of treaties that maintained peace in Europe was very obviously crumbling – witness the seemingly endless stream of international conflicts that were breaking out: in 1905 the Moroccan Crisis, in 1908 the Bosnian Crisis, then the Agadir Crisis (1911), the Tripoli Crisis (1911), the First Balkan War (1912), the Second Balkan War (1913) ...

The First World War was the war to end *those* wars, and all the others that would follow if the boil was not lanced. The author Walter Flex – a sort of German Rupert Brooke – positively looked forward to the exercise of 'those virtues of sacrifice, fortitude, and boldness that constitute the essence of the combatant and that make of the fighting man, with all his excesses and brutality, a type infinitely superior to that shrewd sybarite who finds in the cult of peace the best expression of his sensual concept of life.'

Parliamentary institutions across Europe were proving shaky, their members lazy and venal, their constituencies embittered or just plain uninterested. What better fillip than a war to foster national identity and promote democratic involvement?

'Now, God be thanked Who has matched us with His hour,' exclaimed Rupert Brooke at the war's outbreak. The Italian writer Giani Stuparich burst into tears at the news, he was so happy. For the French novelist Drieu la Rochelle, the news came as a marvellous surprise, the unexpected fulfilment of his youthful ambitions. 'Rejoice, friends! that we are alive,' exclaimed the German poet Bruno Frank.

In 1914, anyone with a shred of historical sense regarded modern warfare as a glorious alternative to war as it had been, war as had decimated and all but destroyed the continent. The End of History beckoned (as it always does): 'History is trembling to its very roots,' wrote the Spanish philosopher José Ortega y Gasset, 'its flanks are torn apart convulsively, because a new reality is about to be born.'

Maurice Barrès welcomed the First World War as a salvation for the French spirit. He noted how, on 4 August 1914, the day of France's declaration of war on Germany, quarrelsome deputies spoke as one. 'Even if it involves the awful lessons of battle, I've wanted nothing more than for Frenchmen to unite around the great ideas of our race,' he wrote. 'So they have. Blood has not yet rained upon our nation and war has already made us feel its regenerative powers. It is a resurrection.'

How are we to take the seam of blood running through Barrès's rhetoric here – or Ortega's, or, heaven help us, D'Annunzio's, who's by far the most sanguineous of the lot?

Come 1927 – and with the benefit of a decade's hindsight on the Great War – the French essayist and philosopher Julien Benda detected, in the growing bloodthirstiness of their pronouncements, a lot of intellectual self-interest. He wrote:

> About 1890, the men of letters, especially in France and Italy, realized with astonishing astuteness that the doctrines of arbitrary authority, discipline, tradition, contempt for the spirit of liberty, assertion of the morality of war and slavery, were opportunities for haughty and rigid poses infinitely more likely to strike the imagination of simple souls than the sentimentalities of Liberalism and Humanitarianism. The pose of a Barrès or a D'Annunzio strikes naïve persons far more than that of a Michelet or a Proudhon.

This is well-argued. Any modern account of the satanic marriage that evolved between mass-murdering dictators and intellectuals starts here.

But the bloody seam we trace in Barrès and D'Annunzio runs deeper than their self-interested posing. Throughout the war, these writers will cheer at the spilling of blood, and rate it a welcome sight. The odd thing is, though, that as the war progresses, it isn't their enemy's spilled blood that they cheer the loudest: it's their own.

In his 'Song of the Dardanelles' of 1912, D'Annunzio lovingly described how Italian soldiers were crucified by the Turks, their bodies cut with an axe, 'with the skin of the chest pulled down like a red apron', their eyelids 'stitched with needle and twine', his purpose here being, obviously enough, to foment revenge, and answer blood with blood.

On first acquaintance, 'Fluctibus et fatis' ('Waves and Fate'), the first of the *Canti della guerra latina* (*Songs of the Latin War*) D'Annunzio composed between 1914 and 1918, seems of a piece with that earlier effort. The urgency is the same, the stakes just as high. The enemy, the '*homme teuton*', is infamous and aggressive, cruel and rapacious, driven by an infernal urge to expand towards Italy: 'A perpetual, malevolent hunger pushes them from their sandy plains and their icy forests towards our vineyards, our orchards, our sparkling cities, our clement coves.'

To resist the invasion of these animals, frothing with lust, is to ensure the survival of the Italian race. The alternative is slavery and eventual extermination.

But something fundamental has changed. The moment battle is joined, the hostile forces of the *Canti* become weirdly abstract: 'the enemy', 'the barbarian', often just 'barbarism', as though blood were being shed in combat with a cosmic force, rather than a body of men.

The blasphemous monster who burns churches, breaks altars and profanes holy relics remains just that: a monster; a shadowy existential threat.

The *Canzoni* of 1912 had been full of real places, real enemies, real steel, real corpses. The battlefields of the *Canti* are metaphorical; their trenches are the freshly ploughed fields of

Elysium, in which Italian men are sown and reaped in earnest of their rebirth through sacrifice and pain:

What horror and what death
and what new beauties
are everywhere scattered in the night?

There's no let-up in the flow of blood – 'We have no other value but that of our blood to be shed' – but the hatred has been put away; transformed, until it looks something very much like religious devotion.

The war depicted in the *Canti* is at its heart a spiritual struggle, a transcendental experience of national purification. It is the death and rebirth of the Latin people.

D'Annunzio and Barrès each discovered in the other this same religious conviction, and so their friendship was cemented, at last and for life. They met often in Paris as the city emptied out and prepared for German invasion: two midwives of history in bloodied aprons. D'Annunzio recalled:

It was just before that victory on the Marne which checked the invasion into France. Those were the days of the sorrowful retreat which followed on the defeat of Charleroi. I read that day on Barrès's drawn face all the anguish of his country. That expression, revealing so much more than personal anxiety, the expression of a man lost entirely to all but the fate of his country, has remained unforgettable to me ... It is a beautiful thing that in the war and in life, two men, made to be rivals, should have understood and loved each other as Barrès and I did.

D'Annunzio moved to the Marais and laid in supplies and prepared to witness the epiphanic transformation of France, his friend's beloved homeland. He followed 'the great tanks that crossed the white street, heading northwards, full of sacrificial flesh and drunken singing, all the men sitting in their red uniforms as if in their own carnage, like that battalion that had been mown down, shot through the groin, lying on the ground in a congealed puddle and still crying out.'

Separating fact, fiction and rhetoric in D'Annunzio's notes at this time is difficult, because D'Annunzio worked so hard to transform these notes, as fast and efficiently as possible, into publishable verses and reportage for papers both in Italy and in France. 'Every night I went to the gloomy stations to greet the wounded, to adore the splendour of blood, to breathe the strength and power of the people, to feel the heroic quiver deify the undernourished mass.'

Did D'Annunzio visit the cathedral at Reims, within range of the German guns, even as it burned? Probably not: D'Annunzio's response to the sight, as he recounts it, is too pat, too quintessentially D'Annunzian. 'I assure you the Cathedral reaches its perfection in flames. One longs to fall on one's knees before such a miracle ... I trust you will take advantage of this unique occasion, to remove from your church some of the frightful paintings which deface its interior ...'

But we know he approached the front, spoke to soldiers, explored the ruins, and 'the nearer danger was, the more beautiful and strong the city appeared to me.'

D'Annunzio's frustration may be imagined, that he was separated thrice over from a war that fascinated and inspired him: first by age (he was now in his fifties); then by circumstance (he was a foreign visitor; this was not his war); finally, by nationality: to D'Annunzio's exasperation, Giolitti's government had declared that Italy would remain neutral.

Neutrality was far from nothing: Italy was after all a

signatory to the Triple Alliance and should by rights have been prepared to enter the war on Germany's side.

But Italy had been looking for a way to renege on the treaty for as long as Austria had been building up forces in the northern Adriatic; and with even greater urgency once Archduke Franz Ferdinand, heir to the Hapsburg throne of Austria-Hungary, had publicly proclaimed his intention to make war on Italy 'one day'. (His assassination in Sarajevo on 28 June 1914 saw Roman crowds literally dancing in the streets.)

German diplomats struggled to keep Italy on side while Austria sought satisfaction for Ferdinand's assassination. On 28 July, and without Italy's agreement, Austria declared war on Serbia. This broke the stipulations of the Triple Alliance. At the time, the affair was minor and even the treaty seemed mendable.

Within days, however, Europe was at war.

D'Annunzio knew Italian neutrality was untenable over the long term, and he believed the only honourable course for Italy was to enter the conflict as soon as possible, on the 'Latin' side. In 'Fluctibus et fatis' he writes about the extraordinary character of Latin culture, 'necessary for the good name of the world, its pulse implicit in every living being'. Presumably, by this logic, the realm of the Teutons is the land of the undead, and sure enough D'Annunzio goes on to characterise the war as a racial struggle between civilised men and animalistic savages:

> We are the valiant, we are the chosen;
> and we'll crush the hideous horde.

D'Annunzio's bellicosity was rather more welcome in Paris now: '... the admirable talent of the author of *L'Innocente* and *La Giaconda* is here displayed in all its force and vigor,' declared the *Figaro* of 13 August 1914, publishing D'Annunzio's 'Ode for the Latin Resurrection'. 'We are convinced that our great Latin sister will welcome with profound admiration this cry of fraternal heroism in honour of France from Italy's greatest living writer.'

This was indeed the reaction that mattered most to D'Annunzio: how would his Italian public respond? He was once again heavily in debt, and desperately needed his creditors to back off so that he could go home and get some work done.

A dinner on 14 February 1915 with Giuseppe Garibaldi, grandson of the great patriot and revolutionary, offered D'Annunzio a tantalising vision of the role he might play, if he could only scrape together enough for the fare home. Giuseppe, like his grandfather in 1870, had raised a battalion of Italian volunteers to fight beside the French. That night, the pair swore that if Italy failed to side with France within six months, they would lead Garibaldi's legionaries to Rome.

One day in March, D'Annunzio threw aside a letter from Ettore Cozzani, editor of the nationalist journal *L'Eroica*, full of the usual blandishments – 'Dear Maestro' and all the rest – and begging a piece for a forthcoming issue on 'all that is noblest and greatest about Italy.' Also something about a statue . . .

It took a couple of days for the penny to drop. Reading more closely, D'Annunzio learned that Cozzani was friendly with the mayor of Genoa, and the mayor had invited him to give a speech at Quarto, a small port to the east of the city. They were unveiling a statue there of Giuseppe Garibaldi.

This was D'Annunzio's golden opportunity – and to think he had nearly missed it! – to return to Italy, not as a private citizen and notorious debtor, but arm-in-arm with Giuseppe's son, the hero's great-grandson, Peppino Garibaldi, and surrounded by a thousand red-shirted volunteers – the very battalion that had been fighting heroically on the Western Front!

It seemed too good to be true. 'There will be any amount of applause and there will be banquets which will terminate in the drinking of countless toasts. And quiet having been restored, we will sail back again to France,' D'Annunzio told Antongini – more to manage his own expectations than those of his long-suffering secretary.

He need not have worried. Thousands waited at the quayside to greet him. Cheering, they followed him to the Hotel du Parc, and the next day, in front of the statue of their national hero, they listened, rapt, as their national poet delivered his first speech on Italian soil for four years:

O blessed be those who have more, for they will be able to give more, to be more ardent ... Blessed be those who, waiting and trusting, have not wasted their strength, but preserved it by means of a warrior's discipline. Blessed be those who shunned sterile loves to keep their virginity for this first and last love of their life. Blessed be those who, having opposed the event [the war], will accept in silence the supreme necessity and will want to be, not the last, but the first ...

He is talking about death, about sacrifice, about war. And, yes, he is lifting every other word from the Sermon on the Mount.

Blessed be the youths who hunger and thirst for glory, for they will be sated. Blessed be the merciful ones, for they will cleanse a luminous blood and bind a shining grief. Blessed be the pure of heart, blessed be those who will return victorious, for they will see Rome's new

visage, Dante's forehead crowned anew, Italy's trium-
phant beauty.

D'Annunzio's poetry of hate is transformed now into a
poetry of sacrifice and love, and is all the more deadly for it.
('Blessed are those who, discovering a deep-seated hatred in
their breast, will tear it out with their own hands.' Fear, above
all other enemies, the one who thinks he's doing you a favour.)
     The crowd's response is as ecstatic as D'Annunzio expects
it to be. He knows what he is doing. He's been practising this.
     For a while now, he's been developing a rhetoric directed
specifically at a Catholic audience. The Pope has come out
strongly against intervention, so it's the Catholics he needs to
convince. (The more secular and politically minded Italians
are already at least half-persuaded that Italy should go to war
on the Allied side.)
     The Quarto speech is of a piece with D'Annunzio's *Canti*,
whose 'prayers' and 'psalms', full of religious symbols, images
and biblical quotations, talk of holy war, the sanctified fatherland and Latin culture. The last of the *Canti*, 'Il Rinato',
describes Christ reborn amid the trenches.
     This is not, nor is it meant to be, any sort of political
argument. It is, instead, D'Annunzio's way of persuading the
masses without patronising or brow-beating them: a rhetoric
of myths and symbols rather than facts. Poetic and melodramatic, D'Annunzio's rhetoric of enthusiasm will tap into the
desire of the crowd to be led in some great action.
     The crowd is aflame and cheering. D'Annunzio considers
his speech a job well done. On the way to his mother's house
(it's five years since he saw her last) he composes a telegram to
his new blood-brother, Maurice Barrès: 'Our two countries
have become one! From French Flanders to the sea of Sicily is
one land. It is poetry which makes this marvellous gift of our

militant friendship. *Fidem signemus sanguine.* Your brother Gabriele.'

D'Annunzio's poetry is powerful fuel. Desperate for D'Annunzio's visible support, activists in Rome send a telegram to Antongini: 'Expect you for dinner nine o'clock Wednesday evening – numerous friends will meet train.'

It sounds a pleasant and useful excursion. When Antongini and his employer reach the city, they find a crowd of 80,000 there to greet them. Quietly catching a train back to France is no longer an option. It'll be a miracle if they ever get out of Rome's train station. In the end they have to make a run for it. They enter the Hotel Regina by the kitchen door and, once up in their rooms, D'Annunzio decides he had better speak to the throng in the street below.

From his balcony he declares, 'Italy is no longer a *pension de famille*, a museum, a horizon painted with Prussian blue for international honeymooners – but a living nation!'

The applause lasts several minutes. Nor do the crowds disperse. They're in six figures by the time D'Annunzio speaks from the Capitoline Hill, and now his task is clear: to humiliate the government into entering the war.

It's pointless. The government has already signed the secret Treaty of London and is committed to entering the war on the Allied side. But that's the problem – the treaty's *secret*. Keeping the news from Austria also keeps it from the crowd, and D'Annunzio, quite unaware, goes at that crowd with all guns blazing: 'Sweep away all the filth!' he cries. 'Into the sewer with all that is vile!'

A week later, when Italy enters the war as an ally of France, it will look for all the world as though this was D'Annunzio's doing; that he shamed the government into it; that it's D'Annunzio himself, not the government, who's shaping the fate of the nation.

Perhaps he is.

The riot following D'Annunzio's speech at the Capitol leads to several celebrity arrests. Marinetti says he has thoroughly enjoyed 'the multicoloured, polyphonic tides of revolution in the modern capital.'

Also cooling his heels in police custody is the newspaper editor Benito Mussolini.

CHAPTER FIVE

i

Benito Mussolini liked to characterise himself as a 'primitive', partly because he liked to play the thug, but mostly in honour of his radical working-class father, and an upbringing that had turned this child from the sticks into one of the best-read men in Italy. (When Hitler, on his uppers, was painting postcards, an equally broke Mussolini was writing and selling essays on philosophy.)

Born on 29 July 1883 and named in honour of three revolutionaries – Benito Juárez, Amilcare Cipriani and Andrea Costa – Mussolini enjoyed a double baptism, inducted both into socialism and irredentism. Benito worshipped his father, and treasured the copy of Victor Hugo's *Les Misérables* that his father read aloud to the townsfolk of Dovia when they gathered in a cowshed on winter evenings. Benito's mother, a schoolteacher, had virtually no influence over the boy's considerable learning.

There was indeed something authentically 'primitive' (or protean, at any rate) about the politics of the Romagna, the region in which Mussolini spent his childhood. The spirit of the French Revolution of the 1790s had found fertile ground here. All through the early 1800s, the 'Carbonari' network of secret societies staged conspiracies and uprisings against despotic monarchs. The region supported the republican Mazzini, but when he condemned the Paris Commune uprising, they abandoned him in droves.

Anarchism and socialism dominated the political conversations of Romagna. The refugee Russian anarchist Mikhail Bakunin visited in 1864, preaching land to the peasants and urging the workers to seize the means of production. 'My socialism,' Benito explained years later, 'was born Bakuninist, in the school of my father's socialism.'

He was horribly bullied at a religious boarding school in Faenza. The other pupils were not too bad, but they took their lead from the monks who were their teachers. The monks did not hesitate to punish Benito for his father's radicalism; they dubbed him 'the son of a people's leader' and beat him regularly, then wrote him school reports that talked about his 'sharp intelligence and singular memory' before complaining that 'his character is anything but stable.'

Mussolini was one of those gifted working-class and petit-bourgeois children who were being educated into unemployment. ('There's your danger: the overproduction of merit!') Soon enough he took his place among literally tens of thousands of primary and high school teachers who couldn't find a job to save their lives and had to emigrate.

Many ended up in Switzerland. Mussolini was among them, rubbing shoulders with political exiles of all stripes, but especially radicals from Russia and Italy. In 1909, his socialist activism got him expelled.

At nine in the evening on 6 February 1909, twenty-six-year-old journalist Benito Mussolini arrived in the town of Trento in the German Confederation, a few miles north-east of Lake Garda. (Anything rather than teach, which had been his living since he got chucked out of Switzerland.)

It was snowing, it was dark, it was dull, and though the snow and the dark abated during Mussolini's eight-month stay, Trento never shed its dullness.

The young man enjoyed a good political scrap, but the all-against-all politics of this place drove him spare. 'There are three daily newspapers here,' he wrote to the lawyer Torquato Nanni: 'Catholic, socialist, national-irredentist. Their journalistic activity boils down to reciprocal castigation.'

He did manage to find worthwhile work, though, and friendship, with Cesare Battisti, who had just established the socialist newspaper *Il Popolo*. The paper reflected the peculiar politics of the organisation he had founded: linked to the Italian Socialist Party, but at the same time agitating for the region's unification with Italy.

The impoverished Trentino region was culturally and linguistically Italian. Until 1796 it had been an episcopal principality, before changing hands between France and Austria three times in five years. It became part of the Tyrol. It was ceded to Bavaria. In 1810 it became, all too briefly, a part of Napoleon's united Kingdom of Italy. Three years later the kingdom collapsed and two years after that, on 9 June 1815, it became part of Austria again. Since 1818 it had belonged to the German Confederation.

Battisti was a member of the Social Democratic Workers' Party of Austria, a representative to the Tyrolean Landtag assembly at Innsbruck, a member of the Austrian Imperial Council at Vienna, and saw no contradiction between socialism and his irredentist campaign.

Supporting such a mercurial boss gave Mussolini plenty to do, and for little pay. In the end – and with what exasperation one can only imagine – he had to offer French lessons just to make ends meet.

One duty was to assist Battisti in editing *Il Popolo,* which meant writing a feuilleton for the weekly supplement – which is how Mussolini ended up trying his hand as a writer of romances. He was good at it, too. His serial *The Cardinal's Mistress* ran in instalments from 20 January to 11 May 1910 and for all that Mussolini later disowned it ('a novel for seamstresses and scandal,' he called it, 'a nasty book') his tale of two lovers, caught up in violence and deceit, bagged at least ten translation deals.

The kindly shade of Alexandre Dumas hangs over the action, which takes place in seventeenth-century Trentino. A cardinal and prince, Carl Emmanuel Trent, loves his mistress of twenty years, Claudia Particella, with great faithfulness and sincerity. Alas, the world is out to get them, and in particular the cardinal's own chief of staff. It's heady stuff, and one contemporary has it that 'the seamstresses, the workmen, the shop assistants of the lovely town at the foot of the mountains rushed every morning to open the newspaper, ready to weep a river of tears over the new floods of ink.'

The Cardinal's Mistress very likely kept *Il Popolo* afloat. When Mussolini threatened to kill it off, Battisti was adamant: 'For goodness' sake don't kill me! It's time for the subscriptions to be renewed. Just a bit more breathing space: the quarter's almost up!'

It was also on-message – a dramatic and accessible working-out of *Il Popolo*'s anticlerical agenda. It was surely more persuasive than the paper's meticulous dissections of church interference and working-class politics.

The eight months Mussolini spent titillating the washerwomen of Trentino made for a pleasant diversion, but the sojourn had a much deeper impact, as revealed in 'The Trentino from a Socialist Point of View', a piece published in 1911 in *La Voce.*

It is one of Mussolini's best articles, and certainly one of the most deeply thought-out contemporary studies of irredentism.

Though persuaded by Battisti's arguments that Trentino belonged culturally and historically to Italy, Mussolini, a good socialist, saw no way that such a unification could be brought about – not, anyway, in a fashion that would benefit the ordinary citizen.

'Trentino is resigned to accepting its fate and does not think about "freeing itself",' Mussolini wrote. 'Its soul is not revolutionary; it is conservative, and averse to anything new. It submits, but it does not create.'

Mussolini wasn't against Battisti's nationalism; he just didn't think it enjoyed a popular mandate. Unless you could raise the consciousness of the working class, there seemed no prospect of success.

This was a long way from the position held by more doctrinaire socialists, who said that national identity was a primitive superstition that should be obliterated.

After his sojourn in Trento working for Battisti, Mussolini returned home to Italy, and to Forlì, where he was offered the editorship of the local socialist newspaper. It was a solid base from which to develop a political career, and his journalism was already in demand. As correspondent for the socialists' national newspaper *Avanti!*, his rise to prominence in the Socialist Party was assured.

Socialism at this time was split between those who, like Mussolini, considered it a romantic political adventure, and those who looked upon it as a species of science. Mussolini was still, in his own mind at least, 'a primitive'.

I am a citizen of another epoch. There was a time in which

socialism was not practical, it was not industrial, it was not co-operative, there were no banks; there was a time when socialism meant selflessness, faith, sacrifice and heroism. I speak of thirty, forty years ago. Then there were Socialists who had fallen in love with an ideal; today there are Socialists — a lot of them, even the majority – who have fallen in love with money. Italian Socialism has now become a huge accounting ledger of giving and getting.

Romantic socialists like Mussolini were drawn to the kind of politics espoused by a young Neapolitan revolutionary, Arturo Labriola. As Labriola saw it, whatever class held sway arranged specific institutions to foster its own interests. Some of these interests were purely defensive; others existed to smooth relations with the other classes and resolve disputes as peaceably as possible. According to Labriola, the bourgeoisie had created parliaments in this spirit: parliaments allowed everyone their small victories, while making major, transformative reform quite impossible.

The working class, once it took charge of the state, would have no use for parliaments. Workers would promulgate their own policies through trade unions. The unions would seize control of production, then federate within and among nations, all the while avoiding the empire-building of elites.

Labriola's brand of politics, which went under the name revolutionary syndicalism, attempted to steer a workable path between capitalism and socialism. In place of the unending conflict between workers and bosses, syndicalism would foster association and consensus. Under syndicalism everyone, whether worker or employer, would belong to a corporation, and these corporations would ensure that everyone's interests were fairly represented.

With hindsight, such a system smacks of totalitarianism.

Indeed, from these roots, totalitarianism would flourish until it dominated twentieth-century politics.

But all this lay in the future. At the time, what Mussolini admired most about revolutionary syndicalism was its espousal of romantic violence. General strikes, industrial sabotage and factory occupations offered a much more direct route to working-class victory than parliamentary reform. Plus there was some truth to Labriola's complaint that parliamentary systems tend to co-opt, if not corrupt, their own would-be reformers. Mussolini could see how Italy's socialist movement was being transformed into just another parliamentary clique.

Nevertheless, Mussolini was not a syndicalist. He thought it was naive of the syndicalists to think that they could prevent elites from dominating their movement. As a socialist, Mussolini did not expect elites to simply dissolve. He expected them to work on behalf of the people. At least until the rosy dawn of the communist utopia, it was necessary to foster elites and train them up to leadership roles, raising the consciousness of the working class.

This is pure Leninism. Vladimir Lenin was adamant about elites: he demanded unlimited power for a small body of professional revolutionaries, trained exclusively for one purpose: shaping the working class into a blindly obedient force held together by military discipline.

But you didn't have to be a Leninist to think this way. Across the political spectrum, you could find well-argued treatises which explained why democracy, the rule of all, tended ineluctably towards oligarchy – the rule of the few. Mussolini, an insatiable reader, read them all, from Le Bon to Vilfredo Pareto (whose theory of elites was, according to Mussolini, 'perhaps the most brilliant sociological theory of modern times') and from Sorel to Roberto Michels, a

German-born Italian sociologist whose 'iron law of oligarchy' was to shape political assumptions for more than a generation. *Political Parties*, published in 1911, contains Michels's starkest expression of his 'law': all forms of organisation, no matter how democratic they are at the beginning, will eventually develop oligarchic tendencies, especially in large groups and complex organisations.

Some of these writers were cultural reactionaries like Le Bon. Some were left-wingers like Sorel (whose drift to the extreme right seems inevitable only in hindsight). Some were and remained on the extreme left: it was from his reading of Peter Kropotkin's *Words of a Rebel*, which he translated for an anarchist newspaper, that Mussolini learned the political necessity and historical importance of small groups.

Against this all-points barrage of received wisdom, the revolutionary syndicalists had only trade unionism to offer. And much as Mussolini might have sympathised with the syndicalists, he could never believe that trade unions on their own were capable of replacing the entire state apparatus.

Regretfully, but without protest, Mussolini observed the expulsion of revolutionary syndicalists from the Italian Socialist Party – an adjustment that took three years to effect, ending in 1906.

Once Italy went to war with the Ottoman Empire over Libya in 1911, the split between the socialists and the syndicalists became altogether starker.

Syndicalists supported the war. They thought it would help modernise the country. Their founding philosopher, Labriola, thought taking Libya was a perfectly sensible step towards Italy's economic maturation. How could Italy ever hope to be communist if it failed to become capitalist first?

Socialists, on the contrary, considered war a product of capitalist avarice, there to serve a narrow caste of profiteers. Patriotism was a sort of opium, a vacuous and illegitimate sentiment, conjured only to narcotise the working classes.

'Self-esteem, national pride, a sense of homeland are all commonplaces, rhetorical devices for intoxicating the public, but if we do not tear away this rosy veil of ideology, we shall find that it means defending economic interests with the brutal use of armed force.' So, anyway, wrote Mussolini on 7 October 1911, with the war in Libya already begun.

The more bellicose Enrico Corradini's articles became, the more ludicrous D'Annunzio's patriotic verses, published in the *Corriere della Sera*, the more exasperated Mussolini grew with 'the poets, short story writers, dandies, pimps and card sharps' whose brand of nationalism had 'arisen in Italy as a caricature of French nationalism'.

'We would have understood and perhaps viewed with sympathy an internal nationalism, a democratic and cultural movement for the improvement, attention and renewal of the Italian people,' Mussolini wrote, commenting on the Italian Nationalist Association's proposed programme of imperialist expansion. 'They should think that, before conquering Trento and Trieste or Tripolitania, there is Italy to conquer, there is fresh water to be taken to Puglia, there is the drainage of the Agro Romano, justice to be given to the South and illiteracy everywhere!'

These were sensible arguments, passionately expressed, and Mussolini rose in the estimation of his colleagues. By February 1912, and at the end of five month's jail time for anti-war activism, Mussolini was the undisputed *de facto* leader of the Italian Socialist Party.

He was too clear a thinker, however, to ever imagine that the Libyan War had vindicated the position of his own party.

The fact was, the longer it went on, the more popular the war in Libya became. Mussolini noted with concern that his own party seemed incapable of getting to grips with this situation. All they did was fulminate.

Mussolini encountered at least one convincing explanation for the war's growing popularity. This came from an old acquaintance, a man he knew from his days in Switzerland, the syndicalist Angelo Olivetti.

In November 1911, writing in his own paper, Olivetti had set out the basic philosophical difference between the socialists and the revolutionary syndicalists.

The socialists were lightweights, whose efforts to patch up the existing system of government only made it more tolerable, and so delayed the advent of revolution.

Syndicalists, on the other hand, were doing all the real work, by mobilising the workers.

War was perhaps the quickest and most efficient way to get the workers contributing to the country's large-scale industrial and economic development. And the socialists' humanitarian scruples were simply getting in its way.

We have no evidence that Mussolini was persuaded by this argument. We do know that he was troubled by it. He spent the five months of his prison term researching the issue. Olivetti's argument was closely echoed by Georges Sorel, who had spent the last few years edging towards a closer and closer rapprochement with the French nationalist leagues. Of all people, *Charles Maurras* now counted Sorel an ally! How on earth had this happened?

Five months in jail was as good as a sabbatical for Mussolini. His favourite writer during these months was Georges Sorel.

On 7 July 1912, at the Italian Socialist Party's congress at Reggio Emilia, Benito Mussolini officially took the reins of the Italian Socialist Party. From the stage of the Ludovico Ariosto Theatre, he denounced the wing of his party that had dedicated itself to parliamentary reform. He summed up their effort in three words: 'absenteeism, indifference and inaction'.

'In expelling the reformist deputies,' reported an admiring Vladimir Lenin, visiting from Kraków, 'they have restored the integrity of the movement.'

To Lenin's way of thinking, the party that had expelled its syndicalists was now getting rid of its rightists. Mussolini was turning the leadership of the Italian Socialist Party into a proper revolutionary clique.

Lenin was not wrong. Mussolini himself said:

Rather than the obedient, submissive, idiotic flock that follows the shepherd and scatters at the first cry of wolves, we prefer the small, resolute, daring nucleus that understands its own beliefs, knows what it wants and marches straight towards its goal. We want the forty sections of our Federation to be Socialist sections, not just a club to meet at on Sundays.

But Mussolini was more sympathetic to the syndicalists than Lenin realised, and when on 1 December 1912 he was appointed editor of *Avanti!*, his more streamlined, more energetic, more focused Socialist Party was invited to entertain some increasingly heretical ideas, as their paper was turned into a forum for syndicalist theory.

Mussolini had grown into something unprecedented: an able writer who was also an able politician. His secret was that he was not a traditional journalist. He had learned his style from his father, whose soapbox speechifying had steered well clear of anything ambiguous, abstract or even mild. The trick, as Mussolini learned it from his father, was to take an idea and personalise it, dramatise it, and turn it into something that would stir a crowd.

Most politicians avoid specifics because, in an ever-changing world, it's all too easy to give hostages to fortune.

Mussolini took the exact opposite attitude. In an ever-changing world, you could not only afford to be inconsistent – you were duty-bound to be inconsistent. To constantly reformulate your own position, to be always re-appraising what you thought: this was the only honest politics. Anything else was prevarication.

Mussolini considered it his job as a journalist to express strong opinions, 'only for one day, but intensely so.' It wasn't so much that he thought the facts did not matter. Rather, he saw that facts did not exist in isolation. Nor did ideas. Both existed to be put at the service of some dramatic argument. Either that, or they vanished.

Mussolini was no more interested in 'balance' than is an attorney in a courtroom. A newspaper was not there to report or to record facts. It was not there to educate. It was not there to facilitate an exchange of ideas. It was a weapon: 'Any party without a daily newspaper in the busy and quick world of today, is a party without a voice, without followers and without a future.'

Mussolini's ambitions for *Avanti!* were that it should become 'propaganda aimed at Socialists'.

The idea that socialists should propagandise other socialists had the more complacent party members clutching their pearls, but 'ours is not a paradoxical claim,' Mussolini insisted, 'since it is Socialists more than anyone else who have the duty to know how one must act if one is to call oneself a Socialist and how one must fight for the triumph of our ideas.'

Mussolini wanted to fashion an elite socialist 'priesthood' – a revolutionary vanguard that would replace the masses' political confusion with religious faith.

This was a world away from the bloodlessness of conventional socialism.

Marxists believed that history was a book already written, and a story whose outcome was inevitable. But if the course of history is set – and feudalism gives way to capitalism gives way to socialism gives way to communism, and there's nothing anyone can do to avert that happy catastrophe – then individual morality means nothing. Mussolini viewed with horror the ethical vacuity of this position.

Mussolini believed in free will, as Marx and Engels never had. He argued that it was the work of socialists to inspire the working classes to construct the future social order.

In *Avanti!* on 18 July 1912, just days after his triumph at the Reggio Emilia congress, Mussolini wrote:

> Why should the proletariat care about understanding socialism, the way you would understand a theorem? Can socialism really be reduced to a theorem? We want to believe in it, we must believe in it, humanity needs a credo. Faith moves mountains because faith gives the illusion that mountains can be moved. Illusion is perhaps the only reality in life.

This is an exhilarating vision. Coming from anyone but Benito Mussolini, it might convince any young progressive.

The problem was not Mussolini's thinking, so much as his idea of how to promulgate that thinking. Mussolini was growing to political maturity under the strong influence of Le Bon and Olivetti and other thinkers for whom public opinion was a threatening novelty. Their anxious attitude shows up readily enough in Mussolini's own writings: 'Our epoch, unique in history – has seen the appearance of the anonymous and multitudinous masses ... on the world scene ... [The] anonymous and immense mass ... is the human material for the new history.'

Here, Mussolini acknowledges the existence of mass opinion, but he seems unclear what to do with it, beyond wanting to shape it (somehow) to his will.

The idea that mass opinion was so much clay to be shaped is a commonplace of the time. Olivetti, writing in 1909, describes revolution itself as a struggle between contending elites 'over the inert body of the anonymous masses'.

Mussolini's crowd psychology was no more sophisticated. He was steering by the handwavings of people like Le Bon and Pareto, the man who in 1901 asserted that 'the greater part of human actions have their origin not in logical reasoning but in sentiment'. Such statements are not so much wrong as dangerously incomplete. With only them to steer by, any political thinker is pretty much bound to end up advocating elitist management of 'the mob'.

Mussolini started out stressing, with Sorel, the 'moral reality of socialism', rather than its mere inevitability. So far, so good – but both men ended up thinking like puppet masters, studying how to influence collective behaviour.

The day that Serbian nationalist Gavrilo Princip assassinated Archduke Franz Ferdinand of Austria and his wife, Mussolini was on holiday. Called back by his newspaper, he assumed, as many did, that the incident could be contained: a 'distressing but understandable' episode in the struggle between ethnic nationalism and the centralising power of the Hapsburg Empire.

Soon it was clear that Europe was becoming embroiled in war, and Mussolini revised his opinion. Under such circumstances, he said, socialists would have to pack away their dreams of a borderless proletarian Europe. It was unreasonable to expect the German Socialist Party not to support the emperor in the war, and once that happened, the association of socialist and labour parties gathered under the Socialist Second International would fall apart.

Sure enough, as the war gathered pace and governments of national unity were formed, the greater part of the international socialist movement dissolved.

On 31 July, a nationalist fanatic murdered Jean Jaurès, leader of the French Socialists. Even under such extreme provocation, the party did not, as expected, take to the streets; shortly afterwards it joined the government.

In Germany, Social-Democrat leaders voted for war loans in Parliament; anything to defeat the czar, they said.

Mussolini was never too proud to change his mind, and what could be more mind-changing for a socialist than the sight of pan-European socialism fragmenting under the threat of international conflict? 'A European war is inevitable,' Mussolini wrote, 'and France will be the first victim if the more civilised peoples do not unite to save her. The defeat of France would be a mortal blow for European liberty.'

This was strong stuff, coming from the head of a party in large part defined by its pacifism.

'Internationalism is dead,' Mussolini wrote on 4 August 1914. 'Was it ever alive? It was an aspiration, not a reality. It had an office in Brussels and published a soporific report in three languages once or twice a year. Nothing more.'

But his party felt differently. Italian socialists would not abandon their position of absolute neutrality so easily, even when Germany attacked neutral Belgium.

Mussolini was exasperated. 'I would like it if the Socialist Party did not lock itself in an *a priori* opposition to the government,' he wrote. Conditional neutrality made sense, so as not to let Italy get dragged into the war on the Austrian side. But what if things got worse? What if France came under attack? Did Italian socialists really think it was not their duty to defend France?

As leader of the party and editor of *Avanti!* Mussolini was duty-bound to defend the party's principle of absolute neutrality. This he did in public, diffidently, while arguing internally for a more flexible policy.

'The struggle would be to make these gentlemen of the party understand these elementary realities,' he complained. 'They are great revolutionaries in word only; but they fear losing their little positions of power and their own skins.'

Others on the left, with less onerous responsibilities and less to lose, argued openly for intervention in the war. Alceste De Ambris, Filippo Corridoni, Angelo Olivetti and the revolutionary syndicalists came out strongly in support of entering the war on the Allied side.

De Ambris (who, like Mussolini, had opposed the war in Libya) thought that intervention on behalf of the Allies in the current war would be truly revolutionary: a heroic defence of civilisation, liberty and social revolution. On 5 October, he split from the intransigent Socialist Party and produced a manifesto, calling for intervention on the side of Britain and France.

Mussolini's position, defending neutrality in public while attacking it in private, could not be maintained for long. On 18 October 1914, he published an article in *Avanti!* arguing that Italy's absolute neutrality was dangerous and reactionary.

The concept of the nation still existed, he said. Pretending that 'the proletariat have no fatherland' was just silly. What about the socialists in Belgium and France, defending their nations? Even Peter Kropotkin, the father of anarchism, had felt compelled to defend his country!

Mussolini was not (yet) saying that neutrality should be abandoned altogether – only that the party's stand on 'absolute neutrality' was dogmatic and unreasonable.

Even this was too much for the party, and on 20 October Mussolini resigned as editor of *Avanti!*

Rejecting the paper's offer of a termination payment deprived him of funds, as well as a mouthpiece, but just three weeks later, he announced the launch of a new newspaper, *Il Popolo d'Italia*. Speaking to the Milanese section of the Socialist Party, he explained his actions:

> It is certain that the nation represents a level of human progress that we have not yet transcended. The sentiment of nationality exists and cannot be denied. The old anti-patriotism has run its course ... Let us see whether it is possible to find an area of conciliation between the nation, which is a historic reality, and class, which is a living reality ... If Italy stays out of it, it will continue to be the land of the dead, the land of cowards! I am telling you that the duty of socialism is to shake up this Italy of priests, of supporters of the Triple Alliance, and of monarchists, and I conclude by assuring you that, despite your protests and catcalls, the war will overwhelm you all.

A fortnight later, on 24 November 1914, the party expelled Mussolini for 'moral and political unworthiness'. It dubbed him a mercenary, a deserter and a traitor.

It was a mistake from which the party would never recover.

Mussolini's paper *Il Popolo d'Italia* was the new newspaper of interventionism. It hit the ground running with good news coverage, intelligent articles, a serialised story and major advertisers. Its daily circulation grew from 30,000 to 80,000 within a few months, and when it ran into financial difficulties, it successfully solicited funds from a wide community, from Belgian socialists to the French intelligence services. It was a telling success, though politically it was not wildly influential. (By the secret Treaty of London, the Italian government was already committed to enter the war on the Allied side.)

Nor was it the storm-wracked presage of jack-booted fascism that later commentators have made it out to be. The national socialism it advocated still closely resembled that advocated by socialist nation builders like Garibaldi and Mazzini.

At the same time, we can see a big change in the way Mussolini was expressing himself. Once Italy's Lenin, he now sounds for all the world like an Italian Maurice Barrès:

The nation has not disappeared. We used to believe that the concept was totally without substance. Instead we see the nation arise as a palpitating reality before us! Class cannot destroy the nation. Class reveals itself as a collection of interests – but the nation is a history of sentiments, traditions, culture and race. Class can become an integral part of the nation, but the one cannot eclipse the other.

Mussolini is no longer addressing 'the proletariat'. He's addressing the people. He knows, now, what the war is good for: it will make Italians.

ii

Mussolini's year was called up on 31 August 1915. (He had tried to join up earlier, but was told to wait.) On 3 September he joined the Bersaglieri, the troop of marksmen with whom he had done his national service. Two weeks later he arrived at the front, most of the way up Monte Nero, a mountain in the Campania. At thirty-two, Mussolini was old to be serving on the front line. His commanding officer offered him a safe spot at headquarters, writing up the regimental diary. He turned the offer down. When not in hospital with typhoid, Mussolini served at the front with the 33rd Battalion of the 11th Bersaglieri. On 23 February 1917, a mortar he and others were using for firing practice exploded. Mussolini was riddled with shrapnel, his right leg shattered and his left arm paralysed. (We should count him lucky; five of his compatriots died in the same incident.)

Returning from the battlefield, Mussolini no longer talked of the 'proletarian vanguard'. He spoke instead of the '*trincerocrazia*' – the aristocracy of the trenches. 'Italy,' he remarked in December 1917, 'is heading towards a two-party system: those who have been and those who have not, those who have fought and those who have not, those who have worked and the parasites.'

Italy mobilised sixteen per cent of its population in the Great War, more than any other Allied power save France. Its casualty rates were higher than those of any other nation. Annealed by the privations, strictures and horrors of war, bonded as brothers as no previous Italian generation had ever been, Italian survivors of the trenches resembled more the heroes of antiquity than the demobbed servicemen of a modern conflict.

Mussolini, changed in himself and a witness of change, returned to political life convinced that in the trenches, he had glimpsed the country's future: a nation organised on military lines, hierarchical, and animated by a grand purpose.

On 1 August 1918 he removed the word socialist from the

masthead of his paper; *Il Populo d'Italia* was now the 'journal of soldiers and producers'.

A new world was emerging: a 'military national socialist' world, according to Mussolini's formulation: 'The old parties are like the corpses you keep as relics and it will not be difficult to drown them all,' he declared.

But he was in no position to dictate the final shape of this new world. At this stage he was just one, and not the most powerful one, of several figures nursing ambitions to realise a new Italy.

There were the returning soldiers themselves. And there were a lot of them. Thanks to rapid battlefield promotions, an army that had entered the war with 142 generals now had 1,246 of them, all drawing good salaries and none of them keen on government plans to reduce the size of the army.

The generals believed that they were the nation's future, and they were more than capable of organising in their own interests. In November 1918 a league of returned soldiers was founded. Soon the Associazione Nazionale dei Combattenti had branches across Italy, providing the Catholics and the socialists with serious political competition. Its manifesto stole shamelessly from the Socialists, who might have found some traction had they not been so entrenched in their dogmatic hatred of fighting men.

When Orlando's wartime government collapsed in June 1922, a delegate to the league's first congress, Francesco Giunta, called for reorganisation under a charismatic leader. Giunta had two names to offer: Benito Mussolini and Gabriele D'Annunzio.

He could as easily have mentioned Filippo Marinetti, whose urban network of Futurist cells had blossomed in 1919, and started cropping up even in peaceful towns like

Palermo, Cassino and Cagliari. Borrowing their peacetime uniform from the Arditi – Italy's celebrated shock troops, modelled on the German *Sturmtruppen* – Marinetti's futurist thugs were the first Black Shirts, and it was they, and not Mussolini's gimcrack '*Fasci Di Combattimento*' (founded in March 1919 and numbering not more than three hundred rather worn-out Arditi) who committed the first violent acts of the new era. On 15 April 1919, Marinetti and a gang of two to three hundred marched in an armed column bearing pistols and burning torches to Milan's Piazza del Duomo, in front of the cathedral. They then marched on to *Avanti*'s offices, which they sacked and burned, killing four and injuring thirty-nine.

In an interview he gave immediately afterwards to the conservative paper *Il Giornale d'Italia*, Mussolini declared the fracas 'the act of a crowd, the act of returned soldiers, the act of the people, stuffed to the gills with Leninist blackmail.'

'We of the *fasci*,' he said, assumed 'full moral responsibility for the episode'.

But he was bloviating. The assault on *Avanti!* was nothing to do with him, and keeping a revolver and several hand grenades on his editor's desk at *Popolo d'Italia* could not altogether conceal the marginal and tin-hat nature of his organisation.

Behind Mussolini's chair hung the black flag of the Arditi, complete with a skull with a dagger in its teeth. But the Arditi were their own masters, and had it not been for socialist atrocities against returning soldiers, they might well have become what so many in the government feared they would: a private army of the political left. They had, after all, promised to 'take apart, clean, lubricate, and modernise all the parts of the complicated political-bureaucratic-judicial Italian machine, or, finding it out of service, hurl it into the melting pot of revolution.'

In a political ferment stirred by the Arditi, by Marinetti and D'Annunzio, and also by established nationalists like Corradini, Mussolini's political relevance was by no means guaranteed. His strongest card was irredentism. Italy needed to control and dominate the Trento-Tyrol to 'block the path of a German invasion for all time'. It needed control of the Adriatic, and for that it needed to annexe Dalmatia. To achieve these aims, Italy needed back all the territories agreed upon in the Treaty of London. In May 1919, speaking in the Dalmatian city of Fiume (now Rijeka in Croatia), recently wrested from Austro-Hungary, Mussolini declared:

> Italy's hour has not yet rung, but fate decrees that it surely will. The Italy of Vittorio Veneto feels the irresistible attraction of the Mediterranean which will itself open the way to Africa. A two-thousand-year-old tradition calls Italy to the shores of the black continent whose venerated relics are reminders of the Roman Empire.

Mussolini's vision of the Mediterranean as Italy's proper and exclusive preserve – '*mare nostrum*', as D'Annunzio would have it – would have warmed the hearts of many in that audience: Fiume's cultural ties to Italy were profound, and as recently as the autumn of 1918, the government of Fiume had declared its desire to join Italy.

But Mussolini was in no position to follow through on his political rhetoric, and when Italy was robbed at Versailles of all the land it had been promised, all Mussolini's 'Fasci di Combattimento' could muster was a small mob, with drums and trumpets, to disrupt a conference on the Fiume question at the Scala Theatre in Milan.

It was D'Annunzio, poet, playwright and rake, who would enter Fiume as the city's liberator and Italy's hero.

CHAPTER SIX

i

The year is 552. The setting: an island in what will one day be called the Veneto.

The people are at loggerheads, steeped in blood feud and poverty. Their leading families, the Faledri and the Gratici, are at war. The Gratici brothers, Sergio the bishop and Marco the tribune, have blinded their rival Orso Faledro, but are powerless against the attentions of Basiliola, Orso's crazed, seductive daughter.

Out for revenge, Basiliola seduces each brother in turn, setting them at odds with each other. Marco kills Sergio, then realises he has been played. As tribune, he sentences Basiliola to the same punishment as her father. But Basiliola prefers death by fire to being blinded. Just before her pyre is lit (clear parallels here with the later *Martyre de saint Sébastien*) a horde of barbarians led by Basiliola's brother beats at the doors of the town.

The invasion is foiled, and the townsfolk rally and unite, and they launch an immense ship, *Totus Mundus*, to carry them off to a new land. There they will found a new city, Venice, who will be undisputed queen of the Adriatic. Sacrificially bound to the ship's prow as a figurehead, Basiliola is borne away to her glorious maritime destiny.

D'Annunzio's *La Nave* (*The Ship*) was a sensation. Those who complain there isn't a single likeable character in it are not wrong, but they're missing that the actual protagonist is Venice herself: Queen of the Adriatic, undisputed ruler of 'Our Sea'.

La Nave, as eloquent a piece of expansionist political propaganda as D'Annunzio ever staged, was first produced in 1908. The national significance of the piece was such that the king and queen, who disliked D'Annunzio on every level, still dragged themselves out to the first performance at Rome's Argentine Theatre.

As the performance ended, the audience, drunk on chauvinism and the spirit of manifest destiny, ran out of the theatre cheering and screaming. Subsequent evenings worked up the cast and crew to such a pitch, their performances frequently ended in on-stage punch-ups.

D'Annunzio's only regret was that his play did not inspire a real conquest of the Dalmatian coast. Writing for the *Corriere della Sera* while in France, D'Annunzio says of *La Nave*:

all my ardent Italian passion is here, *crucified* at not being able to send an armada against this 'fourth shore'. In my play *La Nave*, how gladly did I long to place upon the Admiral's prow a Victory made, not of bronze, but of some new unknown metal from an untried mine ... Destiny demands that this play be acted in Fiume, in that Fiume which, to my childish imagination, has ever been mysterious, since I first saw her loaded brigantines and schooners coming into Pescara harbour ...

ii

D'Annunzio's wartime reputation as an Italian hero rose on rhetoric.

> Enormous, swaying, howling. I feel my pallor burning like a white flame. There is nothing of myself left in me. I am like a demon of tumult ... I see at last my Credo in blood and spirit. I am no longer intoxicated with myself alone, but with all my race ... They sway and are swayed. I ascend to crown them and I ascend to crown myself ... The mob howls and writhes to beget its destiny ... The mob is like an incandescent metal. All the mouths of the mould are open. A gigantic statue is being cast.

He spent years merging the languages of sex and of religious ecstasy, flattering his public into the belief that they were part of a spiritually higher realm. From this Parnassian vantage point, war was bound to seem a holy enterprise.

D'Annunzio rose, too, through politics, for no other figure was so eloquent or so gaudy. Unlike the Catholic Church, which was actually opposed to the Great War, and unlike King Victor Emmanuel III, who was never a figure people naturally gathered round, D'Annunzio embodied in speech and gesture all the qualities of an accomplished martial civilisation.

D'Annunzio rose, above all, through displays of extraordinary personal courage, audacity and ruthlessness. 'One fact will always remain mysterious and inexplicable for me,' Antongini wrote. 'Never did he manifest the slightest need of a little reflection and mental preparation for the totally new existence upon which he was about to embark!'

D'Annunzio's pursuit of glory was sincere. He planned, built and commanded squadrons in the Italian air force. He bombed cities from the air, sometimes with propaganda leaflets he had composed himself, sometimes with explosives. It took him years to establish that the journey was even possible by plane, but he even managed to drop leaflets over Vienna.

'Viennese! We could now be dropping bombs on you! Instead we drop only a salute . . . We Italians do not make war on women and children, we are making war on your government, which is the enemy of your national liberty.'

Printed on red, white and green papers, their suggestion that the government in Vienna wasn't fit to lead its people was a politically avant-garde move.

The French awarded him the Croix de Guerre and the Viennese *Arbeiter Zeitung* wailed: 'And our D'Annunzios, where are they?'

With hindsight, we see that not every audacious triumph was quite what it was cracked up to be. The bombing raid on the Austrian base at Cattaro was a fiasco, as most of the bombers lost their bearings over the Adriatic. The *'Beffa di Buccari'*, a motor-torpedo-boat raid on the harbour of Buccari, deep inside a Yugoslav fjord, succeeded only in firing at – and missing – an old ferry. But these were propaganda missions and, suitably massaged, they handsomely fulfilled their morale-boosting brief.

On 16 January 1916, a warplane in which D'Annunzio was a passenger came in for too hard a landing, and he lost the sight in one eye. (The long poem *Notturno*, dictated by the convalescent in a lightless room in Venice, is the last work of his worth reading.)

In his mid-fifties, barely healed, and at peace with the death he had so narrowly avoided, D'Annunzio made repeated visits to the battlegrounds, delivering impromptu paeans to the dead that had the soldiers weeping and cheering and their officers scribbling nervous letters to command. Long before the troops' day began, he rose to pick his way along boardwalks blocked by corpses. He led men into battle, into danger, into suicidal feats. On one notorious occasion, he ordered the shelling of a party of Italian soldiers trapped and attempting to surrender to the Austrians – a lawful but vicious act.

The prize expected for these acts of national martyrdom was a restored Italy: an Italy that stretched beyond its peninsula and across the Adriatic to Istria, and the cherished lines of the old Venetian Empire. These ambitions were not colonial but historical and ethnic: these territories were demonstrably Italian, and nursed few cultural ties to their Austro-Hungarian occupiers. Their post-war fate was also the subject of treaty, albeit a secret one. The terms of the Treaty of London were clear enough, and had brought Italy into the war in the first place.

At the peace conference in Versailles, Vittorio Emanuele Orlando and the Italian contingent trusted the US president Woodrow Wilson to respect their territorial claims. But Wilson nursed ambitions to fashion a new, more egalitarian dispensation in Europe, and had little time for secret treaties. He intended that the whole Adriatic coast should be incorporated in the new nation of Yugoslavia – a cobbled-together, artificial state that theories of blood and soil predicted would vanish in the first high wind, a place 'without roots in history, language or religion'.

Italy gained Trente in the Tyrol and Trieste and much of Istria. But no colonies in Africa. No territory in the Middle East. Not Dalmatia. And not Fiume.

The national disappointment was visceral. Of the 5.9 million Italians conscripted, half a million had been killed and a million more wounded – and for what? For food shortages, high prices, falling standards of living, and abject submission to the whims of an American president?

In June 1919, Francesco Saverio Nitti formed a new government, only for the US to threaten to withdraw their support for the lira – and this at a time of food riots, when Italy was relying on US grain imports. Crucified on the pole of American intransigence, exasperated Italians found their spokesman in D'Annunzio: 'Oh, Victory,' he cried, on more than one occasion, 'you shall not be mutilated!'

The post-war plight of the coastal city of Fiume encapsulated Italy's frustrations, as it had once embodied its hopes.

It was one of the most prosperous and polyglot cities in the Austro-Hungarian Empire; one of the most argumentative (during the war it had boasted 346 separate journals); also one of the most functional – an essential trading hub for Belgrade, Prague, Budapest and Zagreb.

It was strongly, but not exclusively, Italian: a splendid mutt, for which all claimants could put forward sensible arguments.

Once a client city of Venice, and occupied by Hungary on Napoleon's defeat, Fiume came to be populated almost entirely by Croats until Hungary, nervous of Slavic nationalism, deliberately diluted the place with Italians again by offering Italian merchants all kinds of commercial concessions.

Then, though the nearest Hungarian town was 350 kilometres away, Hungary tried to assimilate the place, at which point the city's Italian speakers filled it with libraries, literary circles, theatre groups and an Italian-speaking university.

Immediately following the war, the Croats claimed hegemony over the city and Fiume muddled through under two competing administrations, the Croat one and the old Municipal Council.

Finally, non-Italian members of the Municipal Council grew so fed up of having to fight off Hungarians and Croatians, they formed a pragmatic alliance with the Italophiles: anything to smooth the wheels of commerce. The Municipal Council renamed itself the Italian National Council of Fiume and announced its desire to be part of Italy.

President Wilson had other ideas. On 18 October 1918, the Allies assumed responsibility for the city. Soldiers under French command poured in to defend Yugoslav interests (France fancied itself as a champion of the new nation) while American and British ships arrived in the harbour to keep an eye on the French. From 17 November, Italian and American soldiers entered the city as part of the Allied force. The French, to retain command of the city, sent in generals of higher and higher rank. The Italians, playing the same game, followed suit. The city's economy ground to a halt and by the summer, French and Italian troops were in a state of constant low-level skirmish.

In January 1919, two days after Wilson declared that the Treaty of London was invalid, D'Annunzio published a 'Letter to the Dalmatians', promising the Italian inhabitants of Dalmatia that they would soon be united with their homeland. Rejected by the *Corriere della Sera*, D'Annunzio's incendiary masterpiece, which attacked the Allied leaders Wilson, Georges Clemenceau and David Lloyd George as quack doctors preparing to amputate Italy's limbs, appeared instead in Mussolini's *Il Popolo d'Italia*.

Italy had no shortage of military men with time on their hands, and early in the spring of 1919, the first concrete plans emerged for unofficial action to wrest Fiume from the Allies. When a passionate Fiuman, Captain Nino Host-Venturi, wrote to colleagues that Fiume had chosen 'Italy or death', the Arditi offered up their piratical services.

In April, D'Annunzio embarked on a series of bellicose speeches. In the crowd listening to him in Venice's St Mark's Square was Walter Starkie, and in his memoir *The Waveless Plain* he superbly evokes D'Annunzio's power:

> The voice of the poet rose sharper in tone in continual crescendo. He played upon the emotions of the crowd as a supreme violinist does upon a Stradivarius. The eyes of the thousands were fixed upon him as though hypnotised by his power, and his voice like that of a shanachie bewitched their oars.

A couple of weeks later, the industrialist Oscar Sinigaglia met Prime Minister Vittorio Emanuele Orlando:

> Who could stop thirty or forty thousand free Italian citizens from undertaking an expedition in the old style, and going to occupy Fiume ...? When forty million Italians want Fiume to be an Italian city, when the entire population of Fiume wants to be united with Italy, who will be able to oppose this union from taking place? Will America launch a military expedition to give Fiume back to the Yugoslavs?

Orlando's silence was tantamount to assent. By June 1919, the number of rumoured plots and conspiracies around Dalmatia had reached absurd proportions. In mid-June General Giardino had to print a public denial in the *Giornale d'Italia*: no, he was *not* plotting with D'Annunzio or Mussolini on behalf of the king's cousin, the Duke of Aosta! No, he was *not* planning to install the duke as the head of a republic of Venice, Dalmatia and Fiume!

In the same month, D'Annunzio met Mussolini face to

face for the first time. They sat in the Grand Hotel in Rome, talking at length about how a new Italian state might be structured. All the ultra-nationalist elements of Italian society were in contact with each other and wanted action. The Dante Alighieri Association. The Trento-Trieste Association. The Veterans' Association. The fascists, the futurists, the nationalists, the Arditi ...

To calm this rapidly escalating crisis, the government seized on any and every distraction. When D'Annunzio was offered the chance to fly off on a record-breaking air trip to Tokyo, generals and admirals queued outside his door – literally *queued*, outside his bedroom door in Venice – to persuade him to go.

The entire situation acquired a new urgency when an Allied plan was published to make Fiume a free state. This would involve the withdrawal of Italian troops currently serving with the Allies in Fiume. Taking Fiume from sympathetic, supportive Italian troops was one thing; wresting it from British and American forces was quite another. If Italian forces were to annexe Fiume, they had to act immediately.

In Fiume, the Grenadiers were ordered out of the city. They came to rest in a new base in the town of Ronchi, some 70 kilometres away. There, seven officers sat down to write to D'Annunzio, urging him to seize the city.

'You who have all Italy in your hands, great, noble, generous Italy, will you not break the lethargy into which she has fallen for so long?'

D'Annunzio's home was by then a clearing house for all manner of correspondence and conspiracy, from Fiume, Milan, Rome, Split, Zara – but this communication demanded an immediate response.

*

D'Annunzio had long been considered essential to any march on Fiume, and these had been in the planning since at least November 1918. No one, least of all D'Annunzio himself, expected him to occupy the city in any serious way. The march was meant to force diplomats to recognise Italian claims to Fiume and Dalmatia.

By the time D'Annunzio arrived in Ronchi, he was sick with the flu. Just 186 Sardinian Grenadiers awaited him, and the trucks that had been promised them had failed to arrive.

The airman Guido Keller went off and stole twenty-six vehicles from a motor pool. D'Annunzio wrote to Mussolini:

> *My dear Comrade,* Alea jacta est! *I am leaving now. Tomorrow I shall take Fiume by force of arms. May the God of Italy come to our assistance. I have just risen from a bed of fever. But it is impossible to delay any longer. Once more the spirit will dominate the miserable flesh.*

It was a cheerful enough opener to what was basically a letter of instruction: 'Summarise the article which the *Gazzetta del Popolo* will be publishing, giving the last section in full. And support our cause vigorously.'

Mussolini, as editor of *Il Popolo d'Italia*, now found himself serving as D'Annunzio's publicist.

At dawn on 12 September 1919 D'Annunzio dragged himself from his sick bed and into his Fiat 501 and, wrapped in rugs, set out for Ronchi.

The comic aspect of the whole affair was by no means lost on D'Annunzio, whose own account of the famed 'march on Fiume' is positively disarming. Government forces were instructed to prevent this stunt at all costs.

But Prime Minister Nitti's bluff failed quite spectacularly. 'Only a few words from me were sufficient to enrol complete companies, battalions and squadrons as we met them,' D'Annunzio recalls. By the time they reached the gates of the city, D'Annunzio and his little party of Grenadiers had acquired a massive column of tanks, armoured cars, trucks, over 2,000 grenadiers, artillery, Arditi, foot-soldiers and numerous cheering schoolchildren.

Outside the gates, D'Annunzio confronted Pittaluga, the Italian general tasked with stopping him. Their ludicrously operatic confrontation was enjoyed by all. First D'Annunzio offered up his medal-covered chest to the general and urged him to do his duty and shoot him on the spot. Pittaluga, knowing the game was up, and having absolutely no intention of shooting a national hero in cold blood, performed a theatrical volte-face that might well have sprung from one of his opponent's plays: 'Great poet,' he cried, 'I hope that your dream will be fulfilled, and that I may shout with you "Viva Fiume Italiana!"'

D'Annunzio entered the city to jubilation. A young girl pressed forward to present him with a bouquet of flowers. On the sash she wore: 'Fiume or Death'.

'In the mad and cowardly world,' D'Annunzio cried, in the first of very many balcony addresses, 'Fiume today is the symbol of liberty. In the mad and cowardly world there is a single pure element: Fiume. There is a single truth: and this is Fiume. There is a single love: and this is Fiume! Fiume is like a blazing searchlight that radiates in the midst of an ocean of abjection.'

Quite how long was this run of impromptu performances supposed to last? On waking the next morning to news that he was to be appointed governor of the city, D'Annunzio's response was, 'Who? Me?'

British and US troops withdrew straight away; the French (who had ploughed more into Fiume, and were more annoyed) followed shortly after. Nitti's government assured Allied forces that they would resolve the D'Annunzio situation in weeks, if not days.

General Badoglio, writing to the government on 15 September, was not so confident:

> *I am compelled to say that the words spoken by Your Excellency in the Chamber, to the effect of classifying D'Annunzio's act as folly or sport, have not found the soldiers and the officers in agreement; on the contrary they are infatuated ... These magnificent troops, who would move at the first whisper against Yugoslavs or against Allies, will they move against Fiume? I doubt it.*

iii

It is late morning on Tuesday, 20 January 1920.

St Sebastian's Day.

In the church of St Vito in Fiume, Europe's most avant-garde city, a place abounding in beautiful girls, pastry shops, ludicrous confectionery, cavernous cafés, illustrated journals, delicious custards, obsequious waiters and perfumes from every corner of the world, the leading women of the city are presenting Gabriele D'Annunzio with a bayonet made of gold and silver. First the bayonet is passed to Padre Reginaldo Giuliani, the priest of the Arditi, who blesses it. Then the women hand it to their liberator, their commandant, their duce (yes, he uses the word) and D'Annunzio, beside himself, rhapsodises upon 'this holy weapon, this blessed bayonet, in which our spirit and our hearts are fused with our meagre gold and silver, so that with it you may carve the word victory in the living flesh of our enemies.'

There's a political point in here somewhere – on 12 September 1919, D'Annunzio took over the Dalmatian port of Fiume, determined that Italy should annexe this fundamentally Italian territory and fulfil the promises made in the Treaty of London. If he and his little insurgent government have to take up arms to achieve this, so be it!

But D'Annunzio was ever susceptible to Sebastian's occult power, and the longer he speaks, the more his words swerve from the point and towards the piercing agonies of the saint's martyrdom:

I want to believe that the blade of this proffered bayonet, my sisters, was made with the steel of the first and last arrows!

The archer of life cried out in his death agony: I die in order not to die.

He cried, bleeding, Not enough! Not enough! Again!

He cried, I will live again, but to live again it is necessary for me to die.

Immortality of love! Eternity of sacrifice!

On and on like this. Nor do his onlookers tire. As D'Annunzio walks onto the piazza to review his 'legionnaires', Antonio Grossich, the city's mayor, exclaims, 'He is a saint!'

iv

Where would the Albanians of Valona be, without the Italians? Scrabbling around in the dirt outside their primitive huts! Imperialism is the natural, the only choice for a young nation, and offers hope to the world. So: annex Fiume! Revise Versailles! Have the courage to develop a 'world policy' ...

In the pages of *Il Popolo d'Italia*, Mussolini drummed up a storm in support of D'Annunzio's seizure of Fiume, calling the occupation of the city a revolution and a blow to the 'sharks' of 'the plutocratic Western coalition'.

But there were limits to what he was prepared to do for D'Annunzio, the elder hero in whose shadow he now languished. He had his eye on the forthcoming parliamentary elections, and involvement in Fiume would only distract from his first attempts at a national campaign.

There was, anyway, only so much he could do: *Il Popolo d'Italia* was a journalistic success but it had not acquired the sway over national opinion that D'Annunzio (taken in by Mussolini's boosterism) imagined it had.

D'Annunzio and the figures behind the march on Fiume had expected their gesture to embarrass Nitti into resignation. They fondly imagined a national uprising would follow, and a national election would bring a new government to power, composed of irredentists and war heroes. A week after his arrival, D'Annunzio had confidently explained to Riccardo Zanella, leader of Fiume's Autonomist Party, 'If I wanted to, I could march on Rome with 300,000 soldiers.' He imagined that, at the news of Fiume's occupation, Mussolini's *Fasci* would leap to the barricades all over Italy.

But the country, preoccupied with bread shortages and a disintegrating economy, failed to ignite.

D'Annunzio railed at Mussolini:

I am amazed at you and at the Italian people. I have risked everything, I have given my all, and I have seized the lot. I am master of Fiume: the territory itself, a part of the armistice line, the ships; and the soldiers who intend to obey no one but me. There is nothing that can be done against me. Nobody can tear me from this place. I have Fiume, and as long as I live I shall keep Fiume, unconditionally. And you tremble with fear!

But the seizure of Fiume was not going to trigger a change of government, never mind foment a revolution. So, rather like the dog who's chased a car and caught it, D'Annunzio, the saviour of Fiume, now had to work out what on earth he was going to do with the place.

Exasperated, D'Annunzio begged Mussolini, his erst-while champion:

At least puncture and deflate that belly of yours that weighs you down so much. Otherwise, it'll be me who will turn up, once I have consolidated my power, and I shan't look you in the face. Come! Stir yourselves, you loafers enjoying your siesta! I haven't slept in six nights and I'm wracked by fever, but I am still standing.

The men who actually ran Fiume – establishment figures like Carlo Reina and Giovanni Giuriati – wanted to force a change of administration, not tear down Italy's parliament. But Mussolini's commitment to the coming parliamentary elections in November had, ironically enough, left the door open for far more radical figures, who rushed to Fiume in the hope of making it over in their own image.

On 16 September 1919 (the same day he tore into Mussolini) D'Annunzio sat down with the terrorist poet Filippo Marinetti and Ferruccio Vecchi, 'the most literate of the Arditi', who had long advocated for the dissolution of the Italian government. On the agenda: was it worth taking action in Italy itself?

Giuriati and the city's military leaders managed to quash the plan, and even the impractical D'Annunzio knew a poisoned chalice when he sniffed one. Marinetti and Vecchi had altogether too much invested in being the most outrageous figures on the political stage. Marinetti wanted to speak to a mass meeting of the Arditi, but as D'Annunzio remarked to a Genovese legionnaire, 'I would have been pleased to listen to a recitation of [Marinetti's poem] "The Battle of Adrianopolis" if he had read to me alone, but it's a good idea not to give the Arditi swelled heads. *I* talk too much as it is ...'

Having been treated to a wild party on 25 September, Marinetti and Vecchi were invited to leave the city.

Mussolini replied diplomatically to D'Annunzio's tirade on 18 September. His cast of mind was hardly different to Giuriati's: it was, he said, too early to make any move on the mainland. Could they trigger a revolution now? Probably. But without preparation, that might just as easily carry the Socialists to power as themselves. Better to hold onto Fiume as a beacon for the new movement. To that end, he would launch a campaign to gather funds.

The campaign was a huge success, pulling in 3 million lire in little more than a month and boosting the paper's circulation into the bargain. Mussolini brought at least some of those funds with him when Attilio Longoni, a celebrated airman, flew him by plane into Fiume on 7 October.

In a one-and-a-half-hour conversation with D'Annunzio, Mussolini discussed what might be done to further the irredentist cause. Like Marinetti and Vecchi, Mussolini favoured a march on Trieste. They should, he said, declare the monarchy defunct, announce elections for a constituent assembly, and organise a new government directorate composed of sympathetic military leaders and D'Annunzio himself.

The next morning Mussolini flew off to the first national

congress of his *Fasci di Combattimento*, arriving in Florence still in his flyer's kit, every inch the modern hero. He explained what his 'anti-party' was not: 'not republican, not socialist, not democratic, not conservative, not nationalist ... a synthesis of all negations and all positives'. Like General Boulanger before him, Mussolini was out to channel all manner of resentments from a wide spectrum of incompatible people.

To foreign observers, a coup now seemed both likely and eminently achievable. US Vice-Consul O'Hara wired his government from Trieste that D'Annunzio was threatening to 'proceed from Fiume to Pola, Trieste and Venice, and [bring about] the complete downfall of Italian monarchy and the establishment of a Republic not later than November ...'

He was not far off the mark. Now leading nationalists Piero Foscari and Enrico Corradini came to Fiume with an even more detailed plan, involving an armed incursion into the Venezia Giulia region. From there they would march on Rome, where they would install D'Annunzio as the nation's dictator.

The only serious flaw in their plan was D'Annunzio himself. Calmly, Giuriati took the visitors aside and spelled out exactly what D'Annunzio's leadership consisted of. The poet, he explained, was an exemplary figurehead. He delivered speeches, swayed crowds, and worked tirelessly to embody the spirit of his little city. And he could do all this because Fiume was administered by a stable, collegiate National Council. D'Annunzio led, but he did not govern. He was a rotten administrator, financially incompetent, incapable of making the simplest decision without rolling dice or staring up at the stars. (Giuriati was not making this up.)

So where, Giuriati wondered, was Italy's national council, who would support D'Annunzio in his dictatorship? Where was the stable group who would actually run the country?

Better to wait, Giuriati said; and if Foscari and Corradini were set on finding a dictator immediately, they were going to have to find someone more capable of actual government.

The Scottish poet George MacBeth reckoned that D'Annunzio 'was the last major writer who could use the Romantic ideal with its full political relevance before it went bad in the hands of the fascists.'

There was nothing dogmatic, or even particularly political, about D'Annunzio's style of leadership. He resembled more a charismatic religious leader, binding together the most contradictory impulses and tapping the talents of the most disparate people: American journalists, Belgian writers, Italian businessmen, anarchists, trade unionists ... His idea, says historian Michael Ledeen, 'was to replace wealth, heritage and power with heroism and genius.' And he was greatly served by his inability to say no to anything, becoming, like General Boulanger, all things to all men.

Unlike Boulanger, D'Annunzio worked tirelessly to actually realise this ideal, witness his ambitious artistic programmes and extravagant political spectacles, his balcony speeches that moved multitudes to cheering and weeping, witness the parades of black-shirted Arditi, their Roman salutes and cries of '*Eia, eia, alalà!*' (the war cry of D'Annunzio's old squadron).

Osbert Sitwell, visiting the city, thought Fiume might under D'Annunzio's beneficent reign develop 'into an ideal land and offer an escape from the normal European misery and vulgarity.'

Though not responsible for the day to day running of the city, D'Annunzio was its absolute ruler, immune from any legal sanction. This dangerous arrangement worked out well, considering. D'Annunzio thought the best of everyone, showed leniency in the most trying of cases, and was tirelessly gregarious. Almost everyone who wrote about Fiume records some intimate conversation with the great man.

D'Annunzio's personal finances were, naturally, a disaster. 'You will have to contrive to get me a commission – some literary or film work in Paris,' he complained to Antongini. We should admire him for this: after all, had he so wished, he had a whole city to plunder – a point not lost on his secretary. 'This is the man who ... while reigning over a city without any possible control from anywhere, wrote to me, overshadowed by the grave preoccupation of having to pay a rent which, all in all, amounted to 2500 lire!'

Fiume might have been made for D'Annunzio: theatrical, hysterical, libertine. Its women had the vote, and its clergy had long been demanding the right to marry. All the place lacked was cocaine, and that not for long. Thanks to visiting aviators, who were using it to stay awake at altitude, the city was soon dusted with the stuff.

'The Fiumans invited the Italian officers to their homes every night for parties that lasted until the following day,' one young Grenadier enthused. 'One ate, one danced, one drank; indeed, it truly seemed that this city, with its life overflowing with gifts, was the reward for all our exertions during the war.'

Léon Kochnitzky, an earnest socialist once dubbed 'the only bore in Fiume', remembers 'a basement, all decorated with polar bear skins; at the back, among incense smoke, unmentionable orgies went on, alternating with Satanic libations: and neither were artificial paradises out of the picture. Cocaine by the barrel-load snowed down on these encounters, and steaming blood was sipped from human skulls.'

Kochnitzky's flights of rhetorical fancy always contain a nugget of real insight. Recalling his first sight of the Duce, he wrote, 'Here is the author of *Laudi* in puttees and spurs, his chest encased in the tight jacket of the Arditi. What a pace he sets! What vivacity in his glance! He is of the age of his soldiers. He is a mere twenty, as are they.'

D'Annunzio had for sure been rejuvenated by his adventure.

'Nearly every day the Comandante harangued the mob from the balcony of the Palace,' Antongini recalls. 'The spiritual communion between him, the Legionaries and the people was complete.'

On 10 October 1919, an Italian cargo ship sailed to Fiume carrying thirteen tons of arms and munitions, bound for Vladivostok and Russia's counter-revolutionary White Army. The captain, Giuseppe Giulietti, leader of the Maritime Workers' Union, had commandeered the ship and brought it to serve Italy's own incipient revolution and its leader-in-waiting, Gabriele D'Annunzio.

Where enthusiasts of various stripes had failed, thirteen tons of guns and bombs propelled D'Annunzio to action. Wary of action on the mainland, instead he set about transforming Fiume itself into a kind of international political theatre: a lightning conductor for peoples outraged by the Versailles settlement.

D'Annunzio's Proclamation of 24 October 1919 was more a statement of intent than a legal declaration, and perhaps not even that: 'a courageous and violent invective,' Antongini calls it, 'directed against the "madness and vileness of the world", and particularly against England' (widely blamed for the failure of the Treaty of London).

All the rebels of all the races will assemble under our sign. And the crusade of all poor and impoverished nations – the new crusade of all poor and free men – against the usurping and predatory nations, against the preying races and the caste of usurers who yesterday exploited the war that they might exploit the peace today, this noble crusade will re-establish that true justice that a frozen maniac [Wilson] crucified with fourteen nails and a hammer lent by the German Chancellor of the 'Scrap of Paper'.

D'Annunzio, who worked best at the level of image and gesture, now conceived the most outrageous political gesture of his career – the creation of an anti-League of Nations, bringing together 'in a compact formation the forces of all the oppressed peoples of the Earth'.

The task of assembling the 'League of Oppressed Nations' was handed to Kochnitzky, who had already been appointed head of the Office for External Relations. Under Kochnitzky, a keen supporter of the Soviets, the League made common cause with other countries 'spiritually murdered by England' – 'struggling Ireland, black-jacked Egypt and down-trodden India'.

Representatives of Sinn Féin and of nationalist groups from India and Egypt arrived, trailed by British agents. Every foreign office in Europe sent observers to the city. Journalists crammed the hotels.

While the 'League of Fiume' generated international head-lines, at home the Fiuman project no longer commanded attention.

In Italy's general election of 16 November 1919, the Socialists triumphed with 1.76 million votes. Winning 156 seats – up from 52 – they became Italy's largest political party.

For Mussolini and his fellow fascist candidates, including Marinetti and the conductor Arturo Toscanini, the elections were a catastrophe.

Of more importance to the fate of Fiume, Nitti remained in charge, and with an increased mandate. Bolstered by the result, he decided to offer D'Annunzio a reasonable deal and finally resolve the Fiume crisis.

Nitti's 'modus vivendi' proposed that, rather than annex the city to Italy outright, Italy would guarantee the people of Fiume their right to decide their own destiny. Italian troops would resist any Yugoslav attempt to take over the city by force, and the government undertook 'not to welcome or agree to any solution which separated Fiume from the motherland.'

It was, by any reasonable measure, an excellent offer. Fiume's National Council was ready to accept it. So was Giuriati. So was Major Reina, foremost among the officers who had first urged D'Annunzio to take the city. Mussolini wrote to D'Annunzio, urging him to recognise the treaty.

For D'Annunzio, however, 'a beautiful thing is about to end. A light is going out'. He could not bear to relinquish this place that he had transformed into his very own national theatre. Tirelessly he had crisscrossed the city, faithfully followed by two camera crews. Tirelessly, he had spoken, from balconies, in plazas, on hillsides, turning every occasion into a parliament en plein air (though these were more occasions for mass hysteria than real debates). And for what – so that he could hand his creation over to regular Italian troops, and leave his Legion of Fiume disbanded?

Fiume was his joy, his 'City of the Holocaust' (by which, one should quickly add, he meant something like 'spiritual cleansing') and he would not let it go.

On 15 December the National Council of Fiume met to discuss the modus vivendi and voted, forty-eight to six, to accept it.

D'Annunzio, fighting a frantic rearguard action, insisted the proposal be put to a plebiscite.

This was held on 18 December, and though we don't have precise figures, it's clear enough the city voted overwhelmingly in its favour.

The next day, D'Annunzio annulled the plebiscite.

After that, the character of the city changed very quickly. Ruling without mandate, D'Annunzio's mania increased (he had discovered cocaine). The city's Italian newspaper, *The Lookout*, now printed every one of his speeches verbatim. Proclamations reflecting his mercurial changes of mind and policy were promulgated up to eight times a day, handed out as leaflets, posted up on walls, even dropped from aeroplanes. According to Father Macdonald, a Scottish Catholic priest and reluctant witness of the Fiume affair, 'the prisons were full to overflowing. The Carabinieri [Italian military police] proved admirable spies and secret detectives, and "adjustments" were nightly carried out by the Arditi.' Censorship increased. Hostile foreign journalists were expelled; they were joined, in January 1920, by more than two hundred socialists.

Workers' groups staged protests against D'Annunzio's rule, and D'Annunzio threatened to execute opponents of his regime. The city's economy collapsed. There were shortages. The city's bands of piratical *uscocchi* went 'completely berserk', sacking towns and villages all along the Dalmatian coast.

The bridges that had existed between D'Annunzio and the Fiuman establishment were now merrily ablaze. Giuriati resigned in disgust, leaving D'Annunzio without a first minister.

No longer reined in by figures who were practised in politics and business, D'Annunzio's rule now took a utopian and millenarian swerve. He turned for support to the leftist forces that – in the shape of men like Kochnitzky and Giulietti – had long been waiting for their moment in the sun.

He had every reason to trust them. While the nationalists – and even Mussolini – had done nothing but urge caution, the left were full of ambition and invention. Kochnitzky had set diplomatic circles ablaze with the League of Oppressed Nations; Giulietti had brought him a ship full of guns and a propaganda campaign on the mainland!

On 5 January 1920, at D'Annunzio's urging, Giulietti sent his brother to Fiume with a proposal: D'Annunzio's Legionnaires should at last march on Rome, shoulder to shoulder with the Maritime Union and the Socialists.

It was a tantalising idea, and it may have succeeded, had the Socialists themselves not dug in their heels. 'The workers of Fiume must not trust anyone aside from the Socialist Party,' ran a pronouncement in *Il Lavatore* on 13 April. 'They must be on guard ... The workers must have faith only in their strength and their solidarity ... with the Socialists. With no one else.'

(Kochnitzky, reflecting on the failure of the Fiume project in his memoirs, regretfully concluded that 'the Socialist Party must bear a tremendous responsibility'.)

D'Annunzio still had the city, though – and when Giuriati resigned, he brought in a man he knew shared his utopian leanings.

The revolutionary syndicalist Alceste De Ambris, secretary of the Italian Union of Labour, was a socialist of the Mussolini sort. He had been strongly in favour of intervening in the war, and he was a keen follower of Georges Sorel. De Ambris not only helped D'Annunzio run the city; he took the lead in drafting its new constitution.

As the summer's heat beat down on the roof of Fiume's Teatro Fenice (turning it, D'Annunzio extemporised, 'into a furnace in which a new order will be smelted') the Charter of Carnaro was read out.

Ostentatiously presented on heavy paper with special inks and ludicrously ornate capital letters, the preserved document appears as eccentric as some of its provisions. It is, nonetheless, one of the purest statements of syndicalist government we have.

There were to be three electoral bodies. One would consist of sixty candidates, proportionately divided between different types of employment: ten industrial workers or peasants, ten employers, five schoolteachers and students, and five public servants, and so on.

The city's corporations were essentially trade unions; the charter would 'give the city into the hands of the workers'.

This was the first and last time syndicalism – the guild-based political arrangement beloved of fascists, socialists and anarchists alike – was given a chance to play itself out in its purest form.

It lasted one season.

De Ambris considered the political transformation of Fiume to be a dry run for the transformation of Italy, and the world. 'In Italy a saviour is demanded and awaited, and the most illuminated identify him as Gabriele D'Annunzio,' he declared.

But no amount of philosophical ingenuity or flowery rhetoric could now bridge D'Annunzio's isolation from the institutions that actually ran the city. Fiume's National Council managed as best they could to govern, though the coffers were empty and trade had come to a virtual standstill. On the mainland, Nitti – with what forbearance one can only imagine – ensured through the Italian Red Cross that the city did not run out of food or medicine.

The situation exasperated De Ambris, and in September he struck up a dialogue with Mussolini, hoping he might be able to resuscitate D'Annunzio's long-promised march on Rome.

The Charter of Carnaro, he wrote to Mussolini, 'defines

our goals with great precision. Just as the liberal uprisings of '21 were accompanied by the cry, "long live the Spanish Constitution", our movement today must have as its war cry, "long live the Fiuman Constitution".'

Mussolini made encouraging noises. He said he would need control over the armed forces of the insurrection, and accepted without comment De Ambris's idea that D'Annunzio should ultimately assume the role of head of state.

The truth was, he was stalling for time.

He had no problem with the Charter as the basis of a new government. Years later, when he proclaimed that he was building a 'corporate state', its categories owed quite a bit to the terms pioneered by De Ambris.

Getting to power was the sticking point. Mussolini wanted parliamentary success and at least the fig-leaf of legality. Marches and coups were unreliable.

And he was right to be circumspect. Though 16 November had been a disaster for his party, its fortunes were on the turn. The Socialists were busily undoing all the good they had done themselves in the election. Strikes, invasions of private property and terroristic rampages across the Italian country-side were alienating the very people who had been tempted into the socialist experiment. In the countryside in particular, loyalties flipped overnight, and from a few thousand, the socialist-baiting *squadri* – belligerent vigilantes, brutalised by war – now boasted more than 300,000 members.

When Giovanni Giolitti succeeded Nitti as prime minis-ter in the summer of 1920, he was determined to bring the Fiuman adventure to an end. Nitti had tried to contain the affair within the domestic realm, and had earned nothing but calumny and insult for his trouble.

So Giolitti upped the ante. If D'Annunzio wanted to play power politics, then Giolitti would oblige. Working with

British and French diplomats, he fashioned a mutually agreeable treaty with Yugoslavia, providing Italy with a generous border. All of Istria would come to Italy, four islands off the Dalmatian coast, and Zara. Fiume became a free state, with a land connection to Italy. The Treaty of Rapallo achieved more even than Nitti's perfectly sensible 'modus vivendi', and it did so at a diplomatic level D'Annunzio could not ignore.

Nor did he: the man who had written to Mussolini on 16 September that 'it would be sweet to die, swallowing the last draught of Fiume's waters', now declared war on Italy.

Everyone had had enough of D'Annunzio by this point: the Italian government, the Italian military (who had to clean up after his Legionnaires' coastal raids), the Legionnaires themselves (many of whom had left to fight the Socialists in the Italian countryside), landowners and businesspeople (who had seen even their working capital evaporate) and above all the people of Fiume.

Diehards remained; in his autobiographical novel *Trilliri*, Mario Carli recalls that the remaining Legionnaires were furious with the Italian government:

in their rage they ripped the Italian insignia from their uniforms, putting Fiume stamps in place of their stars. In Italy no one acted on our behalf, and the parties which had helped us up till then did nothing for us. The whole of Italy was willing to stand by and see us massacred.

But when on Christmas Eve the government ordered military forces into the city, the battle resembled more the climax of an opera than a war. Each side hollered warnings to the other before lobbing their grenades. Italian soldiers ushered civilians indoors, out of the way of the fighting. Live ammunition took its toll – perhaps a dozen died, all told – and when it was clear the Legionnaires would not yield their positions, on Christmas Day the Italian dreadnoughts *Andrea Doria* and *Duilio* opened fired on Fiume. By the standards of the day, it was the most surgical of strikes. A missile sailed into D'Annunzio's stateroom and knocked him off his feet.

On 18 January 1921, D'Annunzio left Fiume, reeling on cocaine.

The press ignored him.

V

In the Italian countryside, the Socialists' attacks on capital (shops, farms, livelihoods) and militarism (returning soldiers) reaped their wholly predictable harvest.

Soon rural Italy resounded to the war cries of the *squadri*. From the Arditi they borrowed the trick of forcing their enemies to drink castor oil – a laxative so powerful it could kill as well as humiliate. Hundreds died in violence; hundreds of cooperatives, cultural centres, libraries and theatres were burned to the ground.

On 21 July 1921 the government blocked a fascist march on the industrial town of Sarzana. Eighteen fascists died and thirty were wounded in the manhunt that followed. Locals strung up fascists wherever they found them – that, or pitchforked them to death.

Under the direction of men like Italo Balbo, a ruthless and violent mercenary, breaking strikes for local landowners and cracking the heads of communists and socialists, fascist *squadri* were flinging themselves headlong into confrontation with both the government and the people, just as hot-headed socialists had done following the November election.

In *Il Popolo d'Italia,* Mussolini tried to bring the movement to order. 'Thousands of individuals have interpreted Fascism as no more than a defence of their own personal interests and as an organizer of violence for the sake of violence,' he complained. This was stupid and futile: there were two million socialists in the country. Did they really want a permanent civil war?

Balbo and his fellow *squadri* regarded Mussolini's circumspection with contempt. Disappointed with his bloodless approach to the leadership, they cast around for a real captain – and lighted on Gabriele D'Annunzio. In August, they visited the poet at the Vittoriale, his newly purchased estate overlooking Lake Garda, and offered him leadership of the 'national forces'.

D'Annunzio thanked them, flattered them, and told them that first he would have to consult the stars. But as the skies that night were overcast . . .

Balbo and his party withdrew, disappointed.

Time and again extreme nationalists of one stripe or another beat a path to D'Annunzio's door, hoping to reawaken the spirit of Fiume. But D'Annunzio had by now determined to retire and focus on his memoirs and his poetry. Deliberately claustrophobic and oppressive, his new home was, he said, 'a bar against the time when I shall be receiving visits from war comrades, who cannot move within the crabbed space of the Vittoriale among things that might drop or break.'

On October 29 1922, Mussolini was summoned to Rome. He was officially proclaimed prime minister the following day. On 31 October, the Black Shirts, who had been waiting for the order to 'march', caught special trains to the capital and paraded before Mussolini and the king.

Four days before this 'march on Rome' Mussolini told an audience in Naples:

We have created our myth. Our myth is a faith, a passion. It does not need to be a reality. It is a reality because it is a spur, it is a hope, it is faith, it is courage. Our myth is the Nation, our myth is the grandeur of the Nation! And to this myth, to this grandeur, that we want to translate into a complete reality, we subordinate all the rest.

This is not a cynical statement. This is the last corrupted gasp of the old nineteenth-century romantic ideal.

A keen student of Georges Sorel, Mussolini believed in the motivating power of myth. As Duce, he worked tirelessly, and with a mythomaniacal intensity, to realise that myth in stone and blood. 'The world is how we want to make it,' Mussolini says, 'it is our creation.'

It is a world entirely at odds with the materialistic conception of happiness, 'which would turn men into animals who only think about one thing: to be fed and fattened, reduced, that is, to vegetative life purely and simply.'

It is a world in which duty, patience and self-discipline are sources of personal joy and civic strength.

Mussolini rejected the bureaucratic model of politics. He turned instead to aesthetics. He wanted something more than the mere 'modernisation' of Italy, and had his intellectuals and artists and designers wed the designs of a Walter Gropius and an Adalberto Libera with the 'spiritual grandeur' of Rome, blending commercial appeal with classical homage.

Mussolini's regime spent twenty years inventing symbols, myths, cults and rituals. It conjured up new ways of dressing, speaking and behaving. It rewrote not only its own history, but also the history of ancient Rome, and fashioned from this story a national religion, founded on faith, belief and obedience.

'Democracy has deprived people's lives of "style",' he wrote, by which he meant 'the colour, the strength, the picturesque, the unexpected, the mystical; in sum, all that counts in the soul of the multitudes.'

And bringing style back to people's lives meant, in the end, giving birth to a new kind of person, 'a new man ... serious, intrepid, tenacious.'

Mussolini cast himself as the artist of fascism, the creator of a 'beautiful' system and 'a doctrine of force, of beauty.'

The crowd itself, for this reader of Gustave Le Bon, was his clay:

When I feel the masses in my hands, since they believe in me, or when I mingle with them, and they almost crush me, then I feel like one with the masses. However there is at the same time a little aversion, much as the poet feels towards the material he works with. Doesn't the sculptor sometimes break the marble out of rage, because it does not precisely mould in his hands according to his vision? ... Everything depends on that, to dominate the masses as an artist.

Mussolini and D'Annunzio – and Maurice Barrès, for that matter – shared a set of political assumptions and sentiments that belonged to their common era and their common experience of politics and war and life.

All three believed in glory. All three discovered, rather late in life, the power of blood and soil. All three worshipped the dead. They each nursed a mania for martyrs, and where no martyrs were available, all three were more than capable of making some up.

In Rome in April 1915, a spellbound crowd stared up into

the sky as D'Annunzio declared that 80,000 dead soldiers were flying over the city, bearing the mountain on which they had perished: 'I see it! Don't you see it too?'

Mussolini's National Fascist Party likewise rose on the shoulders of its martyrs. Mussolini wrote on 20 January 1922: 'No ideal has, like the fascist one, been consecrated by the blood of so many youths.' Speaking in Naples on 16 September 1924, he prophesied that 'the ineffable sacrifice of our 3,000 dead' (a figure exaggerated five-fold) would grant fascism a glorious future.

I believe in the high Duce,
maker of the Black Shirts,
And in Jesus Christ his only protector.
Our Saviour was conceived by a good teacher and an
*   industrious blacksmith.*
He was a valiant soldier, he had some enemies.
He came down to Rome; on the third day
he reestablished the state.
He ascended into high office.
He is seated at the right hand of our Sovereign.
From there he has to come and judge Bolshevism.
I believe in the wise laws,
The Communion of Citizens,
The forgiveness of sins,
The resurrection of Italy,
The eternal force,
Amen.

This outrageous oath, written for Italian children to recite in schools in Tunisia, is pure weaponised D'Annunzio.

Mussolini cast himself as D'Annunzio's natural successor. Blisteringly rude letters from Fiume, heavily edited, become in Mussolini's memoirs D'Annunzio's declarations of brotherly love ('I too had been living this drama – day by day D'Annunzio and I had been close together'). One evening in August 1922, fascist enthusiasts cornered D'Annunzio in Milan and insisted he deliver a speech. Afterward, though the speech had been perfectly anodyne, Mussolini declared D'Annunzio the John the Baptist of fascism. (D'Annunzio, deeply embarrassed, never spoke in public again.)

All Mussolini's ritual, symbolism, mystique and style can be tied back to D'Annunzio: the title of Duce, the Roman salute (adopted on 1 December 1925 by all state civil administrations, including schools), the phrase '*mare nostrum*', the Black Shirts, using the song 'Giovinezza' as a 'national hymn', speeches from the balcony . . .

In the hostile judgement of Angelo Tasca, a founder of the Italian Communist Party, 'The occupation of Fiume . . . furnishes fascism with the model for its militia and its uniforms, the names for its squads, its war cry and its liturgy. Mussolini commandeers from D'Annunzio the whole of the stage scenery, including the dialogues with the crowd.'

Tasca reckoned D'Annunzio was 'the victim of the greatest piece of plagiarism ever seen'.

In his long essay from 1927 'La Trahison des clercs' ('The Treason of the Intellectuals'), Julien Benda anatomises what he sees as the moral collapse of the intellectual ideal. Enlightenment minds, which once championed universal human experience, have taken the emperor's shilling and are now, 'from D'Annunzio to Kipling', state moralists, exhorting people 'to feel conscious of themselves in what makes them the most distinct from others, in their poets rather than in their scientists, in their legends rather than in their philosophies.'

Enlightenment minds urged Europeans to deaden their differences, but Barrès and D'Annunzio and their breed praise instead the differences between nations: fidelity to 'the French soul', the fervour of 'Italian hearts', the immutability of 'German consciousness'.

'A work like [D'Annunzio's play] *La Nave*,' he observed, 'with its national plan as exact and practical as that of a Bismarck, wherein the lyric gift is used to extol this practical character, seems to me something new in the history of poetry, even of political poetry.'

Even as Benda is writing this, in Berlin a young Joseph Goebbels is yet again revising *Michael*, his only novel. For example, the sentence 'By redeeming myself, I redeem humanity.'

Goebbels amends the line to read: 'By redeeming myself, I redeem my *Volk*.'

MAXIM GORKY (ALEXEI MAXIMOVICH PESHKOV)

1868–1936

CHAPTER SEVEN

i

'My sympathies are with the Russian revolution, of course,' writes Mark Twain to the Russian revolutionary Nikolai Tchaikovsky. 'Government by false promises, by lies, by treachery, and by the butcher-knife, for the aggrandisement of a single family of drones and its idle and vicious kin, has been borne quite long enough in Russia, I should think.'

Twain is a favourite of the A Club, a literary club located just around the corner from his home in New York. He often comes in to spin stories through the smoke of his cigar.

In the spring of 1906, the A Club receives news that the celebrated Russian writer and playwright Maxim Gorky is visiting America on a fundraising trip for the Bolshevik wing of the Russian Social Democratic Labour Party. This sounds fine to the members, who can't tell one Russian revolutionary from another.

'In the ten years since his first success,' the A Club's founder Ernest Poole writes, 'Gorky's novels, short stories and plays had sold well in translations all over our land, and to millions of Americans his name had become a symbol of the cause of Russian freedom then so popular over here.' Gorky's reputation was built chiefly on his short stories about the lives, miseries and crimes of tramps. (They've not dated particularly well, though at the time he was spoken of in the same breath as Leo Tolstoy and Anton Chekhov, who both gave him writerly advice.) Then his play *The Lower Depths*, published in 1902, had swept world capitals, propelling him to international celebrity. The first edition of the script sold 40,000 copies in two weeks. Gorky's American publisher claimed that his fame now surpassed Tolstoy's.

Gorky is the voice of his suffering nation. His eyewitness accounts of the atrocious 'Bloody Sunday' massacre of January 1905 have set the world alight. In the US, William Randolph Hearst's magazine *The American Weekly* has been publishing articles by Gorky all about the plight of Russian working people.

So: Twain will chair a committee to organise mass meetings all over the country, and the émigré Ivan Narodny will pay for a grand reception dinner, if only to cock a snook at the Russian embassy.

It's from Narodny that the A Club catch their first whiff of trouble. From a Russian banker friend in Washington, Narodny has learned that Gorky is travelling with the actress Maria Andreyeva, a young widow and star of the Moscow Art Theatre.

Andreyeva and Gorky met about three years ago on the set of *The Lower Depths*. Gorky's separation from his wife Ekaterina has been amicable (the pair will remain lifelong friends and correspondents), and in Russia, this is all old news.

Now, though, the Russian ambassador Baron Rosen, in a last-ditch effort to scupper Gorky's trip, has been handing out photographs of Gorky's 'mistress' and 'deserted' wife and child to the New York press.

'At once we sensed the danger,' says Poole. 'America then was not what it is now. Puritanism was still going so strong that our dream of a million-dollar campaign might all come to nothing if the story should be played up in the way the Russian Embassy hoped.'

On the evening of 10 April, crowds throng the quayside at Hoboken.

'Everything is running, hurrying, vibrating tensely. The screws and paddles of the steamers rapidly thresh the water which is covered with a yellow foam and seamed with wrinkles.' Gorky scribbles notes as the steamship *Kaiser Wilhelm* comes in to dock. 'Sirens wail like fairy-tale giants, angry whistles shrill, anchor chains clang, and the ocean waves grimly slap against the shore.'

Narodny and a few other A Club members head out on the revenue cutter and board Gorky's ship at quarantine. Travelling with Gorky and Andreyeva is Nikolay Burenin, a writer, concert pianist and music collector (also, it turns out later, Gorky's Bolshevik minder, carrying about his person over 170,000 rubles stolen from the Helsinki branch of the Russian State Bank). Narodny has a word with Burenin, musician-to-musician. Instead of heading for the hotel reserved for them, why doesn't Gorky come and stay at the A Club? Andreyeva is welcome in the Staten Island home of John Martin, a liberal English friend. The arrangement is only temporary.

Burenin conveys the message – but Gorky refuses.

In vain, Narodny urges his celebrity guest to approach the problem philosophically. It's outrageous, of course, but what can you do? And what are one man's private affairs against the cause of Russian freedom?

Quite a lot, it turns out: Gorky, fed up of the voyage-long charade of separate cabins, now means to share a bed with Andreyeva.

On the pier, Gorky speaks briefly to the press.

What is his opinion of the promised Duma, Russia's first

ever state parliament? Is this not a sign of a sea-change in Russian politics?

'I do not believe in the Duma nor in the present method of holding elections,' he replies. 'The elections have no connection whatever with the liberation of the people.' The Russian people are bent on revolution; there is no other way forward. 'In twenty-two provinces,' he says, 'the people are starving to death, using, meanwhile, all the money they receive to buy arms.'

Gorky is, if anything, understating the case. In an attempt to put down countryside rebellions, the tsarist authorities have been plying their Cossack forces with vodka and sending them out on punitive missions devoted to rape and lynching. Since mid-October 1905 around 15,000 people have been killed, 20,000 shot or wounded and 45,000 deported or exiled.

But would a bloody insurrection lead to any better consequence?

Gorky's response endears him to all: 'Russia will go the way of the American federation,' he predicts. 'We will follow the road the United States has opened.'

Now, he has to take a break. He's been working twelve hours a day on the voyage, and he needs a few days to recuperate.

Crowds cheer him into his carriage and along the 14th Street ferry slip to 23rd, and wave him to his rest, in a suite in the Hotel Belleclaire, Broadway and 77th.

Leaving nothing to chance, one of the A Club committee, the journalist Leroy Scott, calls the press over and spells out Gorky's relationship with Maria Andreyeva. In Russia, divorce is not an option, and like it or not, ménages like the one Gorky now enjoys with Andreyeva don't even make the Russian papers. Scott points out that Gorky is good for many more headlines, so long as he isn't derailed by scandal straight away.

His audience are sympathetic: no one is running the Russian embassy's story. The evening editions describe Andreyeva as 'Gorki's charming wife'. *The New York World*, the yellowest of New York's yellow press, its circulation driven by sensation, sports, sex and scandal, is enthusiastic to a fault. In a cartoon titled 'Let There Be Light!' the Statue of Liberty bends to light Gorky's torch from hers.

From their suite on the ninth floor of the Belleclaire, Maxim and Maria have views east to Central Park and north across the Hudson. Maxim, who spends the day writing, enjoys the view of the river; it reminds him of the Volga. Exhausted, the pair receive only Russian acquaintances. More than a hundred other well-wishers leave cards.

'Gorky Amazed at New York's Greatness' runs one banner headline, and Gorky writes to a friend:

Well, Leonid, here is where you must visit. I mean it. It is such an amazing fantasy of stone, glass, and iron, a fantasy constructed by crazy giants, monsters longing after beauty, stormy souls full of wild energy. All these Berlins, Parises, and other 'big' cities are trifles in comparison with New York. Socialism should first be realized here – that is the first thing you think of when you see the amazing houses, machines, etc.

Narodny's grand welcome dinner is held for Maxim Gorky on 12 April.

Arthur Brisbane is there, the newspaper editor; Robert J Collier, editor of *Collier's Weekly*; senate whistle-blower

David Graham Phillips; also the socialist Robert Hunter (who will eventually abandon an unsuccessful political career to go and design golf courses).

Hunter speaks first:

> The idea is to assist the Russians in securing the freedom for which our fathers fought, and which we have enjoyed for more than a hundred years – the freedom of speech, of press, of assembly, of ballot, and of religion or conscience – to which are due the peace and prosperity we enjoy.

Across the table, Gorky's adopted son Zinovy Peshkov serves as translator. Gorky nods sagely. He dominates the table as much by physical presence as by reputation: lean and massive, with a pale face, high cheekbones, green-grey eyes, and bushy moustache. He has come dressed in a blue blouse buttoned high up at the neck, and black trousers tucked into high boots: he's every inch the 'bosiak', the Russian itinerant labourer.

To his left, Mark Twain rises to speak:

> If we can build a Russian republic to give to the persecuted people of the Tsar's domain the same measure of freedom that we enjoy, let us go ahead and do it. We need not discuss the method by which that purpose is to be attained. Let us hope that fighting will be postponed or averted for a while, but if it must come . . .'

He leaves the thought unfinished.

'I am very glad to meet Mark Twain,' says Gorky in reply. 'I knew him through his writings almost before I knew any other writer. I was little more than a boy when I began to wait and hope for the meeting which has been realised tonight.'

But sentiment must take a back seat: 'Now is the time for the revolution. Now is the time for the overthrow of Tsardom. Now! Now! Now! But we need the sinews of war. The blood, we will give ourselves. We need money! Money! Money! I come to you as a beggar that Russia may be free.'

To business. A programme of future receptions is outlined. A dinner for the New York literary circle. A meeting in Boston planned by the suffragette Alice Stone Blackwell. Arthur Brisbane of Hearst's *New York Evening Journal* is writing an editorial in support of Gorky's mission which will appear in all of Hearst's papers across the country.

Afterwards, Gorky and Zinovy head to 69 West 93rd Street, the home of Henry Gaylord Wilshire (a land developer who later gives his name to Wilshire Boulevard). This evening, Wilshire is entertaining a special guest of his own: H. G. Wells is in town.

There is no ease in Gorky's manner, no lightness, no tact. Panic sets in among the A Club committee when Gorky writes a telegram in support of two US union workers accused of murder. William 'Big Bill' Haywood and Charles Moyer, leaders of the Western Federation of Miners, have been indicted for the killing of Frank Steunenberg, the former governor of Idaho. Gorky's telegram reads: 'Greetings to you, my brother socialists. Courage! The day of justice and deliverance for the oppressed of all the world is at hand!'

Upton Sinclair begs Gorky not to send it. 'If Gorky supported Moyer and Haywood, he would get no money from the liberal millionaires of New York, the Schiffs and the Strausses and the Guggenheims and the rest, who might be persuaded to subsidise the Russian revolution, but who had no interest in industrial freedom for America.'

But Gorky is an international socialist, and will not stand idly by while two radical labour leaders are railroaded to the gallows.

Poole and his colleagues stiffen their backs but the blow, when it comes, lands from an unexpected quarter.

Angling for the presidency, William Randolph Hearst has for some while been courting the backing of the country's socialists. Gorky has a deal with him to write fifteen articles.

On Gorky's arrival in New York, the *American*'s circulation explodes, and soon every other paper in the city is hurting.

Joseph Pulitzer, publisher of *The World*, has been playing the long game, and keeping Gorky in the limelight as long as he can. But then comes news that they are all going to be gazumped by Gordon Bennett, then living in Paris with a young Russian countess, and proprietor of the famously uptight *New York Herald*.

Bennett has cabled his paper to run an exposure of Gorky's 'mistress'.

On the morning of 14 April, *The World* steals a march on the *Herald*, publishing two front-page pictures: one of Gorky with his first wife, Ekaterina Pavlovna, and their child; the other of 'the so-called Mme Gorky who is not Mme Gorky at all but a Russian actress, Andreyeva, with whom he has been living since his separation from his wife a few years ago'.

The article isn't brutal; it more or less repeats *verbatim* Leroy Scott's explanations on the pier at Hoboken. But the pictures trigger a scandal.

Early in the morning of 14 April, copies of *The World* are delivered to the Bellecourt Hotel and carried up to the guests' bedrooms.

Minutes later there is a queue of outraged men in slippers, banging on Milton Roblee's door. It takes the hotel's proprietor some minutes to figure out what the hell is going on. His Russian guest, it seems, presents an imminent threat to the children and womenfolk of the Bellecourt Hotel.

Gorky's suite has been booked by Henry Wilshire, and it's while Roblee is trying to raise Wilshire on the phone that Joseph Mendelkein, another A Club member, turns up to take Gorky and Andreyeva out for a drive.

This is as well, because soon the hotel is besieged by reporters. Wilshire hurries in – he's already seen the headlines – and is immediately bushwhacked.

'I did not mean to do Mr Roblee or any one an injustice,' he explains, trying to catch his breath. 'I knew Gorky was not married,' he says, 'I thought everybody else knew it.' Wilshire is surprisingly bad at this. 'You have to make allowances for genius,' he says. This does not go down well. 'Bernhardt came here with a trail of scandal behind her!' he protests. 'She was allowed to live as she pleased in American hotels. People who went to George Eliot's receptions knew she was not a married woman. I am not narrow. I am liberal in my views. These things are permitted on the Continent.'

He then takes an elevator to the office floor, where Milton Roblee is there to remind him that they are not on the Continent: 'I don't care what they do in Europe. I'm running an American hotel for American people.'

Wilshire tries it on: 'My lease runs until May 1. Those apartments are mine until that date – I've paid in advance for them!'

'I'll give you your money back,' Roblee replies, 'But you get that bunch out of here.'

Wilshire rushes off – 'on foot, and travelling fast' – and two hours later Mendelkein and his foreign guests, all unaware, pull up outside the Bellecourt.

That reporters are waiting for them does not seem so unusual. Gorky gives them a cheerful salute.

'So do you have any statement to make in your own defence?'

Gorky has no English, but he knows a hostile tone when he hears one. Puzzled, he delivers another military salute, takes Andreyeva's arm and heads for the elevator.

A few minutes later Wilshire returns, resolved to be diplomatic. He and Roblee go back a way. They are both men of the world. 'Look here, old man,' says Wilshire, 'if you only let this great man stay here you'll be made famous.'

Roblee reckons his establishment's had enough publicity for one day.

'The Waldorf would take them in a minute,' Wilshire says.

'Bet a hundred they won't.'

Wilshire is running out of rope. 'Give them until tomorrow morning to leave,' he begs. 'Why, *Charlotte Perkins Stetson Gilman* has just been here to see them. She is proud to know them!'

'I'll give them just long enough to pack their traps and no more,' says Roblee.

Out of options, Wilshire heads upstairs. The cursing that issues from Gorky's suite is terrible. Happily for Wilshire, who doesn't speak a word, it is in Russian.

Wilshire, mortified, wants the couple to stay with him, but Gorky doesn't want to embarrass his host any further. At 4 p.m., the couple leave the Belleclaire and board the El train at 81st. Mr and Mrs Leroy Scott are waiting to meet them at Eighth Street station. They have booked the couple rooms at the swanky Lafayette-Brevoort, on the corner of 5th Avenue and 8th, only half a block from their house.

But as they arrive, the manager is there to meet them: they cannot stay with him. He's not without sympathy, though, and has arranged rooms for them at the boutique Rhinelander apartment-hotel across the street.

The couple, rather shaken, take possession of a two-room suite, snatch a nap, then leave for a socialist rally at the Grand Central Palace.

They return in the rain, exhausted, a little before midnight, to find their trunks stacked up in the lobby of the Rhinelander. They cannot stay, the manager says, and orders their luggage out into the street. Andreyeva – from an old Russian family, widow of a prince, star of the world-famous Moscow Art Theatre – now throws such a fit of rage that even the massive and intransigent Gorky looks nervous.

The Scotts, hearing of this latest debacle, turn out again at once, and bring the pair back to their home.

'My wife is my wife,' Gorky tells reporters the next day, 'the wife of Maxim Gorky. She and I, we both consider it the lowest to go into explanation about this. Every one may say about us what he pleases. For us remains to overlook the gossip of others. The best people of all kinds will be with us.'

Little chance of that. 'I don't want to judge Mr. Gorky,' comments the suffragist and Gorky's erstwhile supporter Alice Stone Blackwell, 'but apparently his views on morality and ours somewhat differ.'

From all corners of New York and elsewhere, notices of cancellation pour in. The writer William Dean Howells abandons the society dinner he was sponsoring with Mark Twain. Mrs Leroy Scott cancels her series of teas.

And after farce: tragedy.

Four days later, news of the San Francisco earthquake hits the papers. The city is on fire. Thousands are dead.

Gorky's mission to the United States counts for little after this. Nicholas II's dissolution of the Duma on 8 July prompts an effort to revive Gorky's campaign. On 28 July he issues a blood-and-thunder appeal to the American public, predicting Russia's disintegration into lawlessness: 'Black blood-soaked wings of death will flutter over the country for months. The exhausted earth will swallow thousands of corpses of men whose only crime is the desire to live a human life.'

But no one is listening.

Gorky and Andreyeva are being handed round from one A Club committee member to another like unexploded ordnance.

Ernest Poole gets a visit from H. G. Wells. 'I've been hunting this whole city to find Maxim Gorky,' Wells complains, 'so I can tell him what I think of this outrage. I've heard he's with you here.'

'Sorry,' says Poole, 'he isn't here.'

Wells knows this isn't true.

Poole, deeply embarrassed, tips his hand a little. 'We're trying hard to keep Mark Twain as chairman of the committee and so save the campaign.' Twain has agreed to remain chairman of the campaign committee so long as Gorky is made to shut up.

'Then let me just say this,' says Wells. 'When you see Gorky, please tell him from me that, when this silly fuss is over and he comes to England, I do so hope that both he and his wife will come and stay with me in my home.'

Poole's embarrassing subterfuge is in vain. The next morning, Twain throws in the towel. 'Gorky is a puzzle and a vexation to me,' he complains. 'He came here in a distinctly diplomatic capacity – a function which demands (and necessitates) delicacy, tact, deference to people's prejudices ... He hits the public in the face with his hat and then holds it out for contributions. It is not ludicrous, it is pitiful.'

Gorky and Andreyeva are finally settled on Grymes Hill in Staten Island, in the home of leading Fabians John and Prestonia Martin.

One evening in May, Ernest Poole and some friends meet Gorky and Andreyeva on South Beach. It is empty at this time of year, lit by clusters of lights twinkling from the harbour of New York. They build a big fire out of driftwood and cook supper. Gorky, gaunt and gigantic, with an old slouch hat pulled down over his blunt face, kneels in the sand and, with Maria translating, tells stories of old Russia.

'And then,' Poole remembers, 'toward the end of the evening, he cited a Russian translation of Poe's Raven; I can still hear his deep musical voice, so dramatic with all its quiet, sounding after each verse the fatal refrain – *"nikogda"*.'

ii

Hell is made of papier mâché painted a dull red and slathered with some fireproof stuff that stinks of fat. Hell is very badly made: a cave strewn with pasteboard boulders, doused in reddish gloom. On one of the boulders sits Satan in scarlet tights, 'rubbing his hands,' writes Gorky, 'like a man who has just brought off a good business deal.'

Various sinners are brought to judgment. A young girl, admiring a new hat in her mirror, is seized by two demons and hurled into a long, smooth chute which descends steeply into a pit in the middle of the cave. Grey vapour issues forth; tongues of red-paper flame rise up. A young man drinks a glass of whisky and vanishes into a hole under the stage. It is stuffy in hell, and the devils are utterly worn out. Gorky thinks they should go on strike.

At the end of the performance, 'the considered work of

some old pedagogue who is worried by the escapades of the children and wants to teach them humility and meekness even through their toys,' a nauseatingly handsome angel sweeps across hell on a wire, blowing a wooden trumpet.

Gorky rises and leaves. Outside, in a brilliant cobweb of translucent buildings, 'tens of thousands of grey people with colourless eyes crawl about tediously, like lice in a beggar's rags.'

Gorky is writing for his Russian audience, for whom the West and Westerners have been a stock target ever since Napoleon's army froze to death on their retreat from Moscow. He writes six essays on America in total, and 'The Realm of Boredom' is one of four that remain untranslated.

The two pieces that do emerge in English are offensive enough. New York's acting city mayor, Patrick McGowan, remarks, 'A few years ago it was the custom of visiting Europeans to go home and write books about us from what they saw in a superficial view as they hurried around the country. I am afraid that Mr Gorky has yielded to this temptation without going home.'

'The Mob', printed in the *Cosmopolitan*, is pure horror. A woman pedestrian is raped to death by a mob. The crowd then reduces a streetcar motorman to 'just a piece of chewed meat – fresh meat – appetisingly dripping with bright-red blood. The black jaws of the Mob carry him along, still crunching, and its arms, like the tentacles of an octopus, twist about this body without a face. The Mob bellows: "Lynch!"'

'The City of Mammon' is less gruesome but even more antagonistic, as Gorky works out of his system all the bile occasioned by the Andreyeva scandal in a barbed sermon on the evils of capitalism: 'This is the first time I have seen so monstrous a city, and never before have people seemed to me so insignificant, so enslaved. At the same time nowhere have I met people so tragicomically satisfied with themselves.'

Writing to his first wife, Ekaterina, Gorky tots up his hate mail. His estimate of 1,200 letters is probably an underestimate. 'I am,' he writes, 'the most terrible person in the country, an anarchist, bereft by nature of any moral principles, and astounding in my hatred of religion, order and finally, of mankind.' But as he writes to his Berlin publisher I. P. Ladyzhnikov, 'What can you do? Americans read only what is written about America.'

'The City of the Yellow Devil' is more hateful yet:

The horrors of East Side poverty are more dismal than anything I have ever known. In these streets, as tightly packed with people as sacks of meal, children search greedily in the dustbins on the sidewalks for rotten vegetables and devour them, mildew and all, on the spot, in this bitter dust and heat. A crust of mouldy bread arouses the most savage enmity among them; possessed by the desire to devour it, they fight like little dogs.

Never mind what you see. Your job as a travelling Russian writer is to convey what you know. And Gorky, arriving in America, already knows what he is going to denounce.

Gorky's 'first-hand' account here is a set of clichés from start to finish. Even the refrain that casts America as the land of that 'yellow devil', gold, will be as familiar to Gorky's Russian audience as an old song. The greedy, gluttonous American capitalists stalking 'The City of the Yellow Devil' are pantomime figures, and offer Gorky's Russian readers pantomime satisfactions.

'The streets are deep ditches that lead people down into the depths of the city, where – you imagine – there is a huge, bottomless hole, cauldron, or frying pan. All these people stream into it and there they are boiled down into gold.'

The West's spiritual barrenness is the stock theme of Russian writers abroad. The purpose of Russian travel writing is not to witness this barrenness, or investigate it, but to catechise it. For years, Russian writers travelling abroad have been denouncing capitalism as a civic duty.

With summer comes another change of location: Gorky and Andreyeva move with the Martins to their summer cottage near Keene, New York, in the Adirondacks. There Gorky makes several stabs at learning English, but he doesn't get very far. 'It's as difficult as pulling out nails with your teeth,' he writes to a friend. 'You have to memorise the pronunciation and spelling of each single word: these sticklers to rules speak the language of anarchists – there's not a single rule in it!'

He also begins *Mat* (*Mother*), the novel that will establish his reputation as a revolutionary writer though it is, by his own account, 'a really bad book, written in a state of resentment and irritation'.

Mother is the story of a revolutionary, Andrey Nakhodka, and Pelageya Nilovna Vlasova, mother of Pavel, a wayward young factory worker who discovers the revolutionary movement. Pelageya, at first worried for him, comes to realise that this movement has the potential to save both her son and her country from perdition.

There is a strike, and Pavel is jailed. Pelageya volunteers to distribute her son's revolutionary leaflets, hiding them under a basket full of bread rolls meant for the factory workers' lunch.

The plot builds neatly enough; alas, with this comes an increase in the volume at which characters address each other.

'You have torn man away from life and disintegrated him,' Pavel tells his judge: 'Socialism will unite the world, rent asunder by you, into one huge whole. And this will be! *This will be.*' When the police finally catch up with Pelageya and her lunch basket, she cries out, beneath their cudgelling, 'You will not drown the truth in seas of blood!' And so on.

Mother was written to be a 'revolutionary' book: a didactic work reflecting not what Gorky had seen of the world, but his important opinions about it. Translations into twenty-eight languages ran into hundreds of editions, and were devoured by millions of readers from India to China.

iii

On 13 October, Gorky and Andreyeva sailed from Hoboken, New Jersey and returned to Europe. Already a wanted man in Russia, Gorky secured permission from the Italian government to go to the island of Capri, but before the couple could settle in, he was invited to London as a delegate to the fifth Congress of the Russian Social Democratic Labour Party.

As special guests of the congress, the couple were given a room at the Hotel Imperial on Russell Square. No sooner had they registered, than they had a visitor.

'I had never met Lenin until that year,' Gorky writes later, 'nor even read him as much as I should have done.'

Lenin dashed round from his own lodgings nearby to ensure his guests' comfort. Barely stopping to shake hands, he rushed over to Gorky's bed, thrust his hand into the bedclothes, and started rummaging around. Reassured, he returned to Gorky's side: 'In London the climate is raw,' he explained, 'and we must see to it that the bedding isn't damp. Especially in your case. We need to take good care of you.'

As they talked, the reason for Lenin's invitation came clear: he had been reading *Mother*. He called it 'a thing useful for the Russian workingman, which summons him to battle against the autocracy!'

Gorky thanked Lenin for his compliment, though in truth he was annoyed. It's one thing to write a 'useful' book, quite another for someone else to find it useful, as though it were a kind of committee manifesto calling for the extermination of the autocracy.

At its inaugural meeting, held secretly on 10 May at the Worker's Friend Club in Whitechapel (and attended by several policemen and agents of the Okhrana, the tsarist secret police), Maxim Gorky took the podium and in a passionate speech, encompassing everything from the exploitation of the peasants to the suffering of political exiles in Siberia, he called for Nicholas II to be deposed.

Being by inclination a pacifist, Gorky envisaged a bloodless coup. The speakers who followed him were more militant. Leon Trotsky snarled and shook his fists, before being upstaged by a series of fresh-faced young women with long plaits who, one after the other, screamed for 'war at any price'.

Afterwards Lenin caught Gorky's eye, came over and seized his hand: 'I'm glad you came. You like a fight, don't you? Well, there's going to be a nice scrap here.'

The organisers of the 1907 London congress saw to it that their distinguished guests, Maxim Gorky and Maria Andreyeva, had a room in an hotel. Lenin and his wife Nadezhda Krupskaya had a cheap room just a bit larger than a compartment in a railway carriage and their landlady served fish and chips for breakfast, but at least it was still in Bloomsbury. For run-of-the-mill delegates – and there were

336 of them, making this congress much bigger than the assemblies in 1903 and 1905 – accommodation was hard to come by. London won praises among the delegates for making them welcome and for championing free speech; less so for the disused army barracks they made available as accommodation. Many found a billet in a notorious doss-house in Dalston, on the western side of London Fields, and walked to and from the congress venue each day along Regent's Canal.

The congress took place in the Brotherhood Socialist Church in Hackney, about which Gorky wrote, 'I can still see vividly before me those bare wooden walls unadorned to the point of absurdity, the lancet windows looking down on a small, narrow hall which might have been a classroom in a poor school.'

Many delegates were wanted by the police in their native Russia. Those delegates who could kept as low a profile as possible, hiding their faces behind umbrellas and homburg hats. Others, from far-flung corners of the Russian Empire, had only their usual clothes: Caucasian sheepskin hats, dark cloaks, tunics, high boots.

Rosa Luxemburg turned up, fresh from a German jail cell; also the future Josef Stalin – then a delegate without voting rights by the name of Ivanov. His attempts to chat up a young Irishwoman on an evening walk by the Thames got him beaten up by navvies armed with bricks and sticks.

Proceedings of the congress were 'protracted, crowded, stormy, and chaotic' – at least, this was how Leon Trotsky described them. The Russian émigré Angelica Balabanoff remembered the event's 'all-absorbing, almost fanatical, spirit of factionalism.' Each morning, the sides would line up like litigants in court. The congress lasted three weeks, and one topic dominated: were you a Menshevik or a Bolshevik?

The split in the Russian Social Democratic Labour Party

(RSDLP) between Bolsheviks and Mensheviks had first appeared in 1903, emerging out of a debate about how to relate to other political groups. One group wanted to establish loose alliances with liberals and others. The other, led by Lenin, wanted to develop a centralised and tightly disciplined Communist party.

The failure of the revolution of 1905 polarised these factions beyond healing. The Mensheviks under Julius Martov (once Lenin's closest friend) wanted to ally with the liberals and get what reforms and concessions they could out of the newly opened Duma.

The Bolsheviks under Lenin disagreed. A second Duma opened in March 1907, and while the Mensheviks worked hard there to encourage reform, the Bolsheviks worked equally hard to sow discord in an effort to expose the Duma as a sham.

Over three bruising weeks in London, Lenin's vision of a tightly organised vanguard party gradually won out over the Mensheviks' reformism. The task, Lenin argued, was not to 'represent' the working class, but to lead the working class to revolution, and that required a vanguard party of trained, educated communists.

But it was a bloody affair. Gorky remarked on how the initial 'festive' mood surrounding the congress evaporated in wrangles over procedure: 'The fury of the disputes chilled my enthusiasm.'

CHAPTER EIGHT

i

Maxim Gorky was a fixer: one of that vanishingly small band of writers who are not only willing but able to run a soup kitchen.

He was born Alexei Maximovich Peshkov in Nizhny Novgorod on 28 March 1868 into a petty merchant family who added to their financial woes by beating each other up, even to the point of murder. Throwing over a lousy job in a lawyer's office, Peshkov famously went walking across Russia, down the Volga, around the Caspian Sea, across Astrakhan, over the Zhiguli Mountains, to the Mozdok steppes, Kazan, the Don, Ukraine, Bessarabia, the Danube, the Black Sea, the Crimea, Kuban, the mountains of the Caucasus – all this on foot, in the company of picturesque tramps, his nights spent around fires on the steppe, in abandoned houses, under rowboats turned upside down.

He learned about Russian life from the bottom, from itinerants and sailors and, most particularly, from peasants, whom he despised. A writer of shocking, fact-based tales of peasant cruelty (his very pen name means 'bitter'), 'Maxim Gorky' arrived at his revolutionary convictions without any of the usual romantic illusions. Poverty and slavery brutalised people, and his countrymen were brutes.

Russian tradition had it that writers were also moralists and social commentators. The aristocratic Alexander Pushkin had supported the Decembrist revolt of 1825. Nikolai Gogol's novel *Dead Souls* was meant to be the first book in a trilogy that would 'restore Russia's soul'. Leo Tolstoy became a notorious moral botherer who sponsored several pacifist sects.

What separated Gorky from this tradition was his attitude towards the peasantry. He knew them too well not to revile them, and much as he wanted to improve their lot, he wanted even more to improve their character.

Once, early on, he had been seduced into thinking that the peasants were crying out for enlightenment and education. In 1888, with the populist Mikhail Romas, he had set up a general store in the remote settlement of Krasnovidovo. They fondly imagined that come winter, peasants would gather there with them to have their consciousnesses raised by progressive ideas. Instead their customers shoved gunpowder into the stove, burned the store to the ground and, armed with pitchforks, pursued these interfering 'white hands' into the surrounding forest.

Three years later, in Kandubovka in the gubernia of Kherson, Gorky got another taste of peasant justice, beaten unconscious after trying to rescue a woman who was being horsewhipped naked in the street by her husband in front of a baying mob.

Gorky contended that the intelligentsia had never understood the peasant, but had merely projected its fantasies upon him.

Any fool can desire to save the poor – but what if the poor don't want to be saved?

Russian writers and intellectuals and do-gooders treated philanthropy as a moral obligation and this, Gorky argued, was completely wrong-headed. It made them weak and moralistic. 'We waste our time on dreams about goodness, but do little about "doing good" in practice,' he complained. Help the poor to help themselves! Show leadership! Show strength!

In the spring of 1898, Gorky's short stories were published. They won instant notoriety. In tale after tale, Gorky introduced readers to a colourful peasant figure and then pole-axed them with a finale that exposed his or her greed and cruelty.

The Russian literary public clutched its pearls. Young men in Moscow and St Petersburg began copying Gorky's dress and mannerisms. (And not just the young; even Konstantin Stanislavsky, director of the Moscow Art Theatre, admitted that 'I often caught myself imitating his pose or gesture.') Phrases and passages from Gorky's poems were circulated as militant slogans: 'To the madness of the brave we sing a song!' 'In the madness of the brave is the wisdom of life!' Third class railway cars – the haunt of vagrants and ne'er-do-wells – were labelled 'Maxim Gorkys', and Gorky's image starting cropping up on cigarette cartons and boxes of caramels.

Within a year, Gorky found himself editing both the journal *Zhizn* (*Life*) and running the Znanie (Knowledge) publishing cooperative – all the while maintaining his image as a barefoot bum, the authentic voice of the people, the first ever writer to emerge from the bottom of society.

The writer Ivan Bunin, whose aristocratic background inoculated him somewhat from Gorky's charisma, remembers meeting Gorky and Chekhov in conversation, and how Gorky regaled his hero with long, melodramatic, 'terribly boring' stories about 'boring, mythical merchants and peasants'.

When at last he relaxed, Gorky's crude, colourful mannerisms fell away, revealing 'not a husky or raging man, but simply a tall and somewhat round-shouldered, chestnut-haired young fellow with green eyes, a duck-like freckled nose, wide nostrils, and a blond moustache which he kept stroking with his large fingers while coughing.'

The press insisted that Gorky was an authentic man of the people (and not what he actually was, a self-taught petit-bourgeois writer who had had the guts to do some real research). As he adapted to his celebrity, Gorky found himself switching at will between bookworm and bum, 'fully entering first into one role, then into the other, and when he wanted to be especially convincing ... he could even easily bring forth tears to his green eyes'.

Nikolai Valentinov, an ally of the Bolshevik revolutionaries Alexander Bogdanov and Anatoly Lunacharsky, recalls Gorky once saying:

> All of us agree that we need a revolution and that it is nec-
> essary to enlighten the people politically. But that by itself
> is not very much ... We must teach the people literacy,
> culture, respect for work, knowledge of technology. It is
> necessary to give them a many-sided education. You see,
> we are hateful, backward Asia. Nothing good will come of
> us as long as we do not extirpate from ourselves the Asiatic
> spirit, as long as we do not become Europe.

It's remarks like this that have given Western commentators the idea (quite wrong, as it happens) that Gorky was a bour-geois at heart, and a believer in liberal democracy.

What Gorky was actually interested in was Western *dis-cipline*: its capacity for work, self-regulation, and sustained effort. Russians of all stripes – the intellectual do-gooder quite as much as the brutish and resentful peasant – needed this infusion of Protestant work ethic.

Being largely self-taught, and an avid reader, Gorky believed that culture, education, and especially reading, could be used to rid Russia of its 'Asiatic' miasma. He believed words could persuade. 'Keep telling a thief that he is an honest man, and he will justify your opinion about him,' he declared on more than one occasion, claiming the line was Edgar Allen Poe's.

Following those devastating early stories, Gorky vacillated between two kinds of writing. In one, he wrote (sometimes brilliantly) about the need to inspire hope and the need to tell the truth, and how these needs, both vitally necessary, could never be reconciled.

At other moments, Gorky tried the beautiful lie out for himself and told thieves that they were honest men, again and again and again, sometimes until their ears bled.

Gorky the artist wrestled with the tragic nature of the human condition. Gorky the conjuror hawked various ways to elude or ignore the human condition.

The conjuror despised the artist.

In 1899, in the novel *Foma Gordeyev* (*The Man Who Was Afraid*), Gorky the conjuror attacked those 'born without faith in their heart,' who 'never felt that anything was true,' forever wandering between yes and no.

He labelled these vacillations 'petit bourgeois', and according to the exiled Soviet dissident writer Andrei Sinyavsky, he later extended the concept of 'petit bourgeois' far and wide, 'casting into it all who did not belong to the new religion: property owners large and small, liberals, conservatives, hooligans, humanists, decadents, Christians, Dostoevsky, Tolstoy.' Sinyavsky adds, coolly: 'Gorky was a man of principle.'

Gorky the conjuror knew that all that is not God is the Devil.

This version of himself was in constant conflict with Gorky

the artist, who would read over the conjuror's work and despair. Of *Meshchane* (*The Philistines*), his first play and his first attempt at a purely political work, written in 1901, he complained to Chekhov: 'Well, the play has turned out to be clamorous, beastly, empty and dull. I dislike it greatly.'

Gorky's next play, *Na Dne* (*The Lower Depths*) was written in reaction to *The Philistines* and gave Gorky the artist full rein. It is a much better play – more a staged piece of lyrical poetry than an actual drama, but powerful for all that, and packing real pathos.

A group of barefoot bums live in a shelter near the Volga. Bubnov says, 'give 'em the whole truth, just as it is.'

Luka, cunning and elderly, says, 'You've been saying we need the truth. But it isn't always truth that is good for what ails a man – you can't always cure the soul with truth.'

To prove his point, he tells the story of a man who believes in the existence of a 'true and just land', until a scholar shows him that it does not exist. Unable to bear this bitter truth, the simple man 'went home – and hanged himself.'

As the play progresses, the bums come to half-believe Luka's tale of that good kingdom, and in their belief, they find that their lives become easier to bear.

After Luka's mysterious disappearance, their lives become mean and terrifying once again.

Opposing Luka is Satine, a Bolshevik in the making if ever there was one, optimistic, belligerent, and devoted to facing up to things as they are. 'Lies are the religion of slaves and landlords,' he declares. 'Truth is the god of the free man.'

Well, maybe; maybe not. At the end of the play, and in a speech which humanises Satine without at all undercutting his convictions, he tells his fellows, who have been abusing Luka's memory, to shut the hell up.

'Silence! You're all beasts! Blockheads ... not one word

about the old man! Yes! He lied – but he did it out of pity for you.'

Full of fury and symbolism, *The Lower Depths* is tough-going, but at the time (it was staged at the Moscow Art Theatre in 1902) it thrilled a theatre-going public only then waking up to the existence of the working class. 'After the first performance of Gorky's play,' Bunin remembers, 'the spectators rose in a body, went wild, and gave Gorky nineteen curtain calls.'

Once Gorky began earning substantial sums of money, he began handing it out. He needed very little for himself. He founded the Society of Nizhny Novgorod Lovers of Art. He edited a short story collection to support the Nizhny Novgorod Society to Help Women in Need and the Nizhny Novgorod People's Theatre. He wrote a collection of essays to fund building a dormitory for the children of public-school teachers. He ran an appeal to organise a skating-rink for the children of the poor, asking for skates, straps and money. He gave a thousand rubles towards higher education for women; a thousand to the Society of Teachers to house abandoned children; a thousand to the Society for the Protection of Public Health so they could build a children's home; five hundred for a public reading room in a Moscow suburb.

In 1902 Maxim Gorky visited the offices of a Moscow dentist, his head and face wrapped up in a shawl, and a huge wad of cotton stuffed inside his cheek.

He did not have toothache. He was hale and hearty, and his lively conversation boomed around the cab. The taxi driver, not at all taken in by Gorky's disguise, promptly reported his conversation to the tsar's police.

Gorky's dental treatment turns up in his file: 'He made on

all of us a wonderful impression,' reads one intercepted letter; 'He very much wants to get better acquainted with our direction, all our publications and practical work, and since his sympathy is solely with us he also wants to help us however he can: in the first place, of course, with money.'

This was Gorky's first meeting with the Bolsheviks.

From then on, whenever Gorky fell particularly under the sway of the Bolsheviks, his writing became shrill, breathless and flat. The second and subsequent editions of his novel *Mother* demonstrate the point. Already a hymn to the power of zeal – which is to say, the power of uncritical thinking – later editions of *Mother* made fewer and fewer demands on the reader's critical faculties.

In the first edition there is a genuinely arresting and difficult section in which our hero, the revolutionary Andrey Nakhodka, kills a police spy. Was he right to do this? The immediate circumstances pretty much demanded it. But what effect will Nakhodka's act have on him? What will it do to the revolution? By furthering the cause, has Nakhodka corrupted it?

In all subsequent editions, the police spy is killed by a person or persons unknown, and Nakhodka's dilemma is no longer merely resolved; it is erased.

So *Mother*, already a simplistic book, became in each subsequent edition an ever more wooden one.

At around the same time as these revisions, Gorky also started churning out a series of 'social' plays – animated political arguments whose hollow characters barked insurrectionary platitudes.

If you're famous enough, turning glib can actually boost your importance. You're not doing anything difficult. You're just producing products that carry your mark. You've become a commodity.

Gorky fought against 'decadent' modernist writers who

'contemplate the vanity of all earthly things and the insignificance of man. And they talk of corpses, graveyards, toothache, and headaches, of the tactlessness of the socialists and other such things which lower the temperature of the air, and of body and soul.'

Alas, this doctrinaire attitude towards the 'usefulness' of literature left Gorky in the end with very few good writers to champion. Settled in Capri, and afraid of losing touch with the Russian literary scene, Gorky wrote to his friend Leonid Andreyev, asking him to come and co-edit his long-running series of Znanie anthologies.

Leonid wrote to a friend, 'Life here is not so good. The only real person is Gorky and even he is not quite right somehow. He has become extremely narrow, and his brains are well and truly messed up.'

ii

On 3 June 1907, immediately after the congress in London, Tsar Nicholas II suspended Russia's second Duma. Sixteen Social Democratic deputies were arrested on trumped-up charges, and the RSDLP effectively ceased to exist. 'We have no people at all,' Lenin's wife, Krupskaya, despaired. 'All are scattered in prison and places of exile.'

In January 1908, with the Okhrana closing in on them and with Finland no longer a safe territory, Lenin and Krupskaya emigrated to Geneva, where, if anything, their depression deepened.

'Geneva looked bleak,' Krupskaya wrote in her memoirs. 'There was not a speck of snow about, and a cold cutting wind was blowing – the *bise*. Postcards with a view of the freezing water near the railings of the Geneva Lake embankment were being sold. The town looked dead and empty ... [Lenin] muttered, "I have a feeling as if I've come here to be buried."'

In Geneva's 'spy-infested shambles' it was easy to imagine that the chance of revolution had passed them by. Lenin listed the party's misfortunes to the London-based socialist Theodore Rothstein: 'The Finnish smash up, the arrests of many comrades, the seizure of papers, the need to remove printing presses and to send many comrades abroad ...'

Adding to his woes was the behaviour of old friends, Gorky included. Losing patience with the (admittedly fairly hopeless) political situation, Gorky and Lenin's erstwhile allies Alexander Bogdanov and Anatoly Lunacharsky were moving ever closer towards syndicalism. Worse yet, they were obsessed with fomenting a 'cultural revolution'.

A cultural revolution would inspire the masses to revolutionary consciousness through myth and ritual and even religion, they said. They had even given their gimcrack pseudo-religion a name: 'god-building'.

To Lenin's eyes, all this was a complete waste of time. For starters, it rested on a false psychology – the assumption that men acted as they did because of conscious beliefs which could be changed by argument.

Marx had shown that people's beliefs and ideals were mere 'reflections' of the condition of their class, and could not alter without a change in their situation. The proper task of a revolutionary was to change the *objective* situation, and that as soon as possible. Lenin, with signature Bolshevik impatience, would settle for troops now over saints later.

Reading the kind of 'drivel' written by Bogdanov and others made Lenin swear 'like a fishwife', as he admitted to Maxim Gorky, and so Gorky, ever the conciliator, wrote to Lenin in mid-January 1908 inviting him to spend the summer with him on the island of Capri. If he could only sit Lenin down with Lunacharsky and Bogdanov, Gorky reckoned he could effect a reconciliation.

Lenin conceded that the idea of 'dropping in' to see his old comrades was 'delightfully tempting, dash it!' He even started teaching himself Italian.

April 1908: Lenin arrives in Capri. The weather is fine and dry, the air heavy with myrtle and pine. Vines and orange groves rattle by the windows of the funicular as it rises from the harbour to Gorky's hillside villa.

Gorky's home, perched high on a cliff above the sheltered cove of the Marina Piccola, overlooks the stupendous Gardens of Augustus. The house has five bedrooms and Lenin is delighted to be given one with a stunning sea view. Once he's rested, Gorky is waiting for him on the balcony. Bogdanov is there, and Lunacharsky. Everything is set for a quite magnificent scrap.

Lenin's visit lasts less than a week. No one gets much sleep. By day, Gorky keeps things civilised with chess matches on the terrace and walks over the volcanic cliff paths to view the ruins of Tiberius's Villa Jovis.

Come evening, the gloves come off. Lenin is determined not to indulge his old friends' 'god-building' claptrap. His sideswipes at Bogdanov, the most mild-mannered of men, are vicious, and when he says he's planning a take-down of the whole god-building project, he triggers a vicious row.

Their gentlemanly debate about which should come first – a cultural revolution or a political one – is forgotten as the combatants discover more and more obscure philosophical points over which they can tear into each other. They even row about the nature of reality.

When they're done – or when Lenin is done with

them – Gorky takes him off to Naples and cools him down with a visit to the ruins of Pompeii, a tour of the National Museum and a hike up Vesuvius. (Lenin bounds ahead while Gorky, a chain smoker vulnerable to TB, all but keels over.) Over seafood suppers, Lenin chuckles at how things got so out of hand on Capri. Gorky is disconsolate.

On 16 May 1908, Lenin heads to London to write *Materialism and Empirio-criticism,* his riposte to this 'ridiculous, harmful and philistine' religion of the masses, this 'god-building' carry-on. Really, how could faith and philosophy possibly substitute for scientific Marxist knowledge?

He brings all the resources of the British Museum to bear on this sketchy and bad-tempered work: physics, philosophy, economics. He talks to nobody. After a day in the library, he retreats to the East End for plates of chopped liver and herring. At the Workers' Friend Club he huddles in a corner, small and intense, drinking Russian tea, and speaks to no one.

He leaves London on 10 June, and *Materialism and Empirio-criticism* is published the following May: three hundred pages of laboured polemic defending orthodox 'scientific' Marxism against the 'deviations' of his spiritually minded friends.

Gorky, writing to Bogdanov, reckons Lenin has written it, not to discover any truth, but merely to prove that he's the best Marxist.

'There is an enraged publicist, not a philosopher here,' Gorky complains. 'Most probably, he will be even more narrow and worse in practice.'

For a while, the god-building faction of Lunacharsky, Bogdanov and Gorky held sway over the Bolsheviks, and Lenin had to follow their tune. When Bogdanov relocated to

Paris in 1908, Lenin, much against his better judgement, had to leave Geneva and follow him, with his wife and mother-in-law in tow.

He attempted to put a brave face on things: 'We hope that a big city will put some life into us all; we are tired of staying in this provincial backwater.' But he considered Paris 'a foul hole': international hub of Russian activism, yes, but also the headquarters of the Okhrana.

They rented a freezing-cold flat in the 14th arrondissement (it took them three weeks to get the gas connected) and Lenin earned what he could from journalism. They were not destitute, but their prospects were nil. Every once in a while a comrade would abandon the Party, or leave the city, or throw himself into the Seine.

In the end, though, the god-builders overplayed their hand. Drunk on their own purity of purpose, blind to the practicalities of politics, they arrived at a meeting of the core Bolshevik group in June 1909 arguing that the Bolsheviks should split from the Russian Social Democratic Labour Party and constitute themselves as a separate party.

In the aptly named Café Caput, Lenin spent nine days explaining to all who would listen what a colossal mistake this would be, dooming the Bolsheviks to sectarianism and impotence, and handing the Party over on a plate to the Mensheviks.

Only Bogdanov and his followers failed to see the logic of this argument, and their refusal to accept that they had been voted down led to their expulsion, ridding the Party of men Lenin by now labelled 'vile scoundrels' and 'swindlers'.

Pursuing interests away from politics, Bogdanov and Lunacharsky seized on Gorky's offer to fund a Party school. (Gorky was once again trying to mend things.) The idea of an institution to train working-class revolutionaries 'up to the level of intellectual revolutionaries' had been bandied about since 1907. Lenin, wedded to the idea of a revolution led by a vanguard party, was particularly keen on the idea.

As it evolved on the island of Capri, though, the 'First Higher Social Democratic Propaganda and Agitational School for Workers' developed rather differently – as a living experiment in revolutionary culture.

Gorky, in a brave if naive attempt to 'unite all constructive elements' of the RSDLP, tried to gather to the island as broad a church as possible: Bolsheviks and Mensheviks, Plekhanov and Trotsky, Karl Kautsky and Rosa Luxemburg of Germany. They all declined (Luxemburg complained the waters around Capri were too warm) but Trotsky did arrange to take the Capri students around the museums of Vienna.

Work began on 18 August 1909. Gorky even invited Lenin over to teach, to which Lenin replied that Bogdanov and Lunacharsky's ideas were 'absurd, pernicious, philistine, wholly priestish, from beginning to end ... I am not going to argue with men who have gone off to preach the fusion of scientific socialism with religion.'

Gorky replied:

My dear Vladimir Ilich, I hold you in great esteem ... moreover, I like you as a person. But you know, you are very naive in your relationship with people ... It seems to me, at times, that everybody is for you nothing more but a flute, that you can play on it one time or another as long as it is pleasing you. You value the individual by whether he is useful to you in realizing your aims, views and tasks. That kind of measure ... will by necessity create around you some kind of void. This in itself is perhaps not very important, for you're strong enough. The main thing is that this attitude will unavoidably lead you to the making of mistakes.

The Capri school survived only a few months before Lenin, who had decided the whole thing must be a factional plot against him, persuaded enough of its students to come to study with him in Paris that the project folded.

It was a miserable sort of victory that alienated old allies, and now Lenin found himself largely friendless.

Lenin was extremely disillusioned: 'Life in exile is now a hundred times harder than it was before the revolution.' It is a measure of Lenin's despond that he even agreed to visit Capri again, and spent two weeks listening to Russian songs played on Gorky's phonograph.

Bogdanov and Lunacharsky were there again, too. They were busy preparing to open yet another new Party school in Bologna – fuel for yet another good scrap, you would think, but the atmosphere this time around was much more subdued.

Gorky wrote to his ex-wife: 'I'm lost in a sort of fog. I get extremely tired and, although it's not that I'm losing my taste for life, it seems that I somehow can't be bothered to live or to think.'

Some measure of Gorky's mood is to be had by reading his play *Chudaki* (*Queer People*), whose central character, Mastakov, is a painfully sharp caricature of Gorky himself in his politically committed guise.

Mastakov is a writer dedicated to optimism; his joy in life is to raise the spirits of his audience. 'I believe that the bright, the joyous, the human will be victorious,' he declares. 'I like to point out to people the bright, the good in life, in man.'

Such is his dedication to positive thinking, Mastakov wanders about completely oblivious to the misery and pain all around him. 'He lives as if in a dream, and believes in his dreams,' his wife Yelena complains, frustrated to breaking point. But she does not leave him – and by not leaving him, it's clear enough that she is sacrificing her chance at happiness.

Mastakov's best friend bangs on, Satine-like, about the truth, and Mastakov doesn't understand him at all: 'Why are they necessary, these little truths, what point do they serve? I've never understood their purpose ...'

In short, Mastakov is useless – and so is everything he writes – because he refuses to speak to life as it really is.

This is the argument of *The Lower Depths*, reprised with better arguments and more sympathetic characters. The spinner of magnificent lies is valued and celebrated, his political usefulness recognised – but his convenient and comforting fictions feel all the more empty for the effort.

The short story 'The Mordvinian Girl' is even sharper: Makov, a romantic revolutionary, finds that the political realities of the movement fall far short of his ideals. His family disowns him, and his comrades offer him no solace at all: 'I tried to talk to them, but they answer by the book. I can read the book by myself!'

Gorky's exasperation with Lenin and the movement is palpable. All they have are rules, theories, dry principles.

They can't even offer an inspiring lie.

iii

In 1913, Tsar Nicholas II proclaimed a general amnesty to celebrate the three hundredth anniversary of the Romanov dynasty, and on 31 December, an agent of the Okhrana in St Petersburg noted '... the famous immigrant, Nizhny Novgorod guildsman Alexei Maximovich Peshkov, arrived by train from the station of Verzhbolovo and was put under police surveillance.'

Gorky's return to Russia was a muted affair. He was certainly a celebrity, but he was not at that time much liked,

having got into a tremendous and heated controversy over
the relative merits of the novelist Fyodor Dostoevsky, that
'evil genius' (according to Gorky) who took a perverse delight
in portraying the deformities of the Russian soul. 'Gorky
against Dostoevsky,' screamed the headlines, 'Gorky accuses
Dostoevsky.'

Nevertheless, Gorky had always kept an open house and
soon his apartment on St Petersburg's Kronverksky Prospekt
reverberated to performances by Rachmaninov and Scriabin,
Chaliapin and, of course, Andreyeva. Guests became house
guests, and house guests became lodgers. The artist Ivan
Rakitsky came to dinner in 1916 and was still there when
H. G. Wells visited in 1920. In a letter to a friend, Gorky conceded, 'Never before have I felt so necessary to Russian life.'

Playing the good host did Gorky good. He eventually
ceased to bark on about 'usefulness' and 'decadence' like
some sort of literary policeman, and discovered – and published – the real talent that had been hiding under his nose:
Mayakovsky, Esenin, Babel.

No longer the darling of the Party, Gorky was concerned
to re-establish himself as a cultural figure, not a political one.

The main task of the revolution, to hear him tell it, was to
arm the people with reason, knowledge and culture: in other
words, to create a revolutionary culture ahead of the revolution itself, lest the overthrow of the tsar 'merely drove the old
disease inside the body'.

The forces of reaction were no more impressed by this
formulation than Lenin was. The chief of police in Petrograd
(formerly St Petersburg; its name was changed in 1914) reckoned that 'Gorky has become "bourgeois", as they say in
Party circles, his glamour as a Social Democrat has grown
dim, and he has altogether discontinued his active work.'

But he was busy enough. He set up the publishing house

Parus (Sail) and its flagship publication *Letopis*, a monthly journal published in Petrograd from December 1915 until December 1917. The idea was that Russian writers who lived abroad would contribute stories about other countries, and alongside foreign writers would 'fight for the interests of international, planetary culture against nationalism, chauvinism, imperialism, and against the current trend of becoming feral'. It generated immense hostility – one socialist, Vladimir Burtsev, accused Gorky of being a German spy – and among established writers, only Ivan Bunin signed up to the project.

Another somewhat unexpected contributor was Lenin, for though Gorky was politically 'always weak-willed and subject to emotions and moods', Lenin had to concede, in a letter to fellow-Bolshevik Alexander Shliapnikov in October 1916:

> *I need some income, otherwise I will perish, I swear!!*
> *Prices are devilishly high, and there are no means of*
> *existence! You must get money, by hook or by crook,*
> *from the publisher of Letopis to whom I have sent my*
> *two pamphlets ... If nothing can be arranged, then I will*
> *not survive. I am very serious, very.*

Through the efforts of Parus, and *Letopis*, Gorky wanted to revive 'Westernness' within Russia. This had a comforting sound to Western spectators of the Russian scene but really it had less to do with Gorky's love of 'Western freedoms' and more with his desire to instil his countrymen with discipline and a capacity for hard work.

With the onset of the Great War, many Marxists discovered their inner patriot. Gorky, on the contrary, waved the flag for internationalism. On 24 March 1917, he co-signed a letter published in Zurich's *Neue Zürcher Zeitung*, condemning

German 'barbarism', but at the same time urging the tsarist authorities to work towards a speedy peace settlement.

'Poor Gorky,' Lenin commented in a letter to Shliapnikov; 'How sad that he has disgraced himself by signing the despicable paper of the Russian liberals.'

Lenin had no desire to see the war come to an early end. 'The war was brought on by the clash of the two most powerful groups of multimillionaires, Anglo-French and German, for the redivision of the world,' he explained in an article dashed off the next day. Suing for peace was pointless, because

> the bourgeois governments either refuse to listen to such appeals and even prohibit them, or they allow them to be made and assure all and sundry that they are only fighting to conclude the speediest and 'justest' peace, and that all the blame lies with the enemy. Actually, talking peace to bourgeois governments turns out to be deception of the people.

Lenin expected this 'predatory' war to bring capitalism to its knees. He wanted the conflagration to continue. He wanted it to consume everything.

Gorky recognised Lenin's growing nihilism. The willingness of Bolsheviks to condone and even encourage the disturbances of February 1917 – when shattered Russian armies, weapons in hand, rolled back over Russia, burning chateaux and committing atrocities – chilled his blood. Even this early warning hardly prepared him for Lenin's 'April theses', however.

Not content with Tsar Nicholas's abdication in March, the Bolshevik leader now declared that the proletariat should overthrow the bourgeoisie, oust the Provisional Government, and take power.

For Gorky, this was the height of irresponsibility: the political equivalent of setting a match to petrol. Armed and hungry peasant conscripts were still bivouacked in the capital's streets, looting to compensate for their unpaid wages. (Zinaida Gippius, who kept a diary of these days, describes inebriated soldiers prowling around people's backyards and firing at their windows.) 'I am very afraid of the soldiers from the local garrison,' Gorky wrote, 'and even more of the Russian peasant. If he does not restore the monarchy, then he will create anarchy ... I do not know and do not see how we will sort out the chaos of the ruins we inherited.'

By 14 June his anxieties had intensified. To his wife he wrote, 'I think that Lenin's insane politics will spawn a civil war soon. He is completely isolated, but his slogans are very popular among the masses of thoughtless and irresponsible workers and among some soldiers ...'

With Lenin deliberately seeding chaos, Gorky even found himself supporting the Provisional Government's attempts to triumph in battle, and so bolster support for their war effort: 'I am afraid, that being a pacifist and hater of war, I will begin to yell soon – "Let the offensive begin!" For activity is necessary; we need an active and lively attitude towards life.'

On 18 June a massive demonstration was arranged in support of the government's offensive. It backfired horribly: half a million people turned up brandishing pro-Bolshevik slogans: 'Down with the Ten Ministers – Capitalists!'; 'Time to End the War!'; 'All Power to the Soviets!'

'What truly Russian idiots they are!' Gorky groaned. 'Most slogans demanded the resignation of ten Bourgeois-Ministers! But there are only eight of them!'

The offensive failed: German troops soon began a counter-offensive that devastated the Russian army.

On 2 July, four liberal ministers walked out of the coalition government in protest. Then the prime minister, Georgy Lvov, announced that he planned to resign as well.

By now there was virtual anarchy in Petrograd. Armed soldiers marched through the streets, firing their rifles into the air and commandeering vehicles, breaking into apartments and attacking wealthy passers-by.

So this was revolution! Gorky watched it with fear and contempt.

If you could only see how entire companies of soldiers threw down their rifles and banners at the first shot and banged their heads against the windows of the stores and doors, climbing into any crack! And this is a revolutionary army! A revolutionary free people! The masses did not realise at all why they crawled out into the streets. And in general, it was a nightmare. The motives behind the mutiny are unknown even to their leaders. But were there any leaders? I doubt it.

The authorities, backed by loyal troops arriving from the front, cracked down on the rioters, and the Bolsheviks, who were fomenting the unrest, were firmly suppressed. Between 18 and 19 July the offices and printing plant of *Pravda* and the headquarters of the Bolshevik Central Committee were destroyed. The next day an order was issued for Lenin's arrest. Those Bolshevik leaders who did not follow Lenin into hiding landed in jail.

The Provisional Government won this battle, but it had lost the war. Wresting political control away from the Soviets – the workers' councils – robbed it of any semblance of being a representative parliament. This, plus Prime Minister Kerensky's determination to continue the war, pushed it past the point of no return. It was now regarded, for all its reforms and promises and good intentions, as an agent of oppression.

Peasants looted farms. Food riots erupted in the cities. On 9 September, General Kornilov, commander of the Russian army, ordered troops towards Petrograd, ostensibly to counter the threat of the Bolsheviks, though it looked very much like a coup.

All factions, apart from the Bolsheviks, were caught up in this supposed conspiracy, while the Bolsheviks wooed Petrograd's workers and soldiers. At this point their takeover of government was not just possible; it was inevitable.

That the coup (the 'October revolution' of song and legend) would be relatively bloodless seemed not at all inevitable at the time. Days before the 'storming' of the Winter Palace, Gorky was predicting in his newspaper *Novaya Zhizn* that

the hideous scenes of July 16–18 will be repeated. That means that once more there will appear motor-lorries jammed with men with rifles and revolvers in their trembling hands, and with these rifles they will shoot at shop windows, at people, at random ... The unorganised crowd will creep out into the streets, hardly understanding what it wants, while under its cover adventurers, thieves, professional assassins will set out to 'create the history of the Russian revolution'.

Novaya Zhizn had first appeared on 1 May 1917 – yet another of Gorky's efforts at 'developing all aspects of culture'. The paper was the nearest Gorky ever came to realising Western notions of free speech, and its determination to reflect all sides of an argument drove its early readers round the bend. On one page you had Martov the Menshevik leader declaring that the Bolsheviks were betraying the revolution;

on the next, an article, sometimes by Lenin himself, saying the complete opposite.

In the face of Lenin's nihilism, however, and his insistence that the war should be allowed to lay waste to the state, *Novaya Zhizn* grew a backbone. It became a paper of strong opposition to the Bolsheviks, with editorials by Gorky under headlines like 'The Breath of Death', 'Demagogy and Impotence', and 'Madness'. He wrote:

> For Lenin & Co. the working class is what ore is to the metallurgist. Let's see whether it is possible to pour off from this molten ore under the given circumstances a socialist state. Apparently not – but why not try? What does Lenin risk if the experiment does not succeed? ... He is working as a chemist does in his laboratory, with the difference that the chemist employs dead matter with results valuable for life, whereas Lenin works on living material and leads the revolution to perdition.

Incredibly, *Novaya Zhizn* survived a whole eight months under the Bolsheviks, all the while promising its readers:

> famine, the complete breakdown of industry, the ruin of transportation, a long bloody anarchy, and, after it, a not less bloody and dark reaction. That is where their present leader is leading the proletariat, and they must know that Lenin is not an all-powerful magician, only a cold-blooded conjuror who will spare neither their honour nor their lives ...

Lenin was not slow to deliver on *Novaya Zhizn*'s darkest promises. On 16 January 1918, the Declaration of Rights of the Toiling and Exploited People made all legal rights conditional: they could be withdrawn by the government were they to prejudice the socialist revolution. When in December 1919 Martov criticised the Bolsheviks' repeated violations of their own constitution, Lenin insisted that 'both terror and the Cheka are indispensable'.

'Dictatorship,' Lenin wrote later, 'means nothing more or less than authority untrammelled by any laws, absolutely unrestricted by any rules whatever, and based directly on force'.

What did that look like? For an answer, we need look no further than the first issue, dated 1 November 1918, of *Red Terror*. (Yes, the Cheka – the Bolshevik secret police – had a house journal.) In it, Martin Latsis, chairman for the Ukraine, writes:

We are not waging war against individual persons. We are exterminating the bourgeoisie as a class. During the investigation, do not look for material and proofs that the accused acted in 'deed' or 'word' against the Soviet power. The first questions that you ought to put are: To what class does he belong? What is his origin? What is his education or profession? And it is these questions that ought to determine the fate of the accused. In this lies the significance and 'essence of the Red Terror'.

At first such papers appeared alongside satirical journals like *Bich* (*The Scourge*) and *Novyi Satirikon* (*The New Satyricon*).

By the middle of 1918, however, all opposition newspapers and magazines were shut down. When Gorky's *Novaya Zhizn* officially closed on 16 July 1918, it was the last independently owned newspaper in the country.

*

Among historians, the few years Gorky spent in Russia, between civil war and famine, tend to define his entire moral make-up. This is good for Gorky's reputation, because his efforts during these years were unquestionably heroic: advocating for those in trouble with the Cheka, 'defending culture' and at last carving out a role for himself as the Bolsheviks' critical friend and Russia's only independent voice.

Whether we can draw any deep political lessons from this period is more doubtful.

One day a young Yevgeny Zamyatin turned up at Gorky's book-filled office with the idea for a new novel:

The scene of action was to be a stratoplane on an interplanetary flight. Not far from the goal, there was to be a catastrophe – the interplanetary plane would begin to fall precipitately. But the fall was to last a year and a half. At first, naturally, my heroes were panic-stricken. But how would they behave afterwards?

'I'll tell you how,' Gorky said, his moustache twitching slyly. 'A week later they will be calmly shaving, writing books, and generally behaving as if they had at least twenty more years to live. And, by God, that's as it should be. We must believe that we won't be shattered, otherwise we're lost.' And he believed it.

CHAPTER NINE

i

How Gorky reached his accommodation with the Bolsheviks in 1918 is not known. Instead we have this pretty little myth about a meeting that probably never happened.

The story goes that when Gorky hears of Fanny Kaplan's attempted assassination of Lenin, all political reservations dissolve and he rushes round to be by his friend's side.

One bullet has ruined Lenin's coat, another has plugged his left shoulder, another has hit his jaw.

Across several bedside reconciliation scenes, the possibility of a truce emerges. Lenin says: 'A union of the workingmen and the "intelligentsia", eh? That's not bad, not bad at all.'

He tells Gorky to tell his friends to come over to the Bolsheviks. 'Do you suppose I dispute the contention that we need the intelligentsia? But – you see how hostile they are. It will be their own fault if we end up breaking the china.'

The details are made up, but there is some truth to this tale. After receiving one petition from his old friend, Lenin really did instruct Soviet officials: 'Comrades! I beg you earnestly, in all cases when Comrade Gorky turns to you with similar requests, give him every cooperation, and if there are any obstacles, hindrances or objections of one sort or another, be sure to inform me.'

In a city without bread or electricity, in an apartment that stank of kerosene, Maxim Gorky kept open house. Actors, artists, musicians, singers, profiteers, former bigwigs, society ladies and sailors: all came to beg his protection from an increasingly predatory regime.

He wrote letters, swore on the telephone; in more serious cases he travelled to Moscow to see Lenin in person. He had no time for his own writing; only endless letters of petition. Interventions, rations, rooms, clothes, medicine, fatty foods, railway tickets, jobs, tobacco, writing paper, ink. False teeth. Baby milk.

He knew everyone who was anyone in government, and this made him the last port of call for many desperate people, and an easy target for the embittered. According to the literary historian Dmitri Mirsky (himself one of Gorky's countless clients), 'Everything that was done between 1918 and 1921 to save writers and other top-ranking intellectuals from starvation was due to Gorky.'

Petitioners, friends, casual callers: people had an unnerving knack of turning up at dinner time, so of course he fed them. If you stayed late enough he would give you a room, or a bed, or at very least a corner and a blanket. First, though, you had to listen to his reminiscences. Though there were a great many of them, eventually they would repeat, and then you finally understood why Gorky's closer friends kept winking at each other and sloping off, one by one.

Business callers: secretaries from the House of Arts, the House of Writers, the House of Academics, World Literature, the Shipovnik publishing house. And in the mix, no doubt some Cheka spy.

In an atmosphere of catastrophe and ruin, Zamyatin recalls, Gorky's cultural enterprises seemed utopian and fantastical, but – 'One must believe'. And, bit by bit, Gorky's faith came to infect the sceptical citizens of Petrograd. Poets, professors, translators, dramatists, all began to work in the institutions created by Gorky, and grew ever more absorbed in them. Gorky's Institute of World Literature set about assembling a dictionary of quotations, a universal dictionary of biography, a rhyming dictionary, a handbook on translation, a series of factual thrillers about crucial moments in intellectual history. This on top of its main business: to publish Russian translations of all the foreign literary masterpieces since the middle of the eighteenth century. The point was not to complete the task, which in a city chronically short of paper was quite impossible. The point was to provide purpose and a pittance for more than two hundred scholars, critics and writers. More than 250 titles were issued before the publishing house closed down in 1924.

For a while, the Bolsheviks accepted these 'concentration camps for the "intelligentsia"'. Some years passed before they thought to break them up, or to co-opt them in the name of the government. Their industrial character, paying writers and editors by the quantity of their output, kept the Bolsheviks happy, but not every writer could hack it. Alexandr Blok, the symbolist poet, came to see Gorky as more of a gangmaster than a saviour.

Gorky never could separate the personal from the political. Now with a private line to Lenin, Gorky imagined that he could play the role of critical friend to anyone in Lenin's circle. When some scholars were arrested on nonsensical charges, Gorky wrote: 'Their arrest is stupidity or something worse.'

In similar circumstances, he wrote to Felix Dzerzhinsky, the head of the Cheka, 'I would like to inform you that I consider these arrests as acts of barbarism, as an attempt to annihilate the best brains of our country.'

Most of those closest to Lenin knew Gorky of old and treated his fulminations with public courtesy and private amusement. Not so Grigory Zinoviev, head of the Comintern and Petrograd's Party boss. And by renewing his friendship with one powerful Bolshevik, Gorky quickly managed to trigger the undying enmity of another.

Gorky wasn't aware of this at first, but Lenin certainly was. A year into the 'truce' and Lenin was writing friendly letters to Gorky suggesting that in the current emergency, there was very little point in Gorky remaining in Petrograd. Indeed, he should leave, 'or else life may become irreversibly objectionable'.

In the end, Lenin got fed up – witness his letter of 15 September 1919, in which he dubs the educated class not 'the brains of the nation ... but its shit'. He writes:

Several times, on Capri and elsewhere, I told you, you let yourself be surrounded by the worst elements of the bourgeois intelligentsia, and you give in to their whining. You hear and listen to the wail of hundreds of intellectuals about their 'terrible' incarceration lasting several weeks, but you do not hear or listen to the voices of the masses, of millions – workers and peasants – who are threatened by Denikin, Kolchak, Lianozov, Rodzianko, the Krasnaya Gorka and other [liberal] Kadet conspirators ... Really and truly you will die if you don't break away from this situation with the bourgeois intelligentsia.

Gorky would not be persuaded.

ii

September 1920.

This is the second visit H. G. Wells has paid to Russia, and the first that's been properly organised – not that you would guess it from their present circumstances, rumbling towards Petrograd at no more than twenty-five miles per hour over loosely bolted rails.

Wells's son George is making the best of things, nose-deep in a Russian grammar. His father would kill for a cup of tea. The nearest they've had to refreshment on this trip is some awful porridge and a cup of moonshine, thrust upon them by curious Bolshevik soldiers.

Wells's first visit to Russia was six years ago, just a few months before the Great War started, and he and Maxim Gorky had somehow failed to connect. This trip will set that right. Chary of his official invitation, aware that the Russian government wants to stage-manage his visit, Wells has declined the offer of a room at Hotel International, the place usually reserved for distinguished visitors. Instead he and George are going to cram into Gorky's apartment on Kronverksky Prospekt.

The 'commune' occupying Gorky's home is not such an unusual ménage any more. Impoverished by war and civil war, two revolutions, famine and plague, the people in Petrograd have moved in together for shelter, for warmth, for security, and for want of anywhere else to go. Everybody looks uncomfortable and nearly everyone is sick, and this in a city bare of drugs and medicines, so a petty ailment can develop into something serious very quickly. The men go about carelessly shaven, which Wells takes at first as a sign of torpor, until a friend mentions to his son that he has been using the same safety-blade for nearly a year.

Petrograd is a fortress under siege. Food is short and life is cheap. If Wells wants to see the real Petrograd, he needs to avoid the official tour. With this comes inconvenience and some risk. The city's wooden pavements have been torn up for firewood. The drains have collapsed. Frost has eaten potholes in the roads so big they look like shell holes. The few cars still running weave between them discharging clouds of pale blue smoke. (They're burning kerosene, and when they start up they make a noise 'like a machine-gun battle'.)

Father and son discover that, should they attempt to board a crammed trolleybus (and they are all crammed), they are as like to be pushed off again. They see a crowd gathering around a child cut in half by a tramcar.

Still, the arrangement has its compensations. Wells gets to catch up with Gorky, a man he considers a democrat, reflecting in his books the ideas of the first Russian revolution of 1905. He also meets Moura Budberg, 'a lady I had met in Russia in 1914, the niece of a former Russian ambassador to London,' a much more able translator than poor George, and soon to be Wells's mistress and 'the last person likely to lend herself to any attempt to hoodwink me'.

Wells is wildly wrong about Moura. She is a triple agent, working for the British, the Germans and the Russians. He's wrong about Gorky, too; he will turn out to be the very antithesis of Wells's freedom-loving liberal.

That Wells mistakes Gorky's politics is understandable. Petrograd has been swallowed by an apocalypse, and Gorky, the inveterate and passionate fixer, is doing everything he can and leveraging every ounce of his celebrity to restore some semblance of order and hope and civic life to the place. When someone is seen to be tirelessly doing the right thing, it is easy and natural to assume that they think the way you do.

Now and again Wells is inveigled into visits that are obvious set-ups. The pupils of one school know far more about Wells's books than about Milton, Dickens and Shakespeare. Wells, smelling a rat, leaves at once, 'thoroughly cross with my guides'.

Most of his official visits are to projects masterminded by Gorky himself: the House of Scholars, the World Literature publishing house, the book and antiquities fund of the Expertise Commission, the House of Arts. Several of these, Wells discovers, are 'salvage establishments' where intellectual workers, previously disowned by the state and on the point of starvation, 'not only draw their food rations, but they can get baths and barber, tailoring, cobbling and the like conveniences. There is even a small stock of boots and clothing. There are bedrooms, and a sort of hospital accommodation for cases of weakness and ill-health.'

The House of Scholars is impressive, but what really stuns Wells is the discovery that intellectual heavyweights like Sergey Oldenburg, Alexander Karpinsky and even the Nobelist Ivan Pavlov are relying on this place for a bite to eat. When he visits Pavlov at home, he finds the family almost starving, growing potatoes and onions in their yard to survive.

Such is the blizzard of impressions raining down on Wells, he perhaps does not spend enough time thinking about Gorky. Gorky is bound to be putting his 'salvage work' in a rosy light; who would not? Gorky makes no secret of his hope that Wells will carry news of Petrograd's beleaguered artists and scientists back to England, and help them reestablish connections with the European academic community. And Wells, for his part, is happy to take on trust what his friend tells him.

Gorky isn't lying about his work. But he is being economical with the truth. He has enemies – in particular Zinoviev. Only a few days before Wells arrived, Gorky offered to resign from all those splendid institutions he created.

However, Wells is Lenin's guest and will be interviewing
the leader for the British press, so Gorky can't afford to let
any cracks show. If he does, Zinoviev will take advantage and
weaken still further his difficult relations with Lenin.

Wells's stay with Gorky culminates on 30 September
with a celebratory luncheon at the House of Arts, which
occupies a huge building on the confluence of the Moika,
Nevsky Prospekt and Morskaia (now Herzen) Street. This
is very much not a salvage establishment. (Writers already
have one of those, the excellent House of Writers, established by Petrograd's local journalists' union in the spring
of 1918.) Rather, it is Gorky's club for Russia's artist elite.
A prospective member needs five recommendations just to
be considered.

Everyone who is anyone in Petrograd's surviving intellectual community attends the luncheon. Gorky is one of several
speakers who cannot decide who to praise more: their proletarian dictatorship (to hear them talk, you would think the
Bolsheviks were some sort of arts council) or their honoured
guest. Wells is being drowned like a fly in honey when all of
a sudden the satirical novelist Alexander Amfiteatrov leaps
out of his seat.

He has a letter he prepared for Wells, and, unable to contain
himself any longer, he's damn well going to read it out loud.

'Amfiteatrov suffered from the usual delusion that I was
blind and stupid and being hoodwinked,' Wells complains
later. 'He was for taking off the respectable-looking coats of
all the company present in order that I might see for myself the
rags and tatters and pitiful expedients beneath. It was a painful and, so far as I was concerned, an unnecessary speech.'

Wells is discomforted. Gorky is livid. There is nothing he
can do; he just has to sit there, staring angrily into the middle
distance, growing ever more pale, as Amfiteatrov kicks all

his careful arrangements to pieces. What on earth will Wells write about them all now?

From that day forward, writes the poet Vladislav Khodasevich in his memoir *Necropolis*, Gorky despises poor Amfiteatrov, 'not because he had come out against Soviet power, but because he had shown himself to be a destroyer of the festive, a *trouble-fête*.'

Gorky has become the very creature he lampooned in *Queer People*: a spiritually complacent Mastakov who lives in terror of destroying festive, elevated illusions. 'Any ruined dream would evoke his disgust and fear,' Khodasevich writes, 'as if it were a dead body, as if he sensed something unclean within it.'

iii

Who doesn't enjoy teasing an old friend? Gorky's renewed friendship with Lenin only made it easier for him to poke holes in him. Invited to contribute to the celebration of Lenin's fiftieth birthday, Gorky wrote an essay for the Communist International. In his final paragraph, he wonders at the temerity with which the Bolsheviks have fomented a European-style social revolution in a country whose peasant class was still hankering for a first taste of bourgeois comfort.

What the peasantry was forced to endure during the revolution seemed to him at the time, Gorky says, 'almost a crime'.

But then he turns the argument on its head, and some of his shuddering hatred for the peasantry bleeds through: 'But now that I see that people know much better how to quietly suffer than to work honestly and conscientiously, I am again singing the praise of the madness of the brave. And among those, Vladimir Lenin is first, and the most mad.'

The nested ironies of Gorky's wry love letter to Lenin fell on very stony ground. A resolution of the Politburo of the Central Committee ensured that after 31 July 1920, nuance was banished from the Communist International. Gorky's literary projects came under attack from various government institutions, and especially from Gosizdat, the Petrograd state publishing house. On the evening of Monday, 3 January 1921, while giving a lecture on the work of World Literature, Gorky lost his thread and his temper, complaining that Russian literature was now 'measured not by its good qualities but by its political direction ... It's the same thing. A writer must be a Communist. If he's a Communist, then he's good. If he's not a Communist, then he's bad.'

In the audience, the artist Yury Annenkov whispered to Korney Chukovsky the poet, 'How Gorky loves to speak through both sides of his mouth.' The great intercessor's habit of talking like a Bolshevik among Bolsheviks, while acting like their fiercest critic everywhere else, was by now a standing joke.

Lenin's suggestion that Gorky would die if he didn't shut up and go away had been mere hyperbole. Then Gorky drove Grigory Zinoviev to a heart attack, and the Petrograd Party boss really had it in for him.

In the spring of 1921, Gorky had received evidence that Zinoviev had fomented the very uprising he had so savagely repressed at the naval fortress at Kronstadt, the base of the Baltic fleet. What had begun as a demonstration about food distribution had rapidly escalated. Several thousand people were killed when the Bolsheviks retook the fortress in March. While Zinoviev had been ordering executions without trial, Gorky had been hiding fugitive sailors in his apartment.

At a meeting of Lenin, Dzerzhinsky and Trotsky, Gorky presented evidence that incriminated Zinoviev as the one who provoked the uprising. Gorky insisted that Lenin confront Zinoviev. As he was being carpeted by Lenin, Zinoviev was seized with excruciating pain. Gorky sneered at Zinoviev's performance: What a faker! Lenin, taking his lead from Gorky, went on shouting ...

Even Gorky, who had a cloth ear for approaching trouble, knew to lay low after this, and it was only with reluctance that he agreed to get involved with the formation of a public famine relief committee.

The crisis was unignorable. Hunger had grown so severe that in the countryside, seed-grain was being eaten rather than sown. Absent any government response, a delegation of liberals and other 'former people' had been going cap-in-hand from Lenin to the Commissariat of Agriculture, offering their services, but of course they were being roundly ignored.

Gorky contacted Lenin on their behalf, with predictable personal consequences. Zinoviev launched investigations into Gorky's activities, ordered that Gorky's apartment be searched and threatened to arrest people close to him. Gorky's mail was censored, and food destined for the House of Scholars, which Gorky had founded, was requisitioned. Now, when Gorky petitioned for the release of this or that intellectual, extra charges appeared on their sheet.

Two failed petitions in particular demonstrated to Gorky just how far he had fallen out of favour. When the poet Blok became ill, Gorky spent six months trying to obtain a visa for him to go abroad. 'Alexander Alexandrovich Blok has scurvy; moreover lately he has been in such a heightened nervous state that his doctors and friends fear the onset of serious psychiatric illness.' In this letter, Gorky asked Lunacharsky, now the People's Commissar of Education, to leave no stone unturned 'so that Blok, with all due speed, may travel to Finland, where I could help him get settled in one of the best sanatoria.'

The visa was eventually granted on 10 August 1921 – shortly after Blok's death.

Blok's funeral summoned all of literary Petrograd. 'By the gateway out in the street a crowd was waiting ... All that remained of literary Petersburg,' Zamyatin wrote. 'And only there did it become evident: how few remained.'

Many in Petrograd held Gorky indirectly responsible for Blok's death. He had failed to protect the one literary great who had freely allied himself to all his many causes.

Zamyatin also recalls how he asked for Gorky's help on behalf of a friend, Nikolai Gumilev, arrested by the Cheka. Gumilev had got caught up in a non-existent monarchist conspiracy, fabricated in 1921 to terrorise intellectuals. Gorky was assured that Gumilev's life would be spared.

He was shot by a firing squad on 23 or 24 August.

Gorky, returning from Moscow, related to a distraught Zamyatin what Lenin had told him: 'It is time that you realised that politics is a dirty business and you had better stay out of it.'

Not much chance of that. Gorky's open letter to American newspapers on 23 July 1921, begging for food aid, got an immediate response from Herbert Hoover, founder of the American Relief Administration (and future US president). By 22 May 1922, fifty-eight steamships had travelled to Russia – arguably the largest relief effort ever undertaken by the United States government – carrying 6,945,000 bushels of corn, 1,370,652 bushels of seed wheat, 9,800 tons of corn grits, and 340,000 cases of condensed milk.

Though it was agreed from the first that the ARA would deal directly and exclusively with the Russian government, the speed, efficiency and success of the relief effort, organised almost entirely by undesirables, was a major embarrassment for Lenin and the Bolsheviks.

Now the British trade representative, R. M. Hodgson, wanted to deal with the Relief Committee, rather than the Soviet government. In Berlin and Paris, rumours were rife that the Committee was a post-Bolshevik proto-government in waiting. In Washington, Pavel Ryabushinsky, advisor to the Russian embassy-in-exile, explained to an ARA representative that the committee might 'finally become the actual governing body of Russia, whether the Soviets desired this or not'. Alexander Kerensky told French officials that the Bolshevik government was in its 'final agonies' and would barely last out the year.

The Bolshevik response was swift. 'The arrests here are terrible,' Gorky wrote to his wife, Ekaterina, on 24 August. 'Hundreds are being arrested. Last night the whole city was buzzing with the cars of the Cheka.'

On the afternoon of Saturday, 27 August, the Famine Relief Committee convened in the hall on Sobachya Square, convinced that this would be their last meeting. Many arrived expecting to be arrested. They did not have long to wait. 'A black snake writhed along the walkway,' Ekaterina Kuskova, the committee's leading light, wrote later. 'One after another, people in jackets with revolvers on their belts ... and so many of them! Now they moved to the entrance. The door opened and into the rooms literally burst this army, the leather-wearing guard of the Soviet state.'

The committee was dissolved, its members arrested and held in the Lubyanka prison. Death sentences were issued, then quickly rescinded following international protests led by Hoover and the explorer Fridtjof Nansen. Many of the accused were exiled the following year.

There was nothing Gorky could do. Any public statement

he made would put the whole famine supply deal in jeopardy. In the Kremlin cafeteria, he ran into Lev Kamenev, the committee's Bolshevik overseer. He spoke bitterly, wiping at his eyes: 'You have made me into a provocateur. That has never happened to me before.'

'You are spitting blood and still do not want to leave!!'

It was Lenin's turn to be Gorky's critical friend.

'This is both conscienceless and irrational. In Europe, in a good sanatorium you will cure yourself [Gorky's youthful suicide attempt had left him congenitally susceptible to TB], and do three times as much work ... Here, there is neither medical treatment nor work – only bother. Purposeless bother. Go away. Do not be stubborn, I beg of you.'

What Lenin was proposing was not exile, nor anything like it. Gorky would have work to do: work only he, with his international celebrity, could accomplish. He was, after all, a unique asset – the best-known Russian cultural figure in Europe.

Vatslav Vorovsky, the Soviet ambassador to Italy, wrote in a similar vein, explaining to Gorky what his presence abroad might accomplish:

It is necessary for you, Aleksei Maximovich, to come, not only because you need to repair your health and eat well, but also because you need to process your distressing experiences and work calmly. I hardly need to mention how useful your presence will be here for establishing a favourable European view of the Soviet Union. Europeans have begun to wonder what this mysterious Soviet Russia is all about.

In essence, Gorky was being invited to take up again, in somewhat more circumspect fashion, the business that had propelled him across Europe in 1906. Promote your country, your revolution, your Party. Give it a human face. Call out the lies of the anti-Bolshevik Whites, capitalists and disgruntled émigrés.

Defend the revolution, not for what it has done, but for what it intends to do. Support the revolution, not for its deeds, but for what they signify.

Talk about how the people have seized power and are maintaining themselves in power over one sixth of the earth! Explain how private ownership, the profit motive, sexual taboos and social prohibitions have been abolished at a stroke, how there are no more rich and poor any more, no more masters and servants, no more officers and men, that husbands no longer lord it over their wives, that parents listen to their children, that teachers learn from their pupils.

Leave politics behind, and moralise.

By now quite seriously ill, at odds with Lenin's regime, ousted by the terror fomented by Lenin and Zinoviev, Gorky needed to remind himself who he actually was.

If he was not to become just another embittered and reactionary exile – and the temptation was very real – then who was he?

Fetching up in Berlin, Gorky set about writing what amounts to his political testament. It is a document so profoundly and universally unwelcome, it made no detectable impact on contemporary Western readers and didn't even see publication in Russia until the era of glasnost.

The essay 'O russkom krest'ianstve' ('On the Russian Peasantry') develops and explores those early and abiding impressions that shaped Gorky's political beliefs. It is very much the work of a disappointed liberal do-gooder, bombed and burned out of his home and pursued by pitchforks. Its thoughts are those of an outraged passer-by, beaten to a pulp by a mob when he tries to save a woman from humiliation. Its argument is formulated by an author whose every story of peasant greed, nihilism and cruelty can be traced to personal experience.

'I have seen and know too much to have the right to be silent. Yet I beg you to understand that I condemn no one, justify no one, I am simply recording the forms resulting from the mass of my impressions.'

The man known worldwide for his work saving the Russian peasant from starvation is going to explain precisely what is wrong with the Russian peasant.

To start, let's draw a clear, thick line between the peasantry as Gorky conceived it, and the peasantry of émigré fantasy. Since before the revolution, in their own writings about Russia, any number of political refugees had harped on about the Russian peasant as a primitive and soulful creature, whose tendency to communal living could serve as an example for the capitalist West.

The mysterious and powerful hold this image had over the West can hardly be exaggerated; witness the number of Tolstoyan communities established in England that combined (with varying degrees of failure) Christianity and anarchism.

This was not Gorky's peasantry at all. For Gorky, peasant psychology was essentially an 'Asiatic' slave psychology, and to it could be traced the manifold failings of the Russian mind. This peasant had invented nihilism and anarchism long before Pisarev and Bakunin, and it was to the peasant that Gorky traced his countrymen's paradoxical mixture of servility and despotism, fanaticism and fatalism, dogmatism and mysticism, 'all adding up to an incapacity to cope with a modern world'.

'We must remodel ourselves or perish,' he says – the implication being that if you want to remodel Russia, you first have to remodel the Russian peasant. And Gorky is clear about the challenge this presents. The Russian peasant is illiterate, ruthless, lazy, deceitful and above all, envious. He finds the solution to all his problems in the sack of cities, the slaughter of townsfolk and the destruction of machinery.

Russian history is chock-full of projects to enlighten and raise the standard of living of the Russian peasant, and yet the Russian peasant remains as he was in the seventeenth century: he has learned nothing. In the recent civil war, peasants watched their churches burn with equanimity (so much for their spiritual nature!) and they weren't even angry; merely indifferent to all lives aside from their own. 'I have asked those who were active in the civil war whether they were at all uneasy in killing one another. No, they were not. "He has a weapon, I have a weapon, so we are equal; what's the odds, if we kill one another there'll be more room in the land".'

This is strong medicine for a nation reeling from unimaginable famine, but Gorky goes even further, criticising the peasants for their own plight.

They have no sense of reciprocity, so is it any wonder that they starve? 'They do not cry in Riazan over the poor harvest in Pskov,' one peasant told him. Another opined: 'It is a great misfortune, and many will die. But who? The weak, the infirm; for those who will remain it will be five times better.' What can you do with such people?

Gorky's parting hope is that the revolution, 'carried out by a numerically insignificant group of the intelligentsia at the

head of several thousand workers it educated', will have fur-
rowed this whole class 'with a steel plough so deeply that the
half-savage, stupid, ponderous people of the Russian villages
and hamlets – all those almost terrible people of whom we
spoke – will die out, and a new tribe will take their place.'

Gorky does not expect these new men to be pleasant, but
they will at least, and at last, be businesslike. 'It will be a
long time before they ponder Einstein's theory or learn to
understand the importance of Shakespeare or Leonardo da
Vinci, but they ... will very quickly understand the value
of electricity, the value of trained agricultural officers, the
usefulness of the tractor, the need to have a good doctor in
every village and the use of highways.'

Europeans, who had always taken Gorky to be a champion of the peasant, were puzzled by the essay, which was
published to no fanfare in Berlin in 1922. The incandescent
reaction of Europe's Russian émigrés may be imagined;
Gorky had besmirched their dearest shibboleth, the soulful
Russian peasant.

More insightful, and more cutting, was the response of
Ekaterina Kuskova, the woman who had co-founded the
Famine Relief Committee, now cooling her heels in exile
in Berlin. Her lengthy rebuttal, 'Maxim Gorky on the
Peasantry', tells a different version of the civil war: how the
government had forcibly requisitioned grain so that while
villages starved, the cities could still enjoy their circuses.

Gorky was painfully aware of the justice in Kuskova's
remarks. But, with his signature belligerence, he was determined to do what Lenin and Vorovsky expected him to
do, and wanted him to do: he was 'getting distance on the
problem', exploring the meaning behind the raw events of
revolution, the better to present them to a wider global
public. On 5 October 1922 he sent a copy of his essay to

Romain Rolland, calling it 'a little book steeped in great sorrow. It was not easy to write it, but it was necessary'.

News of the government's campaign of political repression and executions in Petrograd and elsewhere undermined Gorky's attempts at achieving 'distance'. Believing he might still have a shred of influence left over the Soviet regime, he followed the fifty-day trial of the Socialist Revolutionaries, which began on 8 June 1922, with mounting dismay. Of the thirty-four members of the Socialist Revolutionary Party accused of armed struggle against the Soviet state and other trumped-up charges, twelve were sentenced to death.

Through the Soviet vice-premier Alexei Rykov, Gorky let Leon Trotsky know that any executions would be 'premeditated and foul murder'.

Both Lenin and Trotsky reacted with contempt. For Lenin, Gorky was 'always supremely spineless in politics'. Trotsky dismissed Gorky as an 'artist whom no one takes seriously'.

He was wrong about that. Gorky wrote publicly to Anatole France denouncing the trial as a 'cynical and public preparation for the murder' of people who had fought for the freedom of the Russian people. Anatole France publicly agreed, and the international beating the Bolsheviks received over the trial forced Lenin to 'suspend' the execution of the death sentences. (The twelve remained in prison in a sort of living death until Stalin had them all killed.)

There was no coming back from this one. Gorky and Lenin's long correspondence ends for good at this point, and in July, Bolshevik wits Karl Radek and Demian Bednyi launched a campaign against Gorky and Anatole France in the pages of *Pravda*.

Gorky's health continued to trouble him. He moved to a sanatorium in Saarow, near Fürstenwald, then, in the summer of 1923, moved with his family near Freiburg where, it is said, two teams of spies followed him: a German team afraid he would start a revolution, and a Soviet team afraid he would start a counter-revolution.

December found him in empty, snow-locked Marienbad, fulminating over a publication authored by Nadezhda Krupskaya, Lenin's 'not very bright' wife.

Published in November 1923, 'A Guide for the Removal of Anti-Artistic and Counter-Revolutionary Books from Libraries Serving the General Reader' recommended a policy of intellectual intolerance unprecedented even in Russia. Proscribed authors included Plato, Kant, Schopenhauer, Vladimir Solovyov, Taine, Ruskin, Nietzsche, Leskov and Leo Tolstoy.

Gorky told his friend and confidant Vladislav Khodasevich, 'The first impression I experienced was so strong that I started writing to Moscow to announce my repudiation of Russian citizenship. What else can I do if this atrocity turns out to be true?'

But Khodasevich, with the pitiless vision bestowed by close friendship, saw through Gorky's bluster.

Of course 'this atrocity' was true! Khodasevich had visited Gorky for a few days in Freiburg and Gorky had waved a copy of *that very pamphlet* under his nose!

Gorky was pretending that the matter needed further 'looking into', that he 'could not bring himself to believe', and so on and so on. Gorky's prevarications were, as befitted a man so wedded to honesty, 'the most naïve lie imaginable'.

Krupskaya's pamphlet must for sure have had Gorky hankering to renounce his Soviet citizenship. But it was never going to happen. He could not bear the idea of exile, and he had no desire to stamp his entire life a failure. Instead, he did what he always did: he went on working.

*

In the beginning, the most the Soviet government could hope from Gorky was that he would hold his tongue. Incredibly, he did, and kept his anger and recent disappointments to himself. In February 1924, while he was still in Marienbad, he received a telegram from his wife, Ekaterina: 'Vladimir Il'ich is dead, cable the content of the inscription on the wreath.'

He replied, 'On the wreath write: "farewell friend".'

Gorky had to wait three years for Mussolini's government to issue him a visa before finally settling, in the winter of 1924–5, in Il Sorito, a villa on a bluff created by a recent landslide (which was why the place was so cheap). The Italian government feared Gorky might be out to cause political mischief, and the police's twenty-four-hour surveillance of him can be followed through his file, preserved in Italy's Central State Archives.

The Soviet Union had few friends, and supported the celebrated writer's neutrality as though he were their vocal champion. They spent a staggering 1,010,000 rubles a year on Gorky's colony of friends, ex-lovers, assistants, clients and hangers-on. Dmitry Ivanovich Kursky, the Soviet ambassador to Italy, kept up a close and friendly correspondence, and was forever urging Gorky to help him counteract the misinformation about the Soviet Union that appeared in Italian newspapers.

Gorky was all too aware of how 'our friends the journalists like to gnaw and bite. They hunt me down in every possible way,' he complained, in a letter to his wife, Ekaterina. 'They wait for me outside and on stairways, they click their Kodak cameras and humbly ask me to share my senile wisdom with them.'

Gorky had even less sympathy with the sniping of hostile Russian émigrés, and the more distant his bruising experiences in Petrograd (later, Leningrad) became, and the longer

Lenin lay in his ridiculous mausoleum, the more willing he was to praise the Soviet Union – not for what it was, perhaps, but certainly for what it represented and for what it promised.

Was it not, after all, a messianic prophecy come true? The Government of the Workers and Peasants! The Expropriation of the Expropriators! The Dictatorship of the Proletariat! As Arthur Koestler puts it, Utopia had changed overnight from a bloodless *Bauplan* into a real country with real people, 'sufficiently remote in space to give freedom to imagination; with picturesque costumes and nostalgic songs to feed it.'

In the imagination of some Western intellectuals, Russia had been transformed from a backward nation into a beacon pointing the way to the future, and Gorky was more than happy to entertain such an audience. (Ignoring politics in favour of morality is an old habit with intellectuals.) Whenever Romain Rolland wrote to his old friend with some doubt or other, some accusation, some exposé, Gorky would explain it away; or if he couldn't, then he would pass it on to Genrikh Yagoda, an old friend from his Nizhny Novgorod days and now, of all things, head of the new state security service, the OGPU.

It was easy work, because intellectuals like Rolland wanted to be persuaded. They had been preaching the coming revolution for years, for decades, for more than a century. Looking back on his old political commitments, Koestler says that he and his fellow travellers were as stunned by the Russian revolution 'as a country parson who, after delivering his weekly sermon before an empty church, learns from his curate that the Kingdom of Heaven has been announced on the wireless.'

They had no desire to look their gift-horse in the mouth.

The summer of 1928 witnessed the Shakhty Trial – the first major show trial of the Stalin era. In his article 'To the Peasants and Workers', Gorky defended the government's handling of the trial, and accused the suspected engineers of sabotage and of conspiring with 'foreign supporters' to undermine the construction of socialism. The article makes for painful reading but there can be little doubt that it is Gorky's own work, and we have no evidence that he ever thought differently about the matter.

A flood of outraged correspondence ensued.

'Yes, you are a free writer and in your letters to the Soviet press, using that monopoly, you can say whatever you wish in defence of the Soviet authorities,' wrote one Russian in fury; 'you can harass us without any fear of reprisal. You cannot hear anything from us in reply: our hands are bound and the Soviet gag is forced into our mouths. But knowing this, do you suppose that you are acting as a champion of the free word?'

These letters, which might once have prompted Gorky to action on behalf of the summarily arrested and the falsely accused, now stirred him to irritation. His strained friendship with Ekaterina Kuskova finally broke down in 1929 because she persisted in her carefully evidenced attacks on the Soviet government.

'What is important to me,' Gorky wrote in his last letter to her, 'is the rapid all-round development of human personality, the birth of a new man of culture, of workmen in a sugar refinery who read Shelley in the original. Such men do not need a petty accursed truth in the midst of which they are struggling. They need the truth they create for themselves. I am now one-sided.'

Consciously or not, Gorky is here very obviously channelling the character of Luka from his play *The Lower Depths* – the wily old trickster who says, 'You've been saying we need the truth. But it isn't always truth that is good for what ails a man.'

*

It was always on the cards that Gorky would end up doing this – championing the imaginary future over the difficult present. What finally made him 'one-sided', though, was neither despair nor a want of political courage. What set Gorky on his new and narrow course was a trade fair: the 1928 'Pressa' International Press Exhibition in Cologne.

Pressa was the most comprehensive and ambitious exhibition the industry had ever staged, and the Soviet pavilion was, by popular acclaim, its finest flowering: the work of sixty artists, led by the designer and architect El Lissitzky.

'What a contrast between the English and Soviet Russian rooms!' exclaimed the *Berliner Tageblatt* on 26 May. 'Everything that separates the two finds expression when one sees the two brought together under the same roof. England; pious, aristocratic, and historically reverent, at peace in its confidence ... And Russia ... causing a stir by its enormous steps of progress which are depicted in bold and bragging manner, always in glaring red. Forward! in the struggle and into class consciousness.'

Gorky, on his way to celebrate his birthday in his homeland, visited the exhibition in Cologne and was bowled over.

When the imaginary future can be made this vivid, this visceral, why leave your audience stuck in the unrewarding present?

CHAPTER TEN

i

Gorky turned sixty in 1928, and in Russia, grand preparations were made for his birthday. 'This jubilee begins to make me feel famous,' he wrote, 'like Mary Pickford.'

Come summer he was being led through Minsk and Moscow and down the Volga to his birthplace, Nizhny Novgorod, now called Gorky in his honour.

'Things turned out in a strange way,' Gorky afterwards admitted to his old friend Alexander Kalyuzhnyi; 'I met hardly any of my old personal friends.' But he did get to visit the newly styled 'Gorky Labour Colony', a school for delinquent children to whom he had been writing friendly, encouraging letters for about six years. He got to see his young vagabonds and orphans driving tractors and raising their own food. He considered this the highlight of his trip.

The colony was the brainchild of Anton Makarenko, a Ukrainian social worker whose no-nonsense (and, by all accounts, extremely successful) approach to rehabilitating children had scared the life out of the Bolshevik chattering classes (Lenin's wife Krupskaya had dubbed his colony a school for slaves).

Makarenko didn't shy away from discipline and regimentation. He saw a 'profound analogy between industrial and educational processes'. So did his kids, who essentially ran the place. They enjoyed 'army' games, wore uniforms, performed drill and competed for prizes. The 'Gorky' colony was, effectively, a factory for churning out a new kind of person – capable of self-regulation, concerted effort and teamwork. Gorky loved the sound of that, and in 1925 he had begun an eager correspondence with Makarenko, believing the colony would become a beacon of the country's social transformation.

What he saw on his visit confirmed his hopes. Here was a model institution, capable of re-engineering the flawed Russian soul. He knew he was being shown the best the place had to offer. He wrote quite openly about the colony's being a 'show' institution. But we have no reason to believe he was being hoodwinked, and the enthusiasm of the youthful inmates was real enough.

Felix Dzerzhinsky, 'Iron Felix', one of the most brutish and hated figures of the Stalin era, was also enthusiastic about educational reform. 'Care for children,' he once declared, 'is the best means of exterminating the counterrevolution.'

In 1929, on his second return visit to Russia, Gorky got to visit the Ugresha Monastery, where the OGPU had its own labour commune. Dzerzhinsky had taken the school over from the finance ministry and made it over according to his own theories.

Gorky turned up in time to see some new arrivals at the gates 'in incredible rags, with faces covered with dirt and soot; gloomy, angry, they seemed sick, tortured, trampled by the ruthless life of the city.' A couple of hours later, Gorky writes, he found them 'dressed in clean clothes, strong, as if cast in bronze' and wandering unsupervised around the dispensary building.

There are rhetorical flourishes here aplenty, but they detract little from Gorky's compelling descriptions of the camp, whose youthful inmates are 'already quite skilled carpenters, fitters, blacksmiths, shoemakers. Almost all the guys seem healthy on the outside, well-built, and muscular.'

In Gorky's account we meet fifty boys who are working in a sculpture studio; their instructor is a young artist, himself serving a sentence for embezzlement:

> Some sixteen-year-old, a face amazingly similar to Fyodor Chaliapin in his young years, arranged a so-called 'bio-garden' from a huge cage of wire ... In the cage there are magpie chicks, blind little owls, a hedgehog and a large toad, which he calls Banker. The guy is a dreamer, a romantic ...

Again, we have good evidence that Dzerzhinsky's colony was what it appeared to be: a success.

We should not assume, however, that Gorky's accounts of his travels are simple and straightforward. His visits to countless factories, collective farms, Young Communist League events and workers' meetings during the years 1928 and 1929 were not mere junkets; they were arranged to provide him with material for a series of articles under the heading 'Around the Union', in which Gorky, wryly styling himself a 'foreign dignitary', rose to defend the Soviet system.

Gorky's subject in the 'Around the Union' travelogues is not Russia as it is, but Russia as it will be. He makes no apology for writing about 'model' institutions like the Gorky and the Ugresha. Indeed, of the latter he writes, 'At this colony, builders of such institutions can learn much ... it clearly was founded in order to show the ideal of what a children's labour colony for "criminals" and the "socially dangerous" should be.'

Like Makarenkov and Dzerzhinsky, Gorky is willing the future into being.

Of course, it's not entirely clear to the reader where Gorky's reportage leaves off and his speculative triumphalism kicks in. But Gorky has always been fascinated by this muddying of fact and fiction. *The Lower Depths* is about a character who does little else. And just as Gorky's bums in *The Lower Depths* come to half-believe Luka's tale of a kingdom of rewarded virtue, the Gorky of 'Around the Union' invites readers to suspend their disbelief and imagine their way into the world of plenty ushered in by Stalin's policies of forcibly collectivised agriculture and break-neck industrial development.

To those readers of the travelogues who accuse Gorky of whitewashing or fabrication one may well say, with Satine, 'Blockheads! Yes, he lied … but – he did it out of pity for you.'

In 1929 – as part of the same tour that took him to Ugresha – Gorky visited Solovki. This was the OGPU's prototype concentration camp, located in a former monastery in the far north.

Everything in Solovki had been going to hell in a handcart, but the memory of what the place was supposed to be was not yet dead, and Gorky was perfectly serious when he opined that camps such as Solovki were necessary if the state was ever to do what it had set out to do and abolish prisons.

The prison abolition movement was championed by Fedor Eikhmans, a former Latvian rifleman who had joined the Cheka in 1918. Eikhmans, like Gorky, believed in the power of culture to reform the individual. Under his leadership the first prison camps developed extraordinary cultural programmes.

Eikhmans handed the running of these programmes to convicted members of the intelligentsia. His fellow administrators were appalled: cultural activities in the camps, if they existed at all, should be ideologically committed, and centrally supervised! But Eikhmans defended his policy against all-comers.

His vision for the camps was that, far from punishing their inmates, they would give them new purpose: by colonising Russia's northern frontier, they would be playing a decisive role in the country's industrialisation. Eikhmans would soon have no need to guard his own inmates, for his 'camps', so-called, were nothing less than the seeds – scattered across the ungiving tundra – of future proletarian mining towns. Prisons would become a vestige of the bourgeois past.

Eikhmans's fanciful plan was sanctioned at the highest levels of government. In 1929 Solovki was explicitly mentioned in decrees as a prototype camp that would place economic profit and the settlement of new territory above containment and punishment. (In 1929, Eikhmans was transferred to Moscow, and in 1930 he became the first ever director of the Gulag.)

Alas, the wheels started coming off Eikhmans's revolutionary system almost the moment it was set in motion. His logging camps, which had turned such an impressive profit in their first few years, were hopelessly wasteful, and ran out of trees; which meant they ran out of money; which meant that food rations shrank to almost nothing and typhus ran rampant through the prison population.

Nor, in his desire to reshape prisoners, did it ever occur to him to reshape the guards, who considered their postings a punishment, and took their resentment out on the inmates, with ever more brutal punishments and humiliations. Exhausted prisoners died in numbers; others chopped off fingers and feet to avoid work.

For several years, Solovki had been garnering international headlines of the least helpful sort. In the spring of 1925, a convict, S. A. Malsagov, had escaped. His prison experiences, rushed into print in the US under the title *An Island Hell*, had prompted other former prisoners to set down their experiences, and now a daunting volume, *Letters from Russian Prisons*, was causing an unpleasant stir in diplomatic circles.

Gorky was well aware of these controversies. In a letter from 1927 – two years before he visited – we find Gorky complaining about Britain's decision to break off diplomatic relations with the Soviet Union because of their use of prison labour. He adds: 'The events in London have made me so upset that I felt like going to Russia just so that I could enter into a swearing match with Europe from there.'

The sequence of articles under the banner 'Around the Soviets' was Gorky's way of keeping that promise. The account of a visit to Solovki by a sympathetic 'foreign dignitary' promised to set the record straight – or at any rate rebalance it in the Soviet Union's favour.

The fifteenth-century monastery – once used by the Orthodox Church to imprison heretics – was spruced up for the occasion. New clothes were issued, working hours reduced, guards dressed up as prisoners to make a better impression. As if by magic, a library appeared.

Gorky arrived at Solovka in the company of the secret police, the Cheka. They led him through clean barracks with big windows, 'decorated with personal things: private blankets, pillows; on the walls hung photographs and postcards; on window sills there are flowers.' They sat him down to enjoy a concert and other cultural events. There were newspapers. (Some prisoners turned their copies upside down in protest. Gorky silently turned one of them the right way up: not here, Comrade, not now.) There were 'interesting' conversations with the inmates. A fourteen-year-old boy volunteered to talk to him, left the old man in tears, and promptly disappeared. During the intermission of a theatre show, prisoners thrust notes at him. He kept them, only to lose them all when one of his suitcases was stolen.

In the journal *Our Accomplishments*, Gorky explains how 'socially dangerous people are being transformed into socially useful ones, professional criminals into highly qualified workers and conscious revolutionaries'. Significantly, given what he had already written about the youth camps, he said that in Solovki, 'there is no resemblance of a prison but instead it seems that these rooms are inhabited by passengers rescued from a drowned ship' – passengers described, moreover, as 'healthy lads in unbleached linen shirts and high boots.'

In Gorky's description, it's really only the age of the inmates that distinguishes them from the boys driving tractors around the fields of Makarenko's youth colony.

Gorky is certainly not telling the truth here. A Moscow commission sent to Solovki in 1930 discovered 'chilling facts of mass violence against prisoners'. Murders. Beatings with fire-hardened sticks. Endless, inventive tortures.

But Gorky's account of Solovki is not so much a lie as a fiction: a faithful, detailed, carefully researched depiction of what Solovki was supposed to be like. There really was a library in Solovki, or there had been. The camp journal and newspaper were once among the freest publications in the USSR. Its theatre was still considered one of the best regional theatres in the country. Gorky at one point mentions a little museum – surely a piece of Potemkinite nonsense, fashioned for his visit? But no: the museum was real.

Gorky was not the only one recruited to sing the praises of the camp system. In the same year he visited Solovki, 1929, the filmmaker Evgeny Cherkasov produced *Solovetsky*

Lager (*The Solovki Prison Camp*), a film in which prisoners, unhealthy at the beginning of the film, are considerably fitter by the end: working, reading, playing musical instruments, performing in plays ...

But the film was never shown. The camps ceased to be show institutions, and a few years later, they vanished from the maps.

It is likely that Gorky looked forward to his visit to Solovki quite as much as he had looked forward to visiting Makarenko's reform colony for street children. He had already written about the OGPU's new camps as vehicles for weeding out the 'elemental' in man and in nature. Years after his visit, in 1933, when the camps were well on their way to becoming death camps, Gorky was still full of praise for the administrators.

'*Inzhenery perekovki dush*', he called them. Engineers of the human soul.

ii

Gorky returned to Sorrento – but not for long. Powerful forces were drawing him home

Josef Stalin had been general secretary of the Party's Central Committee since May 1922. Initially governing as part of a collective leadership, he had, since Lenin's death, consolidated power to become, effectively, a dictator.

A critical shortfall in grain supplies in 1928 had prompted him to push for the collectivisation of agriculture. This, together with his plans for more rapid industrialisation and central control of the economy, was alienating rightists in the

Party, and he was not yet powerful enough simply to expunge these dissenting voices.

Who better to champion his cause, then, than Maxim Gorky, arguably the Soviet Union's only international celebrity, and a man whose views on the need to contain and regiment the peasant classes was already known?

That Gorky was no longer quite the draw he had been, and was running out of money, only made Stalin's job easier. He sent the writer chummy, handwritten letters. 'The USSR is going to be a first-rate country,' he scribbled, 'with the biggest technically equipped industrial and agricultural production Socialism is invincible. There's not going to be any more "beggarly" Russia. That's over! There's going to be a mighty and plentiful vanguard Russia.'

Stalin's rightist opponents – Bukharin, Rykov and Kamenev – were also pursuing a flattering correspondence with Gorky, hoping to bring him to their side. (Rykov had Palekh craftsmen craft Gorky a fancy desk set.)

'I was,' Gorky remarked later, 'put into a situation in which I could not fail to come home.'

Settling in Moscow, Gorky asked for a simple, spacious apartment. But the city didn't have many of those and, as he wrote to his secretary Pyotr Kriuchkov on 1 March 1931, there was a rumour going round that a kind of palace or church was being renovated for his use. How would that go down with the proletariat, he wondered, 'who worked like crazy and lived in pigsties'?

The house, No. 6, Malaia Nikitskaya, was an art nouveau masterpiece, once the home of millionaire industrialist Pavel Ryabushinsky. Gorky thought it 'a ridiculous place' and spent most of his time at a dacha in the suburbs.

Stalin's summer home just happened to be nearby. Zamyatin remembers how the neighbours, 'one with his invariable pipe, the other with a cigarette, closeted themselves for hours, talking over a bottle of wine.'

That Gorky eventually came to adopt Stalin's breakneck economic and industrial programme – and never mind the human cost – appalled his western friends and remains a deep, dark mystery to a generation of historians. But there's really no mystery – not if we pay attention to what Gorky actually said. His essay 'On the Russian Peasantry' is explicit: only regimentation and discipline can save the country's twenty million peasants from themselves. Why, given that, would we think Gorky would *not* be in favour of Stalin's collectivisation programme? In an enthusiastic letter to Stalin, Gorky wrote:

This is practically a geological transformation – bigger, immeasurably bigger and deeper, than everything the Party has done so far. A way of life is being destroyed that has existed for millennia – a way of life that created a uniquely ugly creature, horrifying in his animal conservatism and his private property instinct. There are twenty million people like that. The task of re-educating them in a short period of time is the insanest of problems. Nonetheless here it has practically been solved.

(In a hideous way, he was proved right: this calamitous state land grab ended up, one way or another, being responsible for the deaths of twelve million people.)

The promulgation of Stalin's first five-year plan re-awoke all Gorky's hopes for the nation, not to mention several long-nursed personal ambitions. Among the proposals Gorky submitted to Stalin were a newspaper to deal with the life of émigré Russians, a series of popular books about the civil war, and a re-evaluation of anti-religious propaganda (he was god-building again). A complete list of all the projects Gorky launched between 1929 and 1936 would run to many pages. Like Stephen Leacock's Lord Ronald, Gorky 'flung himself from the room, flung himself upon his horse and rode madly off in all directions'.

While some of Gorky's proposals fell on stony ground, Stalin gave his personal backing to dozens of others.

By far Gorky's most impressive project was the Soviet Writers' Union. While he had been living in Sorrento, Soviet literature had fallen under the command – there is really no other way of putting it – of RAPP, the Russian Association of Proletarian Writers, an extreme leftist association whose stated aim was 'to scourge and chastise' their fellows 'in the name of the Party'. They were distinguished less by their literary skill than by their belligerence and Party membership. Nothing good had come of their efforts. Some of the writers subjected to their 're-education' efforts had fallen silent; the works of others betrayed obvious false notes which jarred the least demanding ear, and certainly jarred Stalin's, since he took the arts far more seriously than Lenin ever had, and listened to Gorky's literary opinions.

While living in Italy, Gorky had received many letters from aspiring young writers complaining of their 'literary torments'. RAPP officials had told Vsevolod Ivanov his play *An Armoured Train* was 'not revolutionary enough', and cancelled its production. Leonid Leonov wrote to Gorky complaining that the only subjects left open to writers are 'socialist emulation and the industrial finance counter-plan'.

Gorky, who had kept a note of these complaints, told Stalin that, given command over the Russian literary scene, he could improve the general quality of Russian literature.

Stalin took him at his word. On 23 April 1932, a government decree declared RAPP 'an obstacle to the development of Soviet literature', and put in its place 'a single union of Soviet writers with a Communist faction therein'.

The Soviet Writers' Union had Gorky's signature all over it. Joining the union earned you foreign food and good clothing and maybe an occasional stint at a writers' retreat in the country. If you didn't join, you didn't get published, but members enjoyed a more or less guaranteed income. The union matched writers to publishing houses, and even handed out assignments to journalists. It was the model on which other cultural unions in film, theatre and the fine arts would be constructed.

It is the middle of 1932, and Maxim Gorky has reached the peak of his political influence. The Presidium of the Central Committee of the Party has passed a resolution, 'On Measures to mark the fortieth Anniversary of Maxim Gorky's Literary Work'. Some measures, like the publication of Gorky's collected works and the gift of a summer home in Tesseli in Crimea, are welcome. Some are positively surreal. Many schools, factories and collective farms already bear the name of the writer; now the world's largest plane, the eight-engine Tupolev ANT-20, is christened *Maxim Gorky*.

Others are simply embarrassing, as when the Moscow Art Theatre is renamed the 'Gorky Art Theatre'.

'But Comrade Stalin,' protests Ivan Gronsky, editor-in-chief of the official state newspaper *Izvestia*, 'that is more Chekhov's theatre. And anyway, you've already piled it on pretty damn thick, so to speak.'

'That doesn't matter,' Stalin replies, and leaning over, very quietly, says to him: 'He's an ambitious man. We have to bind him to the Party.'

Little over a month later, on 26 October, Gorky hosts a dinner to hash out Soviet policy towards literature and the arts. Stalin is in attendance, but the floor is Gorky's. In a preparatory meeting with writers, the great organiser was explicit: 'Should we not unite realism and romanticism in a third form that would be able to depict the heroic present in brighter tones and speak of it in a more elevated and digni-fied manner?'

The dinner, at Gorky's grandiloquent mansion on Malaya Nikitskaya, seals the deal. Tables covered with white cloths shine under glittering chandeliers. The dining room is full. All the Kremlin's great and good are here: Molotov, Voroshilov, Kaganovich – and Stalin, of course, around whom the fifty or so invited writers steer their careful orbit.

(No one here doubts Stalin's love of good literature. Mikhail Bulgakov and Mikhail Zoshchenko are numbered among his favourite writers; he keeps them close, on meagre rations, just barely surviving and under constant threat of arrest. Such dangerous talents are Stalin's private vice; need-less to say these men are not in attendance tonight.)

The point of the evening is to set up Gorky's 'third literary form' as the pattern for all future creative production. It's in the nature of projects like this that an inordinate amount of time is spent trying to give it a name. Ivan Gronsky, a gov-ernment spokesman on cultural matters, has been calling it 'proletarian socialism', sometimes, 'communist realism'. Stalin suggests 'socialist realism' (brief; simple; doesn't prom-ise too much). And of course it's Stalin's name that sticks.

The hour grows late. Glasses are emptied and replenished, emptied and replenished. Alexander Fadeyev – formerly of RAPP, now a leading light in the Writers' Union – persuades Mikhail Sholokhov to get up and sing. Another writer stag-gers forward to clink glasses with Stalin. Vladimir Lugovskoi the poet starts shouting: 'Let's all drink the health of Comrade Stalin!'

Another writer jumps up. 'I'm fed up with this! We have drunk Stalin's health one million one hundred and forty-seven thousand times. He's probably fed up with it himself!'

Across the room: a deathly silence.

Then Stalin gets up and shakes the man's hand. 'Thank you, thank you. I'm fed up to the back teeth with it.'

And everyone goes home with a smile on their face. The writers are as proud as punch. Has Stalin not just described them as 'engineers of human souls'? According to Stalin, 'The production of souls is more important than the production of tanks'! (Voroshilov, the People's Commissar for War, objected to that, but no one paid him any attention.)

On 17 August 1933, two weeks after it officially opened, Gorky led a company of 120 writers to see the finished White Sea–Baltic Canal. Several of the period's most important talents came along for the trip, including Mikhail Zoshchenko and Aleksei Tolstoy. Many fully shared Gorky's enthusiasm for 'perekovka' – the policy of human salvage through re-education. Others could not join the writers' brigade because they were already inmates, and labouring on the canal.

The idea of a waterway linking the Baltic and White Seas had been flitting between government offices since at least the seventeenth century. The link would open up Karelia, with its rich supplies of timber, fur and minerals, and protect the Soviet navy should Leningrad experience a sea blockade.

Work began on 'Belomor' in 1931 and by July 1933 the vision was realised. Gorky and his brigade of writers were some of the first to sail through the canal. They did not see many workers on their ten-day excursion; most had already been dispatched to other construction projects. They did, though, get to enjoy a show at the camp theatre.

Gorky, speaking publicly at the site, congratulated the OGPU: 'I am happy and touched by what has been said here, and by what I know – I have been watching the OGPU reform people since 1928 ... You have done a great thing – a very great thing!'

It was certainly a tremendous physical feat: 227 kilometres long, with nineteen locks, fifteen dams and countless dikes and reservoirs. With simple resources – wood, peat, stones, dirt, here and there a dab of cement – workers had rerouted rivers and railways, stopped waterfalls, flooded islands and designed every mechanism in every lock, dam and reservoir.

There is only one way such an impoverished country can accomplish this and similar feats of industrialisation. It used slave labour. The canal was built almost entirely by hand, by around half a million conscripts. Even the engineers were prisoners.

'It's not very big,' Stalin muttered, during the opening ceremony.

It was not very deep, either, and much of it was unlined. But it delivered on at least some of its potential, reducing the travel time between Leningrad and Arkhangelsk from twenty days to eight; years later, it would be the saving of some Soviet ships in the Second World War.

The official book, *Belomorsko-Baltysky kanal imeni Stalina* (*The History of the Construction of the White Sea–Baltic Canal*), assembled and edited by Gorky and composed by thirty-five of the writers who travelled its length, is a surprisingly exhilarating read. The first lock is constructed, and an engineer, examining its handiwork, declares with some surprise that 'wood gates are not inferior to iron ones.' Time and again, the workers' botched solutions turn out to be just what the canal needs: stronger, more versatile and more practical than the West's fancy, high-maintenance iron-work. 'Socialist hydrotechnology' carries the day: 'America and Europe gasped and took off its hat', apparently, to workers armed only with 'rough-hewn pickaxes'.

The camps are humane institutions, staffed by exemplars of the new Soviet man. The OGPU men – valiant champions of social justice – dress as officers but live like monks: 'You never see them drunk, and they don't hang around the girls,' says one prisoner.

There are casualties, of course. The *History* mentions two. On page 274, a prisoner dies in a mining accident for which no one is to blame. On page 335, a female prison worker, receiving a medal for exceeding her production quota, mentions her dear departed father, who also worked on the canal. How he died isn't explained.

The work camp offers redemption through labour. A work-credit system ensures that prisoners who meet their quotas receive a reduction in their sentence. Because prisoners work together in brigades, success is collective, and even the laziest prisoners eventually develop a work ethic. The administration has no need to drive the inmates to heroic acts: they drive each other.

So Belomor becomes, as one prisoner puts it, a 'life factory' where people are remade: 'Yes, strange, unusual transformations are made here. Miraculous transformations, nothing about which you could find even in fairy tales.'

The process of reformation is a violent one. Zoshchenko defines it in medical terms: 'Now we will try a new surgery with the knife, that is, to cut the tissue of the surface.' In his introduction, Maxim Gorky claims that these surgeons of the soul operate 'not to kill as the bourgeoisie does, but rather to resurrect labouring humankind into a new life, and … will kill only when there is no longer the possibility to blot out man's former habits of feeding on the flesh and blood of the people.'

We remember the *History* chiefly for its notorious blend of fact and fiction, detailed reportage and fond fancy. For the writers it was an ambitious attempt to realise Gorky's 'third literary form'. These writers actually got out of their armchairs and went to work in the archive and in the field. The result is a sort of starchy, Soviet-style gonzo journalism, a 'literature of fact', livelier and more edifying than the fiction of the time.

'We decided to write about everything in a new way,' one of the contributors explained to *Pravda* on 7 December 1933:

We worked on the book collectively. We jointly devised a plan for the book. Every line was written by every one of us and discussed by all the others. We added material to each other's stories. In the course of the last ten days we, all together, edited the book that will be a collective whole work.

The *History* was rushed into print to celebrate the achievements of the first five-year plan, and 4,000 copies were reserved for the delegates of the Seventeenth Party Congress. The public edition that year sold 80,000 copies, and another 30,000 in 1935, so someone must have been reading it.

Published in Gorky's series 'History of Factories and Plants', the history of the canal marks the high point of ambition for this kind of sketch writing: often disjointed, sometimes downright chaotic, but indisputably the dominant literary form during the first five-year plan. And what young writer wouldn't want to visit far-flung places and write about them for a decent fee?

Writers under despots may have to take instruction, but they're rarely out of a job. Gorky – enthralled as always with great events and heroes, marshalled writers to write histories of the civil war, of young people, of the five-year plan. Not content with his 'Lives of Great Men' and several histories of the Soviet era, he urged people to write their own histories, testifying to the miraculous transformations being experienced in factories and villages.

Gorky's 'literature of fact' foundered in the end, but not because it ran into literary problems. By the time Gorky's collaborative history of the canal was being pilloried by Western critics for glossing over the deaths of 200,000 indentured labourers, the original (and far superior) Russian edition of the book had already become very difficult to get hold of.

The 1937 Purges, that killed around a million 'enemies of the people', either by execution or during incarceration in the Gulag, anathematised so many of the names contained in this Stalinist bestseller, it proved impossible to revise. It was eventually banned.

iii

In 1920, Vladimir Lenin had suggested to his esteemed visitor H. G. Wells that he should visit Russia again in ten years' time, to witness the country's socialist transformation for himself.

A little late, in 1934, Wells gets his wish.

Now sixty-eight and exhibiting all the barking omniscience of 'a man struggling with a gramophone', Wells arrives in Moscow convinced of two truths. First, that US president Franklin Roosevelt's New Deal is the first step towards America's adoption of socialism. Second, that a Russian branch of the PEN Club, a worldwide association of writers, will, if permitted, quickly supersede all previous peace-building efforts of the League of Nations and all the Internationals – first, second and third. ('The offer,' George

Bernard Shaw sneered in the *New Statesman and Nation*, 'has struck Russia speechless.')

Wells's trip is short – only eleven days – but he manages to bag an interview with Stalin, whom he finds 'easy-going, friendly, and simple. All lingering anticipations of a dour, sinister highlander vanished at the sight of him. I have never met a man more candid, fair and honest.'

He also gets to visit Gorky – by now counted among his oldest friends – at his dacha outside Moscow.

Ivan Maisky, visiting from London where he is Soviet ambassador, sees that Wells finds Gorky much changed, and altogether too calm. 'I remarked with a smile that there was nothing surprising in it,' Maisky remembers. 'Why shouldn't Gorky be calm, when he saw his dreams coming true?'

Wells is not reassured. Gorky seems to him to be quite out of sorts. Why, he has even dismissed the idea of a Russian PEN Club . . .!

Later, Wells writes of his friend: 'Something human and distressful in him, which had warmed my sympathies in his fugitive days, has evaporated altogether. He has changed into a class-conscious proletarian Great Man.'

It's clear enough what's going on. Gorky's prestige is as artificial as it is colossal.

When authorities have difficulty about naming a new aeroplane or a new avenue or a new town or a new organisation, they solve the difficulty by calling it Maxim Gorky. He seems quietly aware of the embalming, and the mausoleum and apotheosis awaiting him, when he too will become a sleeping Soviet divinity.

Gorky is no more taken with Wells: The PEN Club idea is all he will talk about, and this annoys Gorky, who wanted this evening at his dacha to be a rather more triumphal affair, with Wells relating favourable impressions of all the changes he has noticed in the USSR since his previous visit.

When Wells returns yet again to that blasted PEN Club business, frustration gets the better of Gorky: 'Are there fascists among the members of this club of yours?'

Wells blinks. 'I expect so,' he replies.

Gorky finds this deplorable.

Wells finds Gorky tiresome. What is the point of all this political control and restraint? Whence this extraordinary ability to detect capitalist intrigue in every unfamiliar word or suggestion? 'I did not like to find Gorky against liberty. It wounded me.'

Now that the PEN Club is off the table, Wells is at a loss to know what to talk about. Gorky tries to get him interested in the reconstruction of Moscow, and the city's plans for a splendid metro system.

Wells is sceptical. Why not just buy a couple of thousand buses?

Gorky bites his lip and sits in silence, tapping a matchbox against the table edge. He would dearly love to say something cutting, but he has to be hospitable.

When eventually they rise from the table, Gorky invites Wells up to his study. A broad marble staircase leads to the third floor.

Wells stops a moment. 'I remember how you lived on Kronverksky,' he smiles. 'That place was much more modest.' He looks about him: 'Is it good to be a great proletarian writer?'

He's only teasing, but Gorky colours up like a beetroot and says, 'My people gave me this house.'

*

The new union's First Soviet Writers' Congress is held in August 1934 in the immense colonnaded hall of the House of Unions in Moscow. Delegations representing millions of readers are turning up, alongside intellectuals people had forgotten still existed. Thousands of letters are pouring in – congratulations, suggestions, schemes, bad poetry – from workers, collective farmers, students, Young Pioneers. A spirit of freedom winds among the seven hundred writers and seven hundred officials and policemen attending the opening session.

It's an odd sort of freedom, to be sure: established by fiat, administered, centralised, and codified. A few bourgeois hold-outs still wrestle with the idea that creative production has to be unionised at all. But even Maxim Gorky's three-hour opening address cannot altogether extinguish the general enthusiasm.

Picking out the *grand écrivain* from amid the stage dressing – foliage, busts, portraits – including one of Gorky himself – is no small task, made harder when Gorky, blinded by spotlights, snaps at the production crew: 'Get rid of that candle!'

It all begins charmingly enough, as Gorky sings the praises of folklore and myth. Romantic myths, he says, foster the very attitudes that can change the world in practical ways. How might one measure the practical benefits bestowed on humanity by the deeds of folk heroes like Hercules, Prometheus, Don Quixote and Faust?

No one would dispute that literature inspires people. Convinced fellow-travellers in the audience – men like André Malraux (with *Man's Fate*, already a rising French novelist) and Gustav Regler (the noted German refugee) blithely accept Gorky's corollary: that 'pessimism is entirely alien to folklore,' because the collective knows that it will ultimately triumph over all hostile forces.

This, says Gorky, is why tragedy, suffering and neurosis have no place in Soviet literature.

Malraux blinks. *What did he just say?*

'A new type of man is springing up in the Soviet Union,' Gorky declares. 'He possesses a faith in the organising power of reason. He is conscious of being the builder of a new world, and though he still finds life difficult, he knows that the whole aim and purpose of his rational will is to create different conditions. He has no grounds for pessimism.'

Gorky, who says he scorns all philosophies other than Marxism-Leninism, explains that writers imbued with capitalism and imperialism understand nothing about human psychology. The nearest they ever get to a truthful portrayal of the human condition is 'critical realism', which he defines as 'the selfish creation of superfluous people who, too weak to fight their own corner in life, unable even to find a corner to crouch in, and more or less clearly grasping the pointlessness of individual existence, read into their own aimlessness the futility of all civic life and the whole historical process.'

Gorky now takes some cheap shots. How typical of Dostoevsky, that he should have been there at the invention of the detective novel, a form invented by bourgeois capitalists to crush the proletariat's class consciousness! In bourgeois literature, there are assassins and thieves everywhere ...

One by one, and then in a steady stream, Gorky's audience starts slipping out for refreshment. Thank heaven there are many buffets. The exodus builds to the point where the organisers are rushing around telling people that it's rude to leave the room.

But Malraux and Regler aren't going anywhere: they're riveted by the spectacle of Gorky's steady disintegration.

Gorky explains that the hero of folklore, the 'simpleton', always turns out to be wiser than those who despised him.

Who is Icarus (whom the bourgeois libel as a parable of hubris!) but a prototype of the Soviet rocket? What is God, but 'an artificial summing up of the products of labour'?

'Monsieur is a trifle behind the times,' Malraux whispers to Regler, and Regler, close to hysterics, bites his knuckles, hard.

Over the next three weeks – from 8 August to 2 September – in three hundred speeches (none of them, thankfully, as long as Gorky's) literary production is bolted to Soviet power. Every two or three days the secret police – now called the People's Commissariat for Internal Affairs, or NKVD – prepares reports on the mood of the congress. Every speech, the way it's written up, even its position in the schedule, has to be approved by the Central Committee and the Politburo.

Socialist realism is already more than a method. It's the blueprint for an entire bureaucratically centralised culture.

Back in the hall, the temperature is rising. It's like a greenhouse in there. 'Everything's going so smoothly,' the Ukrainian poet Mykhaylo Semenko complains, 'I'm overcome by a simply maniacal urge to take a piece of shit or rotten fish and throw it at the congress presidium.'

Andrei Zhdanov, secretary of the Party's Central Committee, fancies himself a maven of Soviet culture. In an address famous for its public mention of those 'engineers of human souls', he says that 'Soviet literature must know how to portray our heroes; it must be able to look into our tomorrow.'

In ordinary life Zhdanov is a gloomy and heavy presence, but the spirit of the occasion, or possibly the rocketing temperature, inspires him to flights of oratorical fancy. He uses lots of 'R'-words.

Socialist realism is, he says, 'romanticism of a new type,

revolutionary romanticism,' which depicts reality, 'not in a dead, scholastic way, not simply as "objective reality",' but as 'reality in its revolutionary development.'

Socialist realism, in other words, is a myth. Were the radiant socialist future to recede before us all, beckoning to us from an unreachable horizon, then socialist realism will keep us chasing after it.

Anatoly Lunacharsky's exegesis of socialist realism is even more chilling. The 'bourgeois realist' sees that the palace has no roof and gloats, 'Here's your socialism!' Such a person 'does not understand that truth does not sit still. Truth flies, truth is *development*, truth is *struggle*, truth is *the day after tomorrow*. He who does not understand this is a pessimist, a whiner, a swindler, and a falsifier ... voluntarily or involuntarily, a counterrevolutionary and a wrecker.'

The socialist-realist artist, on the contrary, depicts the palace in its finished form with the roof already on. The socialist realist does not accept reality as it is. He accepts it as it will be, 'not to conceal reality but, through stylization, to reveal it.'

As a defence of the white lie, this rivals anything by Gorky.

The few remaining bourgeoisie object. 'I sit and listen in pain,' confides Alexey Novikov-Priboy, who writes nautical adventures. 'According to the speeches and reports, everything's fine, but for anyone, like me, who knows the present literary situation, it's a real impasse. The period of literature's total bureaucratisation is upon us.'

The critic Valerian Pravdukhin agrees: 'Everything that's happening right now in literature is shameless demagoguery and publishing terror.'

Much embarrassment is caused when the congress's distinguished guest André Breton refuses any kind of political control of literature, even in the name of revolution.

But not everyone is as enamoured of freedom as Breton. Gorky is dead against it. When 'Russian writers enjoyed full freedom of creation,' the results were deplorable. The period 1901–1917 'deserves to be branded the most shameful and shameless decade in the history of the Russian intelligentsia'.

'Who has shouted loudest for freedom of expression?' asks another foreign guest, Breton's countryman, the poet Louis Aragon. 'Marinetti – and look where it has led him: to Fascism! We have nothing to hide, and that is why we welcome as a joyful expression the new slogan of Soviet literature: Socialist Realism.'

Rank-and-file writers liked the Soviet Writers' Union. What's not to like about being regularly paid?

But like a state-run factory, a state-run union was not very effective. Bureaucracy flourished; mediocrity was rewarded; talent was stifled. Very quickly, RAPP operators like Alexander Fadeyev and Fedor Panfyorov rose to prominence and, against Gorky's protests, came to form the core of the organisation. Gorky, fed up with having to work with writers he did not respect, tendered his resignation as chairman.

'The "big names" in literature are rich,' Gorky complained in a letter to a friend, on 7 November 1935:

Money is often distributed without due care, taking no account of the actual needs of Union members. It is not unusual for a needy writer to be denied assistance, whilst that same writer's sister might be given five thousand rubles. The government gave money for the construction of a dacha settlement, and 700,000 rubles of that sum has vanished like smoke in the wind. There are many instances of such generosity.

Shortly afterwards he wrote to Molotov, decrying 'these days of the spoilt, the sated, and the indifferent.'

In June 1935 Gorky was visited by Romain Rolland and his Russian-born wife, Marija Pavlovna.

Gorky had long since convinced Rolland that Josef Stalin was necessary for the Soviet Union's survival, and in conversations with the dictator, Rolland tried to explain to him how badly the leader's latest repressions were playing in the West.

Stalin was unbending. Conspirators against Soviet power were everywhere! New plots were being uncovered all the time!

Rolland soothed his troubled conscience with visits to the Bolshoi Theatre, a reception with select politicians and intellectuals, and a workers' gymnastics demonstration in Red Square.

But his disquiet was not so easily smoothed over. 'This was not the Russia of the Civil War,' he later wrote, 'but the Russia of pharaohs.'

This realisation coloured his visit to Gorky's beautiful villa in the suburbs. Rolland spent three weeks with Gorky, who was forever entertaining delegations of one sort or another: Palekh artists, metro workers, musicians, cinema directors, youth from Makarenko's labour commune. ('When a great man is recognised as great,' wrote Lu Xun, China's own Maxim Gorky figure, in 1926, 'he has already become a puppet or a fossil.')

Stalin was a regular visitor, lording it over tiresome lunches, tedious dinners, interminable banquets.

Gorky, against doctors' orders, drank like a fish and kept picking stupid arguments with his fellow diners, even with Stalin. He was never alone, Rolland wrote, but at the same time he was very lonely.

In 1918 it had been given to Yevgeny Zamyatin to spot the secret of Gorky's method: calmly shaving, writing books and generally behaving as if he and everybody else had at least twenty more years to live. Fifteen years on, Romain Rolland got to see the price Gorky paid for devoting himself to the great cause, 'albeit seeing the mistakes, the suffering and even the inhumanity of the cause'.

'His life is being lived as if on the surface of the sea, and not in its depth,' Rolland wrote. 'Gorky is a weak, very weak man in spite of his looks of an old bear.'

Poor old bear! Surrounded by fame, and luxuries that he does not want!

'It seems to me,' Rolland wrote, 'that if the two of us were left alone, and the language barrier would be no more, he would give me a hug and would quietly cry for a long while.'

DING LING (JIANG BINGZHI)

1904−1986

CHAPTER ELEVEN

i

Shanghai, 17 January 1931.

Hu Yepin is in fine form. Today he's setting off for the Jiangxi Soviet, where he'll spend the best part of a year working for the Communist Party leadership. Before he goes, though, there's a meeting of the League of Left-Wing Writers. And he has to meet a friend, Shen Congwen, to borrow some money . . .

'So I'll be back for lunch.' He shucks on his coat. 'Wait for me.'

So she waits.

She sits staring out at the grey sky, their three-month-old asleep on her lap.

The sky grows dark.

Night comes, and the street lights come on.

She waits.

The child is sleeping.

She lays him in his cot and flings open the door and runs into the street. She bolts back and forth along the road, calling for her husband.

No one answers.

In the morning she receives a note – a scrap of yellow paper scribbled over in pencil. Hu says he's been arrested by the British and handed over to the nationalist Kuomintang.

He writes that under no circumstances will he surrender. She must tell them that: the League, the Party.

Take heart, he says.

Take heart!

A local lawyer discovers Hu Yepin has already been handed to the Public Security Bureau. By the time she arrives at the bureau, Hu has been moved again, to Longhua, a Shanghai suburb famous for its pagoda and peach blossoms, but most of all for its political prison.

It snows all day. Messages pass between Shanghai and the Communist Party's headquarters in Nanjing.

Nothing comes of this. Years will pass before the ugly truth emerges: the twenty-odd arrests that day were staged as part of an internal Communist Party coup.

She was born Jiang Bingzhi, but she's wedded to her pen-name now. Easy to remember. Even easier to write – just two strokes for the character 'Ding'. The next day. Shen Congwen accompanies Ding Ling through the snow (it's still falling) to the prison at Longhua. (She's not yet recovered from child-birth; her feet are so swollen she can barely walk.) They turn up with a blanket and a change of clothes but the guards tell them no one is allowed to see the prisoner. They ask the guards to pass Hu a ten-yuan note and to get a receipt. This works – and as they're waiting, Shen glimpses, through barred iron doors, a group of figures emerging into the shadows of the yard. One bends his head, scrawling something on a piece of paper, and Shen (who is a glass-half-full sort of person) nudges Ding and points.

Ding decides this must be her husband. 'Pin, Pin, I'm here!' The figure looks up, but a guard hustles him quickly away.

Shen, being Shen, is convinced things will work out for the

best. The Kuomintang's chief of propaganda is bound to put in a good word for the lad, 'as one writer to another'.

And the snow comes down harder and Ding visits again and is turned away again and by the time she and Shen are riding the train back to Shanghai, on the night of 7 February, she knows it is pointless to hope.

While Ding and Shen are on the train, Ding's husband is being killed. He's left her a letter, written hours before his execution and in seeming ignorance of what is about to happen. Ding receives it on the 10th.

He's not surrendering, which probably means he's in for a two- or three-year term. No matter! It'll give him a chance to write a better novel. No shortage of material in here. Can she get him some paper?

On and on like this. It breaks her heart.

Prior to the Communists seizing power, Russia's educated classes spent at least a century wondering 'what might be done' with their dysfunctional country. Not so the Chinese. All Chinese scholars were, by definition, civil servants, tasked – as a condition of their education – with the running of the empire. This dispensation had held for thousands of years. China's budding intellectuals knew *exactly* what they were going to be when they grew up.

Then, in 1903, came a steady phasing-out of the imperial examination system. By 1905 it was quite done away with.

This left a young generation of trained minds unemployed, unemployable, and wholly alienated from power: a human time-bomb just waiting for a bout of national humiliation to set it off.

In 1905, a Western journalist wrote:

The young men, who already form a class apart in China, are pro-Japanese scholars, who have assimilated a superficial knowledge at the Tokyo schools, and being in a transition stage, with one foot on the rock of Chinese classics, and the other on the bobbing raft of the dangerous New Learning, they must necessarily halt at the treaty ports, and attempt to make for themselves positions which are as yet denied them in the interior. Such men drift into journalism.

The collapse of the Qing dynasty in 1911 ushered in a republic, which fell in a matter of weeks into the hands of Yuan Shikai, a well-armed reactionary who even attempted to set himself up as a new emperor. For young intellectuals, a return to Confucianism was an unbearable prospect, representing everything restrictive about their parents' way of life. The writer Yii Ta-fu remembers:

I nursed the idea of going to Russia and becoming a worker, but I was stopped by my brother in Peking. I embraced nihilism, and wandered along the banks of the Yangtze River, seeking death – but my docile, dull girlfriend talked me out of it ... I've been hanging on for half a year now, and in my heart I feel just as depressed as I did half a year ago. Living in this world, one has to do something. But a superfluous man like me, castrated by advanced education – what can I do?

Bingzhi's long and winding path to unemployability did not deviate very much from this pattern. She was born in Linli, Hunan province on 12 October 1904. Her family – wealthy, feud-ridden, opium-cured and shambolic – might have slipped from the pages of *The Dream of the Red Chamber*.

When her feckless, drug-addled father died of TB, Bingzhi's mother, Yu Manzhen, inherited nothing but debts. With two children to look after (Bingzhi's younger brother did not survive infancy) she made a radical change. Moving back to her home town, Changde, she enrolled as a trainee teacher in the town's newly founded 'normal school for women'.

In 1905 the empire had abolished its ages-old Confucian civil service examination, and public education had become the hobby of elite women who were embracing education for the first time – and 'Western-style' education at that. By blood, Yu Manzhen belonged to this 'elite', though she hadn't two *wén* to rub together.

At home (they lived with relatives) Bingzhi would play with her uncle's slave girls and female servants, or creep up to his attic to read a pile of foreign novels in translation. Most of the time she followed her mother from school to school, making friends outside her family circle – something her mother's generation would never have dreamed of doing.

At Second Girls' Normal in Taiyuan in 1918, Bingzhi copied her classmates and cut off her braids. People pointed and jeered. Later, the poorer ones turned up in night school to take lessons from her. They called her their 'little teacher', which was no more than the literal truth: Bingzhi barely came up to the top of the desk.

In autumn 1919 the fifteen-year-old arrived at Zhounan First Girls' Normal in Changsha. Here, the school newspaper ran essays on the oppression of women by a young Mao Zedong, and a progressive teacher, Chen Qiming, railed against the feudal system in general and fancy, aristocratic language in particular.

Inspired, Bingzhi wrote parochial-language poetry, read everything she could by Guy de Maupassant, joined outfits with names like the Alliance of Girls' Schools and the

Progressive Association of Girl Students, and went on demonstrations calling on Hunan's provincial council to give women property rights. If these demonstrations turned into riots, so much the better.

The following year, with five schoolmates (including Yang Kaihui, who was to be Mao Zedong's first wife), Ding Ling entered Yuyun Boys' School. This early attempt at co-education caused a scandal, and before things got any more out of control, her maternal uncle arranged a marriage for her.

Her schoolmate Wang Jianhong had a better idea: why not run off to Shanghai?

Bingzhi cut off her maternal relatives with a vengeance. She threw off her family name and became 'Ding Ling'. She also libelled her uncle in the local paper, making up tales of embezzlement and darkly veiled sexual offences to ensure that the wedding fell through. Political pressures would hone this capacity of hers for betrayal.

With Jianhong, she attended the Communist-run Common People's Girls' School, and when it collapsed in confusion, the pair went off to Nanjing to make a living.

The world of work was not at all geared to the plight of independent women, and they struggled to survive. They tried teaching, domestic service, factory work – anything they could find. People assumed they were prostitutes.

They were down to their last yuan when they ran into a Marxist theorist called Qu Qiubai, who had just returned from the Soviet Union. He was off to teach at Shanghai University, an institution supported by both the Communist Party and the nationalist Kuomintang. (These political enemies had been drawn into an alchemical marriage by the Soviets, who wanted a stable China on its borders.) If they applied to the university, said Qu, they could study literature with him.

Qu was an excellent teacher. His talks on literature and life ranged across Eastern and Western traditions. He got Ding Ling to read Pushkin in the original. The attachment he formed with Jianhong was even stronger – the pair married in 1924. Jianhong contracted TB shortly afterwards. Qu left her, and she died. Qu's brutal abandonment of Jianhong troubled Ding Ling for a long while, and eventually formed the basis of her 1929 novel *Weihu*. 'I longed to write a story about Qiubai and Jianhong,' she later recalled. 'Although I had a vague idea where his internal conflict lay, in the novel I concentrated only on the conflict between his revolutionary duty and his romantic love.'

In effect, she gives Qu Qiubai, in his guise as Wei-hu, a stock alibi for his desertion. Never mind that Wei-hu's lover Lijia is a wanton spirit 'in whose veins ran the heavy melancholy of Shelley, Byron and Goethe'; after a long night of the soul, Wei-hu finds that 'all that belonged to beauty, love, soft dreams and hopes and pleasure was broken and destroyed. And what he had had before, a kind of endurance and hardening of the will, again seethed in his whole body. He saw the future shining more dazzlingly bright even than blood.'

This fairly formulaic contribution to the 'love and revolution' genre notwithstanding, Ding Ling's disillusionment was profound. She abandoned her leftist associations and moved to Beijing – a shabby place, neglected, clinging to shreds of imperial splendour – and eked out a pitiful life as a largely unpublished writer.

She bit every hand that fed her. Returning briefly to Shanghai to try her hand at the film business, she overheard during her screen test that 'she's pretty enough' and walked out, calling the crew 'rascals'. Tian Han, her former teacher at Shanghai University, was now a film director and invited her along to a party where Ding Ling professed herself mortified by all the modern dancing and transvestites: 'This nauseated me, and I ran away.'

Tian Han even wrote her her own screenplay, *To the People!* portraying the new progressive Chinese woman, but even under make-up Ding Ling could not project herself into the role.

As usual, she blamed other people for her failure. Her first published short story, 'Mengke', is about a sensitive innocent young girl victimised by a corrupt movie industry.

When Ding Ling returned to Beijing, she was no longer alone: she had met Hu Yepin – 'a piece of totally uncut, unpolished jade', she calls him, though he came from a perfectly decent middle-class family, and had paid his own way through Peking National University.

Shen Congwen remembers visiting the pair in their hovel in the Fragrant Hills, west of Beijing. Their house had a well, and buckthorn trees front and back. They were entirely dependent on Ding Ling's mother for funds, and if these were late, Ding Ling would pawn something. Trips to the pawn shop became a fixture of their week. Ten miles of rough road lay between their house and the town, and halfway there they would like as not forget what they were doing, captivated by a clear spring or the whiteness of the clouds.

They were happiest on their own together. Ding Ling spent the days failing to draw, and Hu Yepin spent his failing to write, tearing up one draft after another.

This period is usually portrayed as an idyll of sorts, but Ding Ling winced to remember how purposeless their life was: 'Because of my petit bourgeois illusions I had estranged myself from the ranks of revolutionaries and taken the solitary path of moroseness, vain struggles, and suffering,' she writes. As for Hu: 'he contracted the diseases of melancholy and nihilism. The poems he wrote at that time were filled with these deplorable emotions. Hu buried himself in his poetry, and I passed each day in ennui.'

They drifted from boarding house to boarding house, often with Shen Congwen in tow. Their menage with the irrepressibly optimistic Shen seems to have done them good: in the spring of 1928, their ambitions renewed, the trio headed back to Shanghai, now China's undisputed literary capital, and published two short-lived journals together: 'romantic, reckless adventures' according to Ding.

Shanghai was the most vibrant Chinese city of that time, but it was also the most dangerous. Though a relatively recent creation, the large treaty port was, without doubt, the major city of East Asia, having replaced inland Nanjing as 'the Paris of the Orient'. Travel writer G. E. Miller called it 'the home of the homeless, the haven of undesirables, and the paradise of adventurers' – and though he was talking about foreigners, his words applied just as well to the Chinese, who represented over ninety per cent of the city's population. Here, uprooted people could remain anonymous: refugees, fugitives, disinherited peasants, ambitious young fortune hunters, retired officials on a spending spree.

Most of the city was under Chinese rule, but along the banks of the Huangpu River sat the International Settlement, dominated by the British, and to the west, the French Concession. These were, in effect, colonies within Shanghai, with borders and guards and police, though people did go back and forth between the different areas of the city with relative freedom.

The geographical divisions in Shanghai were picturesque. A Sikh policeman in the international settlement keeps watch outside a marble-clad British bank. A fast car bursts from the driveway of an elegant villa in the French Concession. Coolies haul their burdens, human and otherwise, past signs for Momilk and the latest Hollywood film. Most of the city's huge Chinese majority live in alleyways, straw shacks, reed huts, even boats, but the legends of segregation that have come down to us – for instance about a sign reading No Dogs or Chinese placed outside a British-run public park – conceal a more complex reality.

What really drove the locals mad were the city's rules on extraterritoriality. Foreigners from countries such as Britain and the US could not be prosecuted under Chinese law for most offences committed in China. The patent injustice of that arrangement blew up in the city's face on 30 May 1925, when panicked policemen, Indian and Chinese, shot dead eleven strikers locked out of a Japanese-owned factory in the International Settlement.

The incident galvanised Chinese politics. On the left, the writer Guo Moruo, who had always preached that literature was a personal business, now declared that work which did not promote revolution was worthless. The politically powerful League of Left-Wing Writers was his brainchild.

On the right, Chiang Kai-shek used his influence in the National Revolutionary Army (he was head of the military section at the Soviet-backed Whampoa Military Academy) to gain control of the Nationalist Party, and in 1926 he bound Nationalists and Communists in a campaign to unify China, wresting it from its regionally powerful warlords.

Chiang's 'Northern Expedition' moved up China's eastern seaboard, conquering and cajoling, and in spring 1927 it seized its most prestigious prize, Shanghai – at which point Chiang – whose visit to and training in Soviet Russia had given him a lifelong aversion to communism – decided it was time to shed the freeloaders. Using contacts among

Shanghai's notorious Green Gang crime cartel, Chiang saw to the rounding up and massacre of large numbers of communists and communist sympathisers in the city. A new National Government was proclaimed, and tens of thousands of communists were sentenced to death or murdered.

For the Communist Party, the Kuomintang's 'White Terror' ushered in twenty years in the wilderness. Intellectuals sympathetic to the communist cause continued to operate behind Shanghai's wainscots, but it was a dicey business.

Undeterred, would-be writers and hopeful artists poured into Shanghai by the dozen, by the score, each one hoping to shed the destitution and obscurity of life in the provinces, everyone angling for money and fame. With sufficient resources, and a nose for trouble, you could lead yourself a merry little literary life in this meat-grinder city, sauntering between book shop and theatre, café and restaurant. The essayist Zhang Ruogu remembers lazy hours in Sullivan's coffee shop, or Constantine's Russian café, or the Balkan Milk Store: 'I spent practically all my leisure time in the cafés on Avenue Joffre … Come late afternoon, all of us would gather … and as we drank the strong and fragrant coffee to enhance our fun, we would gently talk our hearts out.'

You were probably over-educated and under-employed, and at dire risk of 'drifting into journalism'. With no imperial examinations to cram for, you might well have travelled to Japan for further study, and be returning with a head full of rather confused Western ideas (socialism, anarchism, liberalism …) and be nursing a messiah complex as big as a house.

The more pragmatic you were, the more likely you were to find yourself writing into a genre marvellously labelled 'mandarin duck and butterfly' (after the traditional emblems of romantic love). Semi-comic and sometimes thrilling, these stories of star-crossed lovers and their hair-raising adventures appeared in serial form before making their way between cheap covers and into the pocket of every halfway literate Chinese in the city.

Nor had you to feel embarrassed: in a culture where fiction had never been thought of as literature, the very fact that you were able to cut it as a professional writer was one in the eye for Confucianism. Leftist writers, too, tried their hand at the form – and did all right by it – once publishers discovered that stories weaving together revolution and love were flying off the shelves of the Kaiming, Beixin and World bookshops.

The formula for 'revolution plus love' fiction was straight-forward: a star-crossed couple do (or don't) get together, depending on which of them does (or doesn't) embrace the coming revolution. There's much heroism on display in these works, precious little sense of a mass movement, and abso-lutely no theory. Qu Qiubai sneeringly referred to these stories as 'revolution by wizard', and may well have had Hu Yepin's novel *Go to Moscow!* (published 1930) in mind.

We know we're in for a guilty treat, the moment we meet Hu's protagonist Xunbai ('truly pure'). Xunbai is a 'handsome communist' 'with ideology, wisdom and personality' who has just returned from Japan with a suitcase stuffed with Russian and Soviet literature. Sushang is the high-born beauty who falls in love with Xunbai and his books. She's unhappily married but, being a New Woman, sees nothing wrong with free love.

Her bourgeois husband, a villainous Kuomintang official, sees plenty wrong, and arranges to have Xunbai arrested and executed. This killing actually goes ahead, whereupon Sushang, woken to the plight of the proletariat, walks out on her marriage and boards a train to Moscow, and a life of revolutionary commitment.

'Do you understand everything you're writing about?' a sceptical Ding Ling once asked her husband.

'Understanding Marxism is quite easy,' he replied. 'The first thing you need to do is believe him, then you just adopt the same attitude.'

Ding Ling found her husband's work full of a kind of left-wing infantilism. To be sure, her own writing was far more sophisticated.

She had followed 'Mengke', her hate letter to the movies, with a series of stories that turned her unpromising mental state, full of 'moroseness, vain struggles, and suffering', into fiction of fragile genius. In these stories, Ding drew on her experiences to depict the plight of women who, having broken with tradition and clan connections, find themselves living on the fringes of a frequently hostile urban society.

Her most famous story, 'The Diary of Miss Sophie', is a superb self-deconstruction, capturing the inner life of a young woman who, according to one contemporary critic, is 'selfish, emotional, frustrated, depressed, obsessive, lost in a mystical delirium, and pursuing bodily pleasures in order to forget her anxiety'.

Ill with TB, Sophie lives alone in a small room. Her main source of entertainment is a would-be boyfriend named Wei. She leads him on and humiliates him constantly. 'If you want to cry, go back home to cry,' she snaps. 'Tears get me down.'

Then she meets Ling Jishi, a stuffed shirt if ever there was one, but tall and devilishly handsome, and as she falls for this cheap, ordinary soul, she can't quite believe her own shallowness. She longs for love, but now it's arrived, all she feels is a 'tasteless jealousy'. Appalled at herself, she turns her back on her whole life in Beijing.

It takes a writer of real depth to plumb the uncharted shallows of the human personality, and with the publication of 'The Diary of Miss Sophie' Ding Ling became famous almost overnight (though not much richer).

But then, even as her star was rising, something extraordinary happened. Her husband, Hu Yepin, became a hero.

The failure of their journals *The Red and Black* and *The Mundane World* had thrown Ding Ling and Hu Yepin into debt yet again, and in February 1930 Hu had taken up a teaching post at the Shandong Provincial Senior High School in Jinan. When Ding Ling followed him, a few weeks later, she was startled to discover that Yepin was much in demand.

There was no Party to speak of in this Kuomintang-controlled district, so Hu was the nearest thing the students had to a communist guru. The same students who kept him up talking late into the night were at his digs again at daybreak, waiting for him to get out of bed. They couldn't get enough of him and his long, simple, riveting discourses on Marxism, dialectical materialism, proletarian literature, and whatever else he could rustle up from his readings of Plekhanov and Lunacharsky.

His materials were cobbled together, but his delivery won hearts and minds. Even the college principal and proctor changed the tone of their lectures. Hundreds rushed to join the students' literary research association, and on 4 May – that charged anniversary of national humiliation at Versailles (when China failed to regain territories lost to foreign powers in the previous century) – the school blew up. Students marched to Hu's house seeking leadership, the provincial authorities scrambled to contain the protest, and Hu and Ding fled town on the next night train, narrowly escaping arrest.

Back in Shanghai, Hu's enthusiasm was boundless. He joined the League of Left-Wing Writers and took on as many responsibilities as he could. That summer he taught at a workers' summer school, was elected to the Executive Committee, and chaired the League's Board of Correspondence with Workers, Peasants and Soldiers. It felt like useful work, and it was a sight more enjoyable than writing.

Ding Ling kept her distance because she was avoiding another League member, the critic Feng Xuefeng, with whom she'd had a brief but torrid affair that had very nearly broken Hu's heart.

She spent her time writing. The two parts of 'Shanghai, Spring 1930' neatly capture her political development. She's still poking gentle fun at her naive husband's expense, witness Part II's portrayal of Wang-wei who, in committing to the workers' cause, must throw over his vain and possessive girlfriend. Wang-wei's romanticism, his belief in 'revolution by wizard' is pure Hu Yepin.

> He was a little excited and he could not help it. He saw, as it were, the surging waves which are rising with a force to overthrow the mountains and upset the seas. He saw, too, an erupting volcano, throwing out roaring flames to burn down this city ... And he – he would move the storm and throw the torch!

All this seconds before poor Wang-wei gets unceremoniously bundled into the back of a police car.

But at least Wang-wei has a cause to believe in. A running theme in both parts of 'Shanghai, Spring' is the sense of failure felt by so many writers in the progressive 'May Fourth' movement. They had devoted themselves, in the main, to reforming the language, replacing classical Chinese with an 'accessible' new diction, combining vernacular Chinese with Western syntax. But they had got themselves into a terrible tangle. Their earnest experiments gathered dust in the warehouses of the Commercial Press and Zhonghua Book Company, while hackneyed 'mandarin duck and butterfly' potboilers proved far more accessible and popular among the people.

'Where is the way out for [these writers]?' wonders a side-character in Part II:

> They can only sink deeper and deeper day by day into their own gloom, not seeing the connection between society and their sufferings. Even if they could improve their language, and produced some essays and poems that may win praise from some old writers, what good, I ask you, is it to them? And what good to society? With regard to writing person-ally, I am ready to give it up.

Ding Ling herself had absolutely no intention of 'giving it up'. She believed her political commitments and the dangers of the times were drawing her ever closer to lived reality, and to a social vision broader and more real than anything she had depicted before.

'Some say that having discussions with two or three friends and reading a few novels in translation constitute the entire culture of our writers,' she once complained. There had to be more to the writer's life than that!

In Part I of 'Shanghai, Spring', we get a glimpse of what this broader, more committed life might feel like.

Mei-lin is bored and overly dependent on her boyfriend Zibin, a dried-up and narcissistic writer. She casts about for something to bring some purpose to her life – and comes face to face with the inequality and exploitation in Shanghai, where 'pot-bellied businessmen and blood-sucking devils, wizened and shriveled from overwork on their abacuses, were going full-tilt in the careening money market, investing and manipulating to increase their exploitation of the laboring masses and to swell their astronomical wealth.'

So far, so much leftist hokum. (Gorky turned this sort of thing out by the yard. For example, 'The City of the Yellow Devil'.)

But Ding Ling takes Mei-lin's development further: 'Action had become an instinctual need. She wanted to be with the masses, to try to understand society, and to work for it.' Mei-lin's old life feels vacuous and lonely in comparison to this new world of clasped hands and close comradeship.

Ding Ling is not exceptional in discovering, in rather wide-eyed fashion, what it is like to leave the desk and pay attention to real life. She does write exceptionally well about it.

Ding Ling joined the League of Left-Wing Writers in May, but was not so nearly involved in its workings as her husband. What had begun as a bit of light literary bureaucracy had for Hu taken on the shades of conspiracy. He went to meetings on the third floor of an affluent foreign home, its windows firmly shut against eavesdroppers, and shared nothing of this business with his wife, who teased him mercilessly.

Anyway, Ding Ling had enough to think about. On 8 November 1930, their son Zulin was born. Hu got to the hospital in time for the birth, but headed straight off again to another meeting. The next day he told Ding Ling that he had applied for membership of the Communist Party.

Just how politically committed Hu Yepin had become is reflected in his story 'Sacrifice', in which a revolutionary, snowed under with clandestine meetings, sorts out an abortion for his wife.

'Don't feel sorry,' she took his hand and said. 'We do love each other. You are not to be blamed; you have already exercised enough self-control ... Even though we could afford to bring it up, we should not allow it to see the light. Once there is a baby, our work will be hindered.'

It's a chilling document to have come from the pen of a young father.

On 17 January 1931, Hu Yepin was arrested while attending a Party meeting in Room 31 of the Oriental Hotel. On 7 February he was executed.

We don't know the exact time of Hu's execution. It must have taken a while. Digging your own grave. Being shackled to your fellow prisoners. Lined up to face the machine guns. Then comes the actual business of dying. No *coup de grâce* for conspirators. Several were still alive as they were being buried.

ii

In November 1930, a group of Chinese communist students known as the 'Twenty-eight', led by the dogmatic intellectual Wang Ming, returned from the Sun Yat-sen University of Moscow, intent on seizing the reins of the Party.

They were an unpleasant lot who had won their spurs conducting witch-hunts against their fellow students at the university.

Four days after Wang was made secretary of the Party, older members, trade unionists and regional delegates met at the Oriental Hotel to foil the planned takeover. Among them were Hu and four other members of the League of Left-Wing Writers.

The same day, anonymous phone calls were received by both the Kuomintang and the police of the international settlement. Communist agents in the police department quickly called the Party to warn them that the Oriental Hotel meeting was blown – but no action was taken.

Hu Yepin may have died against a Kuomintang wall, but it was Wang Ming, the new secretary of the Communist Party, who had pulled the trigger. Decades would pass before this ugly truth emerged.

Ding Ling was assured that her husband had died a revolutionary hero. This had a profound impact on her. Through her former lover Feng Xuefeng, she finally approached the Communist Party and put herself at its service.

She took risks – lecturing at universities, taking part in demonstrations, pasting up slogans, working among factory strikers – but the Party soon put her to better use, editing a 'neutral' periodical called *Big Dipper*.

The idea was to draw people in to the communist movement by stages. Come for the selection of new writing; stay for the politics. It didn't really work; by the third issue, *Big Dipper* had already attracted the attention of the authorities. Ding Ling was harassed, her publisher Hu Feng was briefly arrested, manuscripts and letters were confiscated or intercepted.

Understandably, Ding Ling's own writing at this time was all over the place. She kept embarking on grand epics – *Flood*, *Eventful Autumn*, *Mother* – only to abandon them part way through. Everything she did came out slipshod or aborted. Frustrated with herself, she threw herself into political action.

On 18 September 1931, the Japanese, who wielded semi-colonial control over a large swathe of north-eastern China, now seized this territory for themselves: 1.3 million square kilometres of Manchuria were lost to Japan. Four months later, on 28 January 1932, on the pretext that their citizens in Shanghai needed protection, Japanese army officers triggered the infamous "Shanghai incident". Ordinary life came to an

abrupt halt as heavy fighting consumed the heartland of the
League of Left-Wing Writers. Lu Xun – the grand old man
of the literary left, and the nearest China had to a Maxim
Gorky – fled for shelter to the Uchiyama Bookstore. *Big
Dipper* ceased publication.

These were the kinds of national emergencies Chinese
writers lived for. Though they claimed to have shaken off the
shackles of Confucianism, their sense of national obligation
was deeply ingrained. Straight away the League of Left-Wing
Writers, the Dramatists League and the Social Scientists
League got together to stage a competition to see who could
produce the largest amount of patriotic and revolutionary
work. On the roster for the League of Left-Wing Writers,
between mid-March and the end of April: twenty pieces of
revolutionary literature, two story books for the 'Soviet areas'
(communist enclaves in the countryside) and 300,000 words
on the theme of anti-imperialist and anti-landlord struggle;
also, twenty-seven dissertations. Not content with that lot,
Ding Ling and three other members of the League's secretariat
(Ding Ling was made Party secretary of the League in March
1932) held a competition among themselves to see who could
edit the most, introduce the most new members, and give the
largest number of public speeches.

And how quickly and cheerfully these writers put their
shoulders to the wheel! It was an abiding characteristic of
Chinese intellectuals that they hardly debated at all. They
almost never shared personal visions of what a better society
might look like. Instead they travelled in packs, and as a pack,
a plenum, a league, they produced bulletins and newspapers,
each expressing a unanimous view.

Nor did it ever occur to any Chinese intellectual to throw
up their hands in despair and abandon political service altogether. There's not one writer at this time who challenges the

Confucian notion that a scholar, 'the first to worry and last to rejoice', should carry the burden of Chinese culture into the future.

There is, however, another side to all this cheerful, ego-less co-operation in the service of the greater good – and that is an almost total inability to handle disagreements when they do occur.

This too was an inheritance from Confucianism, which holds that disputants must crush or be crushed as swiftly as possible to maintain the peace.

This attitude struck even Bolshevik agents dumb. Arriving from the international organisation Comintern to take a hand in Chinese politics, they couldn't quite believe that they were working with people more belligerent than they were.

The celebrated leftist writer Lu Xun, though a strong public supporter of the League of Left-Wing Writers, never had much confidence in its members. He once wrote to his editor Yang Jiyun about the 'real threat' presented by the League's 'so-called "comrades-in-arms" who say one thing and mean another. It is very hard to guard against them ... in minding my back, I have to stand slantwise and thus cannot stand facing the enemy.'

He had in mind, in particular, Zhou Yang, a translator and literary critic who had returned from Japan in the summer of 1932. He was a theorist, not a writer. But he knew Russian literature backwards (his translation of *Anna Karenina* was highly rated), he was a close reader of Maxim Gorky, and he understood, better than anyone else in China, the ideas behind 'socialist realism'. Zhou Yang replaced Ding Ling as the League's Party secretary in late 1933; he later became secretary of the Cultural Committee, and Party secretary of the

General Cultural League. Holding all these responsible posts, he emerged as the Party's spokesman in cultural matters.

Also emerging in the League of Left-Wing Writers was Hu Feng, whose bookshop had doubled as the offices of Ding Ling's magazine *Big Dipper*. Hu Feng had gone to Tokyo in 1929, returned at the end of 1932, and only narrowly avoided being made head of propaganda for the League. He'd returned to Japan, where he was arrested for involvement in that country's leftist literary scene, briefly imprisoned, and expelled back to China.

In the end, Hu felt he had no choice but to take on a leadership role in the League. He got on with Zhou Yang at first, but his growing friendship with the celebrated Lu Xun caused friction.

It's not entirely clear what, if anything, Hu Feng did to drive a wedge between the League and Lu Xun, its revered champion. He handled Lu's financial contributions. He had a habit of glossing and 'improving' Zhou Yang's views when reporting them back to Lu. Really, it was only his character that could be held against him: League founder Guo Moruo said he was 'rather intransigently ambitious' while even Lu conceded Hu's hypersensitivity and petty-mindedness.

On 21 September 1934 a poet, Mu Mutian, recently released from Kuomintang custody, claimed Hu Feng was a Kuomintang agent from Nanjing. Zhou Yang seized on this wild accusation, and Hu had little choice but to resign as League secretary. At this shoddy treatment of his friend, Lu Xun washed his hands of the League. It was better not to join, he said.

Further splits followed.

Zhou Yang, as Party secretary of the League, naturally took his orders and his lead from Wang Ming, the chief secretary of the Party. But in the countryside, a new power was brewing. From the Jinggang Mountains in Hunan, the young revolutionary Mao Zedong had built up a soviet 'state within the state' and an army that, by the skin of its teeth, had survived a rout by Kuomintang forces – an episode remembered as the Long March. Now Mao's forces could either prosecute an unequal struggle with the Kuomintang, or ally with the Kuomintang to fight the Japanese.

Feng Xuefeng, Ding Ling's friend and former lover, had been on the Long March. Now he was back in Shanghai, under cover, to establish a united anti-Japanese front between the Party and the Kuomintang.

Feng explained all this to Lu Xun. When he approached Zhou Yang, however, Zhou refused even to open the door to him.

Mao Zedong eventually met up with Wang Ming, his rival for control of the Party. The men nursed different priorities regarding a united front with the Kuomintang, but their rift proved easy enough to heal. Zhou Yang, though, had got into such a bitter and bloody battle with Lu Xun, that the communist celebrity now categorically refused to join any organization or movement that had Zhou at its head.

Years later, these factional disputes blew up in the writers' faces. All the League's literary lights (except for Lu Xun, who by then was dead) would eventually face political ruin.

4 May 1933.

Ding Ling has given her baby son over to her mother, and is part way through a novel about her.

Footsteps thunder on the stairs. Four Chinese men in Western suits muscle into her room, their hands in their pockets, their weapons concealed. Five minutes later, Feng Da enters, accompanied by two more gunmen.

Feng, an eager student of literature, has been helping Ding

Ling with the research for *Flood*, her aborted novel. He's already her lover (and Hu not yet cold in the ground – friends are shaking their heads), and he wants her to know, categorically, that 'this address was not betrayed by me but by others'.

Ding Ling doesn't believe him.

They're bundled into the back of a car, which speeds away from the international settlement. They ride in silence. Eventually they're dumped, under guard, in a third-floor hotel room. Ding Ling snaps at Feng Da: 'I never thought that *you* would be the one to sell me out.'

The next morning they're given a soft sleeper coach for their rail journey to Nanjing. This doesn't reassure Ding Ling one bit. The Kuomintang killed her husband. Now it's her turn.

Sure enough, in Nanjing they're dumped in another old hotel. They're kept there for weeks. Their guards make cheap threats. And at midnight on 31 May, Ding Ling is driven out to the suburbs and through a maze of unlit streets. The car turns down an alley. At the end there stands an old house with high walls. Moss grows through cracks in the floor. The air smells mouldy.

She's still alive, and it dawns on her that if these goons were going to kill her, they would have done so by now.

Held prisoner in this damp, dark, forgotten place – no lights, no running water – it occurs to her that if the Kuomintang are not going to do away with her, she's going to have to do away with herself. Feng Da finds her hanging from a beam by a rope she's made from a torn sheet. Frantically, he cuts her down.

'How dare you?' she says.

The Kuomintang have no intention of killing Ding Ling. According to the man who ordered her arrest – Xu Enzeng, director of the Central Investigation and Statistics Bureau – it's all been an unfortunate mistake: 'I gave the order to arrest her, hoping very much that she would use her talent in creative writing and become a contributing cultural worker for our Party.'

The guards move out of Ding Ling's rooms, and the house is thoroughly cleaned, repaired and put to rights.

Xu says her arrest has proved an embarrassment for the Kuomintang. The League for Civil Rights can protest till doomsday, that doesn't bother the Kuomintang, but now Henri Barbusse and Romain Rolland are kicking up a stink abroad. The sooner the situation can be normalised, the better for everyone.

Promised that she will now be left alone to lead a normal, quiet life, Ding Ling agrees to make a written statement: 'Returning home to care for mother. Will not participate in public activities.'

No one's quite sure how to take this; most are convinced Ding Ling's already dead. There have been tributes, memorial publications of 'Not a Love Letter' (an actual love letter to Feng Xuefeng), 'Sophie's Diary, II' (not a patch on the original) and her unfinished novel *Mother*.

And her life is anything but normal. Ding and Feng are transported to Mogan Mountain, an exclusive summer resort near Hangchow. Summer is over, and all the little tourist shops are boarded up. The leaves are turning, falling. The sky is a yellow swirl. Residents are laying in supplies of food and kindling. One good snowstorm will seal off the mountain for the winter.

Ding Ling wants to go out walking. No one stops her, and soon she discovers why. There's only one route up and down the mountain and it's patrolled by security guards. There are innumerable trails, and innumerable young women, 'maids', who pop out of the bamboo thickets at regular intervals, giggling, asking her where she's going.

Winter bites hard, snow covers the trees and fills the gullies and even walking becomes impossible. The hearth is warm and Ding Ling succumbs and by the time she and Feng Da are returned to Nanjing, she is pregnant again.

Now life is *almost* normal. The guards are gone, at least, and Ding Ling can move about freely within the city. Her mother appears, with Zulin, the son she has not seen for three years. But life does not stay still. On 3 October, her daughter, Zuhui, is born. Feng Da agrees to translate for the Kuomintang to bring in some money. The way he sees it, if he repudiates the communists, things should go more easily for Ding Ling. But he's almost straight away struck down with TB, the promised 100 yuan does not appear, and soon Ding Ling has a sick husband to care for as well as two children.

Ding Ling tries to get her writing started again, and in the spring of 1935 they relocate to a place hidden away in the countryside, where Ding can concentrate and Feng can convalesce. All that happens is that Ding Ling contracts typhoid. She's in hospital until the autumn, Feng Da's TB is very bad, and the medical bills are mounting.

Feng Da is hospitalised. Ding Ling fully expects him to die and when that happens, it's almost a relief. She keeps saying that he betrayed her to the Kuomintang, though there was never any reason why he should, and there's never been any evidence that he did.

While Feng Da is breathing his last, Ding Ling is planning her escape. During a brief period of release, she meets Party contacts in Beijing who help her plot an escape later in the year. On 18 September 1936, she catches a train to Shanghai, carrying a man's briefcase and wearing a woollen overcoat of the latest cut.

She disappears.

iii

From the window of her train carriage, Ding Ling gazes across the North China plain, stretching to the horizon, still and flat as a chessboard. Along the southern reaches of the Yellow River, people sit fishing under the willows. The fields are brown, the wheat has already been harvested.

In the ancient capital of Chang'an, she billets at the house of a sympathetic foreigner. Herbert Wunsch, an Austrian dentist, is a refugee from fascism. When Wunsch and his sick wife leave for Shanghai, they leave Ding Ling behind to keep house, feed the chickens, and walk the dog (who answers to the name of Hitler).

Ding Ling is bound for Bao'an in Shaanxi province, but the journey will be difficult. She cuts her hair, puts on a grey cotton army uniform and, never having ridden a horse before, she practises mounts and dismounts by climbing up and off the brick fireplace.

On 1 November, Ding Ling leaves Chang'an. She travels with a small caravan, leading donkeys along treacherous passes in the mountains. Arriving in Bao'an eight or nine days later, she finds the place razed to the ground. The entire communist apparatus is housed in a line of caves.

But the welcome is warm. Mao Zedong and the Central Committee hold a dinner in her honour, and afterwards, the wives of the committee are always finding some excuse to invite her round. Mao, too: by one account, Ding Ling spends three days with him, staying well into the night.

Everyone pulls their weight in Bao'an, and Ding Ling isn't slow to find herself a job.

Since the early days of the Long March, the Red Army

has been using drama and music to win over and educate the peasantry. The Chinese People's Anti-Japanese Drama Society has about thirty troupes travelling the countryside, and runs a drama school.

Ding Ling wants to set up an organisation to centralise and orchestrate all this effort: an Association of Literary Workers in the Border Regions. It's an idea whose time will undoubtedly arrive – but political events are moving fast.

Mao has made repeated attempts to broker an end to the conflict between the Kuomintang and the Chinese Communist Party, and Chiang Kai-shek's reply has always been the same: not until every communist is in prison and the last Red soldier is dead.

Such is the mounting Japanese threat, however, Chiang's own generals have had enough of this attitude. On 12 December 1936, they kidnap their own leader and sign a telegram demanding an immediate end to the civil war, so that armed resistance to Japan can begin. By 20 December, an agreement in principle has been reached between the two sides, and Ding Ling asks to visit their united front.

She joins a unit headed north-west along the upper reaches of the Luo River. She's more than an observer; she's a literary worker, there to treat with the countryfolk and explain the war by any means at her disposal. (Poetry is popular. The Party exhorts: 'Do not let a single wall in the countryside or a single rock by the side of the road lie free and empty!')

In his cave, Mao Zedong writes: 'Gently billowing the red flag on the city wall, the West Wind envelops the lonely city. New men and women suddenly arrive, and a banquet is held in the Yaodong caves to receive our released prisoner.'

'The Immortal from Linjiang' is a poem dedicated to Ding Ling, Mao's powerful new weapon in the war for communism.

'To your elegant brush, who can compare? For your brush

is like three thousand crack troops wielding rifles, advancing in formation towards Longshan Mountain. Yesterday you were a literary lady, today you become a martial general.'

Mao Zedong was born on 26 December 1893 in Shaoshan, Hunan, the son of a rich peasant whom he never ceased resenting.

Around the time of the 1911 revolution, he moved to the city of Changsha and became involved in a discussion group, the New Citizen Study Society. Widely read in Western and Chinese history, Mao became rapidly disillusioned with the Chinese Republic. By 1920 he was saying that only a 'Russian-style revolution' could save China. In May 1921 he was invited to attend the founding meeting of the Chinese Communist Party in Shanghai.

In the early 1920s, while the Party was working in collaboration with the Kuomintang, Mao edited the Kuomintang's *Political Weekly*. He also studied revolutionary tactics. He came late to the belief that would later come to define his dictatorship: that the peasantry could drive the revolution all by itself. His first experiences of peasant militancy were not positive. Ordered to coordinate a rural uprising in Hunan in late 1927, Mao suffered a total defeat.

He led the survivors of his army to the Jinggang Mountains, and there organised the Fourth Red Army with the former warlord and communist convert Zhu De. On the borders of Fujian and Jiangxi, the two founded the Jiangxi Soviet, the largest territory of the unrecognised Chinese Soviet Republic.

Military disaster followed upon military disaster. To stop the population of their little state-within-a-state defecting to the surrounding Kuomintang, Mao and Zhu orchestrated a campaign of terror. Armed squads were sent in pursuit of those trying to flee, and killed them on the spot. Seven hundred thousand died, either murdered as class enemies, or worked to death, or dead by their own hand. The Kuomintang later uncovered numerous mass graves throughout Jiangxi.

Mao applied much the same methods to maintain discipline within the party. Two thousand army members were shot in a single week. If you refused to help carry provisions, if you stayed away from mass rallies, if you failed to show up for Party meetings, if you complained about the Party in your sleep, you were labelled an 'Anti-Bolshevik' conspirator, and your guilt was established primarily through torture, your skin burned with incense sticks, your bones broken by savage beatings, your palms nailed to a table and bamboo splints jabbed under your fingernails. Suspects' wives had their breasts slashed open and their genitals burned. Even as Mao's first purge wound down, between 1932 and 1934, perhaps a hundred people were being shot every month.

In 1934, the Kuomintang wiped out the Jiangxi Soviet, forcing the Red Army to embark on its Long March to regions in the north-west. Chiang Kai-shek fully intended to wipe out the Red Army and very nearly succeeded.

Mao settled his band of survivors in Shaanxi in the autumn of 1935.

Most of the province was mountainous, a sprawling landscape of peaks, valleys and desert sandstone, with gorges and ravines cut by powerful rivers. To the east, winds carried in dust from the Gobi Desert. There was farmland to the east and in the central part; the north-west was dotted with cacti and chunks of wind-eroded gravel.

Mao's forces numbered barely 13,000 when they moved from Bao'an to the more easily defended south-central city of Yan'an, huddled at the base of the Loess Plateau, and surrounded by mountains on all sides.

Yan'an's many caves made a temporary base for them. Living conditions were cramped. Almost everyone lived two, three or four to a 'room' chiselled out of the rock walls. Water was rationed to five gallons a week for each family. Everyone was on the same diet – some millet, the occasional vegetable – and stomach troubles were common.

By 1937 there was talk of finding somewhere better. No one imagined they would be stuck here for another eight years.

The US journalist and activist Agnes Smedley remembers a dusty frontier town with a mere 3,000 residents.

Another visitor calls it 'the quaintest and most picturesque little fortress city imaginable'. Others talk about the flies, the shit-filled streets, the roads that turn to impossible quagmires in the rain. A single bridge spans the River Yan, which flows through the centre of town. It shakes when you cross it.

The streets are rough and unpaved, lined with two-storey mud-brick buildings. There is a single street market. The surrounding hills are mostly barren and treeless.

High winds. Freezing temperatures. The rainfall in summer here is higher than the regional average.

For Mao's younger followers, Yan'an is a promised land: the fabled 'crucible of revolution'. Fleeing the 'effete' and 'corrupt' Nationalist regime, these young idealists embrace the frugal collective life afforded by the caves of Yan'an. At Resistance University, they train to be cadres in the guerrilla areas behind Japanese lines.

Ding Ling arrives in Yan'an around late January or early February 1937. She is assigned accommodation at the university, even though there are no more classes. The few students left behind by the general mobilisation are fretful and restless. One day half a dozen of them turn up at Ding's door with a plan for how they, too, might contribute to the war effort.

The initial idea is that they should all go and report from the front. By the evening, though, their plans have expanded to include drama, songs, cartoons, lectures . . .

Ding Ling will lead them.

The Northwest Front Service Corps will bring 'large-scale propaganda' to the region 'through such forms as plays, music, lectures, cartoons and slogans'. Both soldiers and civilians will be taught 'the meaning and goals of the national revolutionary struggle'.

Ding Ling manages to scratch together a budget. Two yuan a month per person, over and above living expenses. A one-piece summer outfit and a suit of cotton for the winter. Seven fen a day will be enough to cover a few luxuries: vegetables, oil, salt, soy sauce, firewood.

On 19 August, the Front Service Corps marches out of Yan'an, leading seven overburdened donkeys west along the Yan towards the Yellow River. The town's schoolchildren come out to wave them off. The cliffs shine in the sun. The cadres sing as they march along. Their red flag snaps in a fresh breeze.

At Gangu Station (already a recipient of communist aid: illiteracy has been reduced and the buying and selling of brides eliminated) the corps invent some short jingles and variety acts and teach the villagers patriotic songs. A red curtain is hung and wild flowers are used to decorate the village hall. At the end of their evening concert, the performers add a 'Defeat Japan Dance', jumping from the stage into the audience.

Then dinner, then speeches, and still the audience, many of whom have walked miles in the rain on the promise of entertainment, refuses to budge. More speeches and another play tire them out at last.

A few miles further into their journey, the corps begin scaling their first mountain. Donkeys and the ablest lead the climb, and soon put several miles between themselves and the rear guard.

Ding Ling, bringing up the rear, finally catches up with the front-runners and reads them the riot act. 'We oppose this sort of vanguardism!' she protests, grinning. 'It alienates the people from the masses!'

By 9 October, the corps have reached the outskirts of Linfen, a large city and a favourite target of Japanese bombers.

'We are in danger of becoming rats,' Ding Ling writes to a friend, 'hiding during the day and coming out at night.'

By the time the corps arrives at the town's war temple, the place is packed solid. Old hands now, they soon have around 5,000 audience members eating out of their hands.

At 11 p.m., and with the performance still in mid-flow, a cable arrives. They have one hour to get to the train station.

The next day, Japanese forces overrun the badly battered Chinese positions.

The corps is exhausted. The weakest are taken by train to Fenyang; Ding Ling is told she can head south-east if she wants, to find a Manchurian guerilla unit and stay with them.

Just before Christmas, an observer for the US Navy called Evans Carlson visits the HQ of the Eighth Route Army (the name the Red Army goes under, while part of the Second United Front against Japan) and stumbles on a party of soldiers, singing at the top of their lungs:

We have no food,
We have no clothes,
But the enemy will send them to us!

In their midst stands Ding Ling, 'the Immortal from Linjiang' herself, 'a striking figure in the olive drab of a captured Japanese overcoat.'

CHAPTER TWELVE

i

In the face of Japanese invasion, the Second United Front established rules for how the rag-tag communists and the Kuomintang would cooperate. Both sides agreed that a communist-dominated 'special district' would exist, but no one for a second doubted that its existence would, sooner or later, restart the civil war.

While the communists fought guerilla skirmishes in the mountains and expanded their foothold in Shaanxi province, Chiang Kai-shek's forces faced Japanese incursions head-on, in Shanghai, in Nanjing, and finally in the strategic central city of Wuhan. By the end of 1938, Japan occupied all coastal and Yangtze valley cities, and Chiang had retreated to his wartime capital of Chongqing, far in the interior.

For the Kuomintang, the resurgent communists were now as much of a looming threat as the Japanese. Despite promises that their 'special district' of Shaan-Gan-Ning (named after the three provinces which it covered: Shaanxi, Gansu and Ningxia) would be run under joint authority, it was effectively an independent state.

The two sides finally came to blows in early 1939, and communist Shaan-Gan-Ning shrank rapidly in the face of Kuomintang assault. 'For a while,' Mao later recalled, 'we were reduced almost to the state of having no clothes to wear, no oil to cook with, no paper, no vegetables, no footwear for the soldiers, and in winter, no bedding for the civilian person-nel.' In January 1941, Nationalist forces almost wiped out the communist troops in southern Anhui. Shaan-Gan-Ning was now effectively a refuge, hemmed in on all sides by hostile armies and impassable mountains.

It was the Jiangxi Soviet experience all over again, the stage set for a second and yet more terrible purge.

Nonetheless the Shaan-Gan-Ning Border Region was booming. Yan'an's population had increased at least ten-fold, partly because the military had been forced into this tiny pocket of territory, but also because thousands of stu-dents were flocking to Resistance University and Yan'an's other schools.

Some, when they crossed the border, prostrated themselves and kissed the earth, their heads full of Edgar Snow's *Red Star Over China* and Fan Changjiang's *The Northwestern Part of China* and *Scenes on the Frontier*. The poet Ke Zhongping compared Yan'an to Dante's Paradise.

Most were 'intellectuals' in name only (though Mao, desper-ate to enlist new blood, befriended any number of 'promising' writers and 'fledgling' artists). Few had actually studied in a university. Even fewer had learned anything of practical use. All believed the communist enclave offered them freedom and the opportunity to live a meaningful life, devoted to a cause.

This time, rather than terrorising the local population (what would have been the point? North Shaanxi villagers were considered the most backward folk in China) Mao and the central committee opted instead to educate, discipline and weaponise their new recruits.

*

The Northwest Front Service Corps taught basic directing, make-up and singing, and churned out scores of trained personnel for dispatch into the countryside. In 1940, the Taihang Mountain region alone boasted a hundred drama clubs.

'We encourage revolutionary writers and artists to be active in forming intimate contact with the workers, peasants and soldiers,' Mao wrote later, making the policy explicit in his 'Yan'an talks' of 1942, 'giving them complete freedom to go among the masses and to create a genuinely revolutionary literature and art.'

On 10 April 1938, the Lu Xun Arts Academy (with Zhou Yang as dean) was established to train 'artistic cadres'. Ding Ling's Service Corps provided the model for the academy: trainees were sent in groups into the countryside or interned on the front lines.

Not every cadre took this business seriously. 'They treated their assignments as if they were just taking a bath,' one critic complained.

Ding Ling was ranked a middle-level bureaucrat, and junior to Zhou Yang, who had arrived from Shanghai some years earlier. She taught periodically at Party universities, wrote about the popularisation of the arts, advised on women's policy, lobbied for family reform and edited the literary section of the Party's official government newspaper, the *Liberation Daily*. She also encouraged young writers. The two-year programme of her 'Weekly Literary Garden', held outdoors in front of the Yan'an Culture Club, served to channel the spare-time literary and artistic activity of those who hadn't made it into the Lu Xun Academy.

That creative writing classes were central to the class struggle in Yan'an, and were organised at the highest level on paramilitary lines, will seem a sight more peculiar to

Western readers than to Chinese ones. In China, mastery of certain texts and political power have always gone hand in hand.

It's also worth remembering that cultural work groups, service corps, interview teams, battlefield news stations and literary and artistic campaigns were – since the loss of Beijing, Shanghai and Nanjing to the Japanese – the only surviving outlet for self-expression in the country. There were no independent newspapers or journals. There was no publishing industry of any kind. As a writer, the choice was simple: you escaped to Yan'an and worked for rations, or you languished.

Veterans of the Long March, who had at first welcomed the influx of new blood, became steadily more resentful of all these students of nothing much who couldn't be made to stand still in a straight line, never mind point a gun.

Receiving news and hearing about the lives of city-folk was a novelty that soon palled: many old-timers had never been to a city, and had lived too long up-country, cheek by jowl with folk who feared intellectuals.

The deeper hunger and poverty bit down in Yan'an, the less time the heroes of the revolution had for freeloaders. Heaven forbid you should ever criticise them: 'Our comrades at the front are shedding their blood and sacrificing their lives for the Party and the people of the whole nation,' General Wang Zhen raged, following the publication of a series of critical articles in *Liberation Daily*, 'while you people are condemning the Party after stuffing your faces in the rear lines.'

General He Long was even more forthright. He called Ding Ling 'a stinking bitch'.

Yan'an's writers and artists, for their part, came to regard Yan'an's veteran cadres and military men with disgust. Not only did they know nothing of culture and Marxist-Leninist theory; they saw no point in learning! Some Utopia these thugs were building! Servile to their superiors and imperious to their subordinates, they were constantly sticking political labels on others in order to shut them up. What was happening to Yan'an's spirit of fraternity? Where was the old equality, based on 'comradely love', among the revolutionary ranks?

The fiercest flashpoint between the two communities was sex.

Young intellectuals pouring into Yan'an were painfully unaware of what life had really been like in the Jiangxi Soviet. All they really knew about were the exciting new regulations that had been imported to the soviet from Russia, and in particular a radical code governing marriage and divorce.

Marriage regulations promulgated in Jiangxi in 1931 had allowed men and women to divorce on the petition of one party alone. To those trapped in miserable arranged marriages, this measure was nothing short of a godsend.

Eventually Yan'an's new recruits came to learn about women's actual experiences in the Jiangxi Soviet and on the Long March. Sexual abuse and the rape of women was certainly less common in the Red Army than among the private armies of the surrounding warlords, but it did occur – and the more senior an officer you were, the more lenient your punishment if you were caught.

Some women had joined the army, and the Long March had included a women's regiment; alas, most of its women were killed, and those who survived had been married off to the local Muslims. Not one woman soldier reached Yan'an.

In Shaan-Nan-Ging, meanwhile, women (and there were few enough of them) mostly served a male military, making shoes and socks, washing and darning clothes. The old guard, survivors of history's most harrowing retreat (nine in ten died), considered themselves entitled to the pick of the womenfolk, and arranged regulations accordingly. In the army, only regimental officers twenty-eight years or older with five years' Party membership were permitted to marry, and army women could not divorce their husbands. Countless veterans, including Mao, discarded their peasant wives in favour of some bright young 'intellectual' blow-in.

Yan'an's idealistic young had dreamed of establishing a land of free love. But what arose, in those fag-end months of the 1930s, was a highly regulated society, founded on hierarchies and discipline.

Simple living, meagre salaries and grinding poverty were all very well while they added savour to Yan'an's heady egalitarian dish. But old-timers had begun angling for preferential treatment, and leaders were adopting the privileges of leadership. Important Yan'an cadres were being assigned bodyguards. Their families were assigned nannies and servants, even cooks, even grooms. Bodyguards waited at the school gates to see the Party leaders' children safely home. And that ambulance splashing through the muddy puddles of Yan'an, paid for with donations from overseas Chinese? Even children could tell you that was 'Chairman Mao's car'.

Zhou Yang's ability to quote Marx, Lenin and Stalin had endeared him to Mao Zedong, who had forgiven him his spat with the revered Lu Xun. Zhou now governed cultural activity in Yan'an.

His 'rule' over artistic affairs was not oppressive, and his article 'Remarks on Literature and Life', published in *Liberation Daily* in July 1941, wasn't particularly censorious. He merely restated the old League of Left-Wing Writers line that writers should experience at first hand the lives of the people they were writing about. He wrote:

> The turning of former culturally backward areas into centres of culture does not at all mean packing the former culture of the big towns in boxes and carting it out intact to the villages; it means transforming the old culture which, relatively speaking, was suited only to the big towns and restricted to bourgeois circles, into a culture fitted to the vast countryside and to the wide field of the war.

Zhou flattered Yan'an's writers, calling them 'the flesh and blood of the revolution'. Still, he said, they are unable to keep up with all the changes happening in the consciousness of workers, peasants and Red Army soldiers. Intellectuals are at risk of falling behind! Zhou's solution is 'Frontlinism' – writers should get stuck into the lives of others in order to deepen their understanding.

Ten days later a rebuttal appeared. Xiao Jun, a popular young novelist from Manchuria, wrote that while he didn't exactly disagree with Zhou, he was sick to death of hearing the same old exhortations trotted out whenever writers were caught expressing an uncomfortable opinion.

Under the sarcastic title 'Collected Remarks for Zhou Yang after Reading Remarks on Literature and Life', Xiao took Zhou to task for the silent assumptions that underpinned his good-natured but ultimately rather patronising article.

In the section titled 'Eating Meat, Collecting a Salary, and the Lack of Reading Material', Xiao asks whether it is any wonder that writers are 'falling behind' when they haven't any means of earning enough to eat? Zhou was dismissive of that claim in his article, calling it an 'interesting explanation' of why writers aren't producing anything worthwhile.

Xiao meets this head-on:

Of course, we'd like to have some evidence to use against
such gluttons (who need meat and vitamin C) that would
support Zhou Yang's correct denouncement of them ... In
Yan'an there are only three kinds of people who don't want
to eat meat: those who don't like it; those who can't eat it
for medical reasons; and those who, like Zhou Yang, have
their own private kitchens and get enough meat at the banquets given by certain organisations. If you don't believe us,
take a survey some time.

'No one in Yan'an,' says Xiao, taking the gloves off, 'right
down to the little messenger boys, came here to eat meat or
satisfy his vitamin C requirement, just as Zhou Yang didn't join
the revolution just to become an academy dean, have his own
private kitchen, or have his own horse available at his doorstep.'
   Pondering the economic and social gulf that was opening
up between the leaders and the led in Yan'an, Xiao called
for immediate and practical reform. Zhou in his article had
graciously admitted that Yan'an had its problems. Well, what
was being done about them? To admit there were 'black spots'
in Yan'an without criticising them only legitimated their
existence. 'Soon,' Xiao warned, 'people will actually begin
to praise them.'
   Whatever else you might have to say about it, this argument
was a lot livelier than the rest of *Liberation Daily*'s content.
And now that the paper was a daily (up from weekly since 15
May) its editor Bo Gu was desperate for content. For some
weeks he had been stuffing pages with reheated wire-service
reports and far too much fiction (Ding Ling's bailiwick). And
the articles he did run were really just op-eds, attacking the
Kuomintang from a distance.

Together, Bo Gu and Ding Ling had been looking for a way to bulk out the paper, and found a solution in the sharp, lively, often very funny fulminations of Xiao et al. Why not give such writers their head, and turn the literary pages of *Liberation Daily* into a sort of 'loyal opposition' to the Yan'an authorities, pointing up problems and driving reform?

There was an unimpeachable literary precedent for the effort: half a dozen years after his death, Lu Xun was now considered the literary father of the communist movement. One of his favourite forms – which he had more or less invented – was the *zawen* or critical essay. The trick was brevity: Lu's pieces never ran to more than 1,000–1,500 characters. Social ills could be targeted, but there was usually some literary sting in the tail: an argument about telling the truth and avoiding cliché. No one ever wrote *zawen* quite like Lu did, though the magazines of Shanghai boasted many imitators.

On 23 October 1941, Ding Ling tried her hand at the form, in a short article titled (with a nice circularity) 'We Need *Zawen*'.

Everywhere, people are creating factions and talking behind people's backs. They don't seem to understand what freedom of speech means. Well, says Ding, 'I think it would do us most good if we emulate [Lu Xun's] steadfastness in facing the truth, his courage to speak out for the sake of truth, and his fearlessness.'

As for the discomfort such work might cause: 'It may be in human nature to be intoxicated with small successes or to hate to be told that one is sick or that one needs to see a doctor about it. But that is also a sign of indolence and cowardice.'

It took until March 1942 for other writers to get up the confidence to express themselves in *zawen* of their own, but the material Ding Ling and her colleague Chen Qixia began publishing from that date, by writers both inside and outside the Party, caused a sensation. Xiao Jun's piece 'On Love and Patience toward Comrades' was personally polished and revised by Mao Zedong. Ai Qing's 'Understand and Respect Writers,' and Luo Feng's 'It is Still the Era of *Zawen*' encouraged the effort.

Ding Ling's best contribution was published the day after International Women's Day. 'Thoughts on March 8' bemoaned the lack of women's rights in Yan'an, including the right to remain unmarried. 'It is virtually impossible for women comrades to become amicable with a male comrade,' she writes, 'and even less likely for them to become friendly with more than one.' Married women, meanwhile, were expected to please everyone. If you had no children, why on earth had you married? If you had children, you were obviously too busy to participate in political life and could be divorced for 'political backwardness'. Marriage legislation, Ding argues, ought to protect vulnerable women from the social and economic catastrophe of divorce, and yet in most cases it is still the husband who seeks to break the marriage bond. (She was inspired to write the essay, she said much later, because the husbands of two of her friends were planning to divorce them and marry younger, prettier girls.) Abortions are usually of the back-alley kind, and by secretly swallowing potions, women risk punishment and even death. In closing: 'It would be better if there were less empty theorising and more talk about real problems so that theory and practice would not be divorced, and better if all CCP members were more responsible for their own moral conduct.'

With hindsight, writing such material (never mind publishing it) seems a very brave move. But the *Liberation Daily* staff weren't naive. They believed that by publishing these *zawen*, they were furthering the work of the Party leadership.

Mao Zedong and Kang Sheng, head of the Party school in Yan'an, had recently been censuring cadres for terrorising those with opposing views. Mao had complained publicly about those who studied 'Marx, Engels, Lenin, and Stalin abstractly and aimlessly': 'They do not inquire about their connection with the Chinese revolution. It's merely theory for the sake of theory.'

Ding Ling assumed that the Party's efforts to instil discipline within its vastly inflated ranks was part of a more general campaign against stuffed shirts, martinets and bloviating academics. She mistook the character of a movement that had yet to show its true colours – a movement that went under the then innocuous-seeming label of 'rectification'.

ii

In his speech, 'Reconstruction of Our Studies', on 5 May 1941, Mao explained that rectification would bring everyone, even apostates, back within the communist movement. Only the most intransigent and hostile would be considered an enemy. (To those veterans who were in the know, this marked quite a change: intra-Party struggles up to that point had been met with expulsion, imprisonment or death.)

'If a person who commits an error, no matter how great, does not bring his disease to an incurable state by concealing it and persisting in his error,' Mao explained, 'and if in addition he is genuinely and honestly willing to be cured, willing to make corrections, we will welcome him so that his disease may be cured and he may become a good comrade.'

Run into trouble with the Party, and you absolutely could save yourself. The Party *wanted* you to save yourself. All you had to do was demonstrate complete acceptance of group values.

Mao grew sufficiently confident about this approach that, a year into the campaign, on 8 February 1942, he waxed lyrical about it: 'The first step in reasoning is to give the patient a powerful stimulus: yell at him, "You're sick!" so the patient will have a fright and break out in an overall sweat; then he can actually be started on the road to recovery.'

Outside observers have been rather less sanguine about rectification and its methods. The American psychologist and China-watcher Robert Lifton called it 'probably the most profoundly controlled and manipulated group environment that has ever existed.'

'Rectification' was a kind of schooling – a blisteringly fast form of indoctrination that, at a time of Kuomintang incursions, droughts, famines and crop failures, churned out thousands of committed communist operatives, each capable of carrying out orders and following the Party line even when assigned to a lonely outpost or behind enemy lines.

'Students' were split up into small groups who were assigned set texts for study, among them works by Lenin, Stalin and Mao Zedong. Lectures and other Party publications explained how these revolutionary texts were to be interpreted.

To really get to grips with this material, you then had to apply it to your own life. What concrete examples could you think of that illustrated what the text was about? What did the text teach you about yourself and your past behaviour? What did it teach you about your fellow students, and how they behaved?

Steadily, the focus of the course would shift from the text to the students. The classroom became the hermetic setting for an epic three-act psychodrama that dwelled upon past evils ('criticism and self-criticism'), demanded confession ('struggle') and culminated at last in confession and the expiation of sins.

Silence was not an option. Declaring yourself a good revolutionary was not enough. You had to criticise yourself, bare yourself, anatomise and criticise every doubt, every uncertainty, every shaky commitment. Those who did this demonstrated that they had taken the text on board; they 'passed the test'. (Anyone who's scraped through some HR department 'investigation', or successfully disarmed in the face of a social media pile-on will know what a proud moment *that* is.) They were then admitted to the next round, performed again with a new cast of characters.

It was a painful process, but (and this was its brilliance) it was not *unremittingly* painful. To an alienated bourgeois intellectual, 'thought reform' offered much to fill the emotional vacuum. Subjects experienced a 'great togetherness' as they participated in this 'moral crusade', this 'struggle for peace'.

Round by round, successful students got the idea that they were enhancing their common knowledge, gaining insight and becoming adept in a new political language, full of arcane prescriptive codes: 'three principles'! 'eight points'! 'five changes'! If this sounds Orwellian to you – well, so it was. Robert Lifton again: 'Orwell – in a Western conception – saw milieu control accomplished through mechanical means, such as the two-way "telescreen". But the Chinese have done it through a human recording and transmitting apparatus, extending their control more deeply into the student's innermost world.'

'Rectified' students came out of this process chattering like demons – or rather, *like copies of the same demon*, all their individuality locked away beneath a new, formulaic language.

Those who fell by the wayside (and they had invariably had their cards marked from the beginning) became scapegoats: criticised, harassed, publicly disgraced – pariahs cast out by their fellows.

The de Torquemada of this secular inquisition was Kang Sheng. Kang had been trained by the NKVD in Moscow at the height of Stalin's purges. A 'returned student' who owed loyalty to Wang Ming, his rise to favour in Yan'an was a masterpiece of deft political manoeuvring. 'Mao's pistol' took his soubriquet seriously: he dressed like an NKVD man, in a shiny black leather jacket, black breeches and boots. His black horse and black Alsatian were affectations no one would dream to snigger over – not given his overriding purpose in life, which was to make people confess, whether they were guilty or not.

'Why does the Communist Party make so much effort to rescue you?' Kang writes, explaining his methods:

Simply because it wants you to be Chinese, and not be cheated into serving the enemy. Those of you who have lost your way, be conscious, take a firm decision, repent to the Party, and cast off the special agent's garb, cast off the uniform of the fifth column, put on Chinese clothes, and speak about the deception, the insults, and the injuries you have suffered, and confess to the crimes you have committed.

From February 1942, just as *Liberation Daily*'s *zawen* were being published, Kang Sheng broadened this 'education movement for senior cadres' to encompass the Party as a whole.

At educational institutions across Yan'an, precise timetables were provided, and a list of twenty-two key texts were prescribed for study. Participants were to read them, take notes, and debate them in small discussion groups. Central Committee members and workers from the Propaganda Bureau were dispatched to moderate these groups. The campaign would last three months (two months in the Party schools), followed by a period of investigation, criticism and self-criticism. By early June, more than 17,000 people were participating in the rectification campaign in Yan'an. Work hours were reduced to make time for study. Thousands were questioned and criticised until they dropped with exhaustion. Anyone who could, left.

Between May and June 1943 almost all artists and writers were gathered into the Third Department of the Central Party School, where they underwent rigorous political vetting. By July, seventy per cent had been deemed unreliable. Torture and intimidation were commonplace.

Pyotr Vladimirov, a visiting Soviet journalist, was appalled. Writing in his diary on 27 February 1943:

> *For more than a year already all studies have been called off in all the educational establishments. This is the result of the rectification campaign. Many offices also barely function and are open only half the day. Everyone is occupied at meetings or is studying the '22 Documents'. In the Press and in speeches Mao Zedong is extolled and the 'dogmatists' are branded.*

All Yan'an's publications and cultural organisations came under the jurisdiction of organs Zhou Yang controlled. Peer publications were shut down, and artists and writers were absorbed into the Party administration.

The rectification of Yan'an's writers had begun in May 1942, almost as soon as the campaign was extended to the Party as a whole. The figure Mao chose as scapegoat and hate-figure for that campaign was a relatively obscure (and for that reason disposable) translator called Wang Shiwei.

The first part of Wang Shiwei's 'Wild Lily' had appeared in *Liberation Daily* four days after Ding Ling's own *zawen* 'Thoughts on March 8'.

From a purely literary standpoint, Wang's *zawen* was streets ahead of everyone else's, and the closest anyone had come to realising Lu Xun's ambition for the form. It began with a moving portrait of the woman Wang had loved:

> As I walked alone by the river, seeing in front of me the old-fashioned cotton shoes of a female comrade suddenly reminded me of those of Comrade Li Fen, the most beloved first friend of my life. Whenever I think of her my heart pounds and my blood thickens.

Li Fen is a revolutionary martyr, but Wang refuses to consign her to a pedestal. That kind of bloodless thinking is all too prevalent, he says – and so his incendiary feuilleton against Yan'an's corruption begins.

Yan'an is no utopia! It is not even egalitarian. Frankly, it's callous. Why is clothing divided into three ranks? Why are there five grades of food?

Why? *Because the leadership hates the people.* Yan'an's leaders complain that something of the old Yan'an spirit is missing? Well, they should look in the mirror!

Between the publication of the first half of 'Wild Lily' and the second (which appeared on 27 March), *Grain Rain*, the journal of Ding Ling's Literary Resistance Association, published Wang's essay 'Statesmen, Artists', in which he argued the case for forthright criticism.

Borrowing from Stalin, Wang calls writers and artists 'engineers of the soul', whose job it is to expose and purge the spiritual 'filth' that obstructs the success of the revolution. Wang's essay is moralistic. He's not at all arguing for

Western-style 'freedom of expression', still less is he defending art for art's sake. Like John Milton in his seventeenth-century Puritan pamphlet *Areopagitica* (and with the same level of self-importance) Wang wants to bring his high ideals to bear; he wants a high-minded revolution, and he and his kind – the writers, the intellectuals – are, he reckons, the ones to ensure its moral integrity.

When Mao read Part I of Wang Shiwei's 'Wild Lily' in the *Liberation Daily*, he pounded at the newspaper. 'Who is in charge here, Wang Shiwei or Marx?' He went straight to the phone and told *Liberation Daily*'s editor Bo Gu that he expected the paper to engage in an in-depth self-criticism. Then, hearing of a recent fracas around a wall newspaper posted up at the Central Research Institute (where Wang was a special research fellow) Mao went to read the document for himself.

The newspaper pasted up on the wall of the Central Research Institute had taken up Wang Shiwei's call for moral renewal. It called for 'absolute democracy' and declared that 'whoever hinders democracy will surely shed blood after colliding with this wall.'

Wang's fate was sealed.

At a (public, potentially violent, always humiliating) 'struggle session' at *Liberation Daily* on 31 March, more than seventy writers and critics met with Mao Zedong to listen to Bo Gu's tortured self-criticism. The next day Kang Sheng's wife turned up – all of a sudden she was a literary critic – and delivered a detailed and devastating criticism of both 'Wild Lily' and Ding Ling's 'Thoughts on March 8'.

Then the old general He Long stood up to say that Ding Ling had maligned the Party and the leadership. Ding took his criticism on the chin. Some collateral damage was only to be expected from an assault like this. By the time the eighth speaker stood up to criticise her, however, it was obvious that she, too, was a target. Struck dumb, she shook in her seat. Bo Gu came to sit beside her to offer a bit of moral support: 'Are you all right?'

During his summing up, Mao let Ding Ling off the hook: 'Although "Thoughts on March 8" contains some criticism there are also constructive recommendations,' he opined. 'Ding Ling is different from Wang Shiwei. Ding Ling is a comrade; Wang Shiwei is a Trotskyite.'

But this was hardly a ringing endorsement, and Ding Ling knew she was in trouble.

On 7 April a struggle session at the Central Research Institute took the campaign against Wang Shiwei to the next level. In a way, the session ran itself. Cadres who had originally supported and sympathised with Wang Shiwei now changed sides, desperate not to be caught up in the gears of rectification.

Some, with tears rolling down their cheeks, confessed that their standpoints had been insufficiently stable or that they had been duped and misled. Others quickly rewrote history and claimed that they had always considered Wang 'anti-Party' and 'anti-leader'. Amid mass hysteria and calls for severe punishment, Wang's crimes were steadily inflated until by June's forum, 'Democracy and Discipline in the Party' (somewhere between a rally and a show trial, and convened at a sports ground), he was labelled a 'ringleader of an anti-Party clique', a Trotskyite bandit and a Kuomintang spy.

'This kind of person,' stammered Mao's secretary Chen Boda, 'is like a spineless leech! He is as tiny as a mosquito – the kind that sneak in silently to bite you.'

Ai Qing – a renowned poet, now equally famous as the father of the artist Ai Weiwei – called Wang Shiwei's viewpoint reactionary, 'and his remedies are poisonous. This

290 ENGINEERS OF HUMAN SOULS

individual does not deserve to be called "human" let alone "comrade".'

On 8 June, a thousand 'cultural troops' drawn from schools and organisations across the city gathered for an all-out attack. They were reminded of their revolutionary duty to turn against even family and friends, if they held on to incorrect ideas.

Then it was Ding Ling's turn.

'We tried everything to pull him out of his latrine,' she said of the writer she had just published, and who by now was too ill to stand. Riddled with TB and exhausted by constant interrogation, he was sunk into a canvas reclining chair. 'But he wanted to drag us down with him! This is outrageous. Now, we should declare: Wang Shiwei has one last chance to climb out of his counterrevolutionary latrine.'

She urged people to banish all sympathy, 'all petit-bourgeois sentimentality, humanism, and unprincipled, abstract, and self-regarded feelings of "justice" toward Wang Shiwei'. To borrow a phrase from Lu Xun, people must be willing to beat a drowning dog. The fact that she had published this obscure figure (hardly a *writer*; 'Wild Lily' and 'Statesmen and Artists' are the only things she's ever seen of his) was a mistake she would never live down, 'and I will forever regard it as a warning'.

As for her own 'Thoughts on March 8', Ding Ling renounced it completely:

I need to tell all those who sympathise – this is a bad essay ... Much as I have poured out my blood and tears in that article and infused it with the bitterness and fervent hopes which I have held for years, nevertheless the essay showed that as in the past I had only spoken for a portion of the people and had not taken the position of the Party as a whole. That essay was one-sided; it only pointed out some of the darker aspects and neglected to affirm the bright road ahead.

In the end, it was all about her: 'I feel what Tang Sanzang [Tripitaka in *Journey to the West*] felt when he was standing by the river on the border between heaven and earth – a feeling of suddenly realising the whole truth. I walk forward with steady and sure steps.'

Few eluded Kang Sheng's nets for long; but few if any spies were ever caught. Kang later admitted that less than one in ten of those who 'confessed' were actually enemies of the Party.

But the campaign had never been about investigation or prosecution. It was about terror.

From November 1942, Wang was placed in solitary confinement. Every now and again he was hauled out in front of foreign journalists to denounce himself and praise the Party's open-mindedness. The rest of the time he spent writing self-criticisms. Years later, in the face of a Kuomintang advance, Wang was evacuated to the Jin-Sui Border Region, which was under the control of He Long. On 1 July 1947, the old general had him beheaded.

CHAPTER THIRTEEN

i

The only story worthy of being written and painted is the story of man's power to change the world through a revolutionary force of will, with which each heart struggles to conquer its treacherous individualism, and all combine together to triumph over the chaotic forces of nature – including the chaotic forces of men who have failed to understand the need for change.

On 2 May 1942, and in the midst of the Party's scapegoating of Wang Shiwei, Mao Zedong took Party writers aside to explain their duties.

The Yan'an Forum on Literature and Art was held in the pleasant, modern central auditorium at Yangjialing. It was a private affair. No official minutes survive, and *Liberation Daily* did not cover the event.

It was, in the midst of the hysteria of rectification, a chance to bring writers into line and establish the policy they were supposed to follow. There hadn't been a policy before. ('What policy on literature and art?' Mao had initially retorted, when the idea was first mooted. 'Right now we're busy with the war and planting millet.')

Over three weeks, the Yan'an forum thrashed out the Party's 'socialist realist' approach to creative work. Zhou Yang, Mao's cultural spokesperson, expressed this line best when he drew a distinction between 'old realism' and 'revolutionary realism'. Old realism is critical, even sceptical. Revolutionary realism looks for the bright side; it writes about the positive, the growing, the developing side of reality, the side with a future. 'Brightness is not an abstract concept, it concretely and actually exists. To demand that the writer write about the bright side is to demand that he write about something already contained in reality, or new and about to be born.'

China's emperors had always employed writers as teachers and bureaucrats. To this traditional view of writers as state servants, Mao then added his especially trenchant version of Marxist-Leninism. In the two talks he gave at the forum, Mao explained that love, freedom and truth were abstract ideas that had no reality outside of a particular social context. There was no 'human nature', either: only particular kinds of human nature belonging to different classes.

Consequently, it made no sense for writers to express their 'love of humanity'. 'We cannot love our enemies or social evils; our aim is to eliminate both. How can our artists and writers fail to understand this common-sense view?'

The job of the writer was to distinguish between social classes and point up their differences – not to obscure them by dwelling on imaginary universals.

There was plenty of positive work at the forum, about how to address an illiterate population and how to reflect the realities of rural experience and all the rest of it. Nonetheless, the main lesson of the forum was that you either found a way to weaponise your work in the Party's service, or you found something else to do.

On the last day of the forum, 23 May, the discussion stopped before dinner. The sun was setting but it was still bright enough for a photograph. Eighty or so people crowded together for a group shot, Mao Zedong naturally taking the middle seat in the front row.

All of a sudden Mao stood up, went to Ding Ling, and ushered her into his seat. 'Let our woman cadre be in the middle,' he said. 'We don't much want to be ticked off again, come next March 8th.'

Ding did her best to join in the laughter.

The rectification campaign saw Ding Ling leave her post as literary editor of the *Liberation Daily*. She spent the next two years in study and reform work at the Party school and in the countryside.

In early 1944, she was assigned to the Border Regions Cultural Association to concentrate on her writing. A posting to Mata village near Yan'an gave her the opportunity to experience rural life, and she was delighted by the abundance of source material around her: 'It's just the right thing for an article!'

Did this period mark a decline in Ding Ling's fortunes? She certainly didn't see it that way. 'We still have to learn good reportage,' she wrote:

Well written, fascinating newspaper reports about life and work ... are more important than literature at present. The 'literary' people don't like this kind of work, while the journalists don't have the necessary training to write well enough. I want to develop a new style of reporting ... and I'm learning and teaching it at the same time.

A month later came her fictionalised portrait of peasant co-operative director Tian Baolin. As reportage, 'Tian Baolin' is not bad at all, full of detailed information, production statistics and place names. As literature, it seems to have abandoned characterisation entirely, as though people were simply their job titles.

Only public activity counts. Tian Baolin is a hero, a model for emulation, the embodiment of his community. ('My every thought was for the people,' claims this rustic hero. 'If it is to their advantage, they will support you; without them nothing will succeed.')

He keeps saying 'I am not a capable man', but it turns out he can do almost anything. He starts a co-op and within six months it blossoms; eight pack animals become sixty-four; the business earns nearly 100,000 yuan.

The day after this story appeared in the *Liberation Daily*, Chairman Mao invited Ding Ling over to dinner. He was delighted by her 'new literary direction'. 'Very good, isn't it?' he enthused to a Yan'an cadres' conference. 'Writers should write for workers, peasants and soldiers.'

A fairer test of Ding's 'new literary direction' was to follow. Faced with such a wealth of raw material, the writer of nuanced, melancholic short stories conceived a work of quite staggering scale: a three-part epic built around the experiences of rural villagers who are finally reclaiming their land from greedy landowners.

Life and politics got in the way of Ding's grandest schemes, but *On Sanggan River*, the first novel in the planned sequence, was achievement enough: a quarter of a million words covering just a little over a month in the life of a village that's throwing off its traditional past for a revolutionary future. Its forty representative characters collide and intersect, argue and collaborate, in a choreography of political change that, though not very deeply felt, is still vividly realised.

'Originally I wanted to go to Manchuria,' Ding Ling explains in the preface to the 1979 edition, 'but because the Kuomintang had launched the Civil War, for a time transportation came to a halt.' Stuck in newly liberated Kalgan in north-western Hebei, Ding Ling suddenly began to long for the villages. She had got to know such places quite well, but still fretted that she had no deep knowledge of rural life. 'I wanted very much to return and live once again among the people ... and to work with cadres who were "country bumpkins".'

It was the summer of 1946, and the Party had just promulgated its directive on land reform. Ding Ling immediately put in a request to join a land reform team, 'and after a quick look at several villages I finally lingered a while in Wenchuantun'.

The novel is based on fact, describing the drastic ethical and economic changes that follow the arrival in the village of a land reform team. There's mention of the Kuomintang, the Eighth Route Army, and even 'that American general Marshall' (who visited China in December 1945); the Japanese occupation is skated over, and reserved mostly for flashbacks.

'Real people' have finally seized the power from those inhuman creatures the landlords, who have always oppressed them. At the novel's climax ('The Final Combat', no less) 'Schemer Qian', a local landlord and notorious bully, is hauled to a mass meeting to face his former victims.

A man leaps from the crowd and rushes up to him: 'You murderer!' he screams.

'You trampled our village under your feet! You killed people behind the scenes for money. Today we're going to settle all old scores, and do a thorough job of it. Do you hear that? Do you still want to frighten people? It's no use!

There's no place for you to stand on this stage! Kneel down!
Kneel to all the villagers!' He pushed Qian hard, while the
crowd echoed: 'Kneel down! Kneel down!' The militiamen
forced him to kneel down properly.

Qian attempts to cool things down by making a full confession. His wife begs for mercy: 'For the sake of our son in the
Eighth Route Army,' she pleads, 'don't be too hard on him!'
But the people have received anything but mercy at Qian's
hands over the years, and one feeling animates them all:

'Vengeance! They wanted vengeance! They wanted to give
vent to their hatred, the sufferings of the oppressed since
their ancestors' times, the hatred and loathing of thousands
of years; all this resentment they directed against him. They
would have liked to tear him with their teeth.'

In June 1948, Ding Ling made a copy of her newly finished
manuscript and delivered it in person to Mao's secretary
Hu Qiaomu.

On 15 June, Ding Ling was told to come to Xibaipo village in Pingshan County, the Party's new command centre,
and consult with the Party about her future role. No sooner
had she arrived at the new encampment then she saw another
vehicle coming from the opposite direction. Out of the packed
vehicle stepped Mao, older than she remembered him, and
carrying more weight, but healthy and cheerful. Abandoning
his wife Jiang Qing and a score of children, he invited Ding
Ling to take a walk with him.

He had heard good things about her novel. He asked her
about her work, and said he was looking forward to reading
the first draft. She was one of the people now, he said. He
wanted her to represent them at an upcoming congress in

Budapest, the Second International Congress of Democratic Women's Federations. At dinner that evening, he grew even more fulsome, comparing her to Lu Xun, Mao Dun, Guo Moruo ...

Ding Ling had also given her manuscript to Zhou Yang, and of course Zhou, her arch-rival, had hated it and had done what he could to prevent it being published. But Mao's opinion was the one that mattered. So long as it passed muster with the Central Propaganda Committee, it could be published. In July 1948, the Committee pronounced it 'the first and best book depicting class struggle in China's villages'

Once Ding Ling had revised the manuscript, *On Sanggan River* was rushed into print in time for her to take it with her when she left for Hungary on 9 November 1948 – her first trip abroad.

ii

Budapest. In the parliament building, where the emperor once received guests, amid national flags and flowers and carvings, three hundred women from over fifty nations are gathered for the Second International Congress of Democratic Women's Federations. Ding Ling is overwhelmed.

At night there is a big political demonstration. Standing amid a sea of torches, with all other lights extinguished, she hears the masses cry: 'Long live Stalin!' and encouraging cries follow the Chinese delegation wherever they go. 'Cracking job of beating Chiang Kai-shek!' 'Don't be afraid of American imperialism!' 'You're all heroes! All the women in the liberated areas are heroes!' 'Mao Zedong is amazing!' 'Long live China!' And now – 'an extremely familiar name, a name shouted in unison by a hundred thousand people, by so many foreigners and in a foreign tongue' – 'Long live Chairman Mao!'

Tears fill Ding Ling's eyes as she chants along with the crowd: 'Long live Mao Zedong! *Lija* Mao Zedong!' The women of the delegation fall into one another's arms, weeping.

> In the past I only knew how the Chinese felt, how grateful they were to Chairman Mao and how they praised him. Even the mention of him put people in a cheerful frame of mind. But only now did I realise the significance the name Mao Zedong had in the world.

Every face is smiling, smiling at *her*, and '*Lija* Mao Zedong!' rings in her ears.

'All I could think was to rush back to China to share this new discovery with the Chinese people, and tell all of those who love him.'

Look at Ding Ling: she has become indestructible.

Martyr figures like Wang Shiwei were the exception, not the rule. Rectification destroyed a few in order to raise the many, rebuilding them in the Party's own image.

From this point on, no matter how badly things go for her, no matter how poorly the Party treats her, Ding will cleave to her iron-clad faith. Even in the face of history, a changed culture and different attitudes, she will prove almost embarrassingly unshakeable: the Party's very own 'red clothes priest'.

Secure in her faith and thoroughly rectified following Kang Sheng's 'rescue campaign' (which killed barely a hundred, but brought an entire generation to heal), Ding Ling racks up triumph after triumph. Her novel is getting a Russian translation (and acquires an oriental flourish: from now on it's *The Sun Shines over Sanggan River*). No less a literary lion than Alexander Fadeyev, author of *The Rout* and *The Young Guard* and chairman of countless Soviet policy committees, dubs her 'an engineer of human souls'.

Back home, on 16 March 1949, she delivers a speech to a literary conference in which she humbly sets aside that dangerous title:

> To be an 'engineer of the human soul' and yet remain unconcerned about the whole of Mankind, to ignore the battle at the front or production in the rear … and only be concerned about oneself, one's fame and position, how would it be possible to merit the name? Fundamentally I think it would not fit! When one's own soul is vile and ugly, how can you talk about reforming and teaching other people?

But such is her reputation now, she cannot help but be placed first among equals. In April she's in Prague, attending the First World Peace Conference, when the morning papers carry the news that 300,000 troops of the People's Liberation Army have crossed the Yangtze. A couple of hours later – at noon on 23 April 1949 – the conference chairman announces that Nanjing, China's capital for the past twenty-two years, has been liberated.

'Long live Mao Zedong!'

'Long live China!'

'Long live Stalin!'

The Chinese delegation is mobbed. Ding Ling is lifted into the air.

*

In Moscow's Red Square, Ding Ling steals a moment to once again rejoin the masses. She's been flown in, witnessed the May Day troop review, and spent her evening at the theatre.

But now, at last, she's where she belongs, in the crowds flooding a square so brightly lit, it might as well be day. No one recognises her, or understands her, and yet she has never felt closer to the people. Someone puts his arm around her. She hugs him back. The people around her form a circle. She passes from one group to another, dancing and whirling like a child.

She returns to China to spread the good news. How must the writer reform? How wash away old petit bourgeois influences and become more pure? This is the only question left for the writer to answer; the only question that matters.

She's appointed chief editor of the *Literary Gazette*, official organ of the Writers' Association. She becomes Party Secretary of the Association of Literary Workers, and vice chair of its Standing Committee. In September 1950, Mao asks Ding Ling what she wants to do – write, or be an administrator? – and she opts to nurture young writers at the newly opened Central Literary Research Institute.

In the spring of 1951, Ding Ling attains the most prestigious position she will ever occupy: head of the Literature and Arts Section of the Central Propaganda Bureau. Even the bigwigs are by now getting a little fed up with her conservatism, her dogmatism, her doctrinaire approach to socialist realism; but Mao Zedong is happy. With Luo Ruiqing, minister of Public Security, he visits her to discuss what can be done about the country's few remaining petit bourgeois intellectuals.

Ding Ling cannot escape the demands of her many offices, even if she wanted to.

North Korea's Soviet-supported invasion of South Korea in June 1950 has raised the spectre of a nuclear response from America. The Chinese state responds by tracking down and attacking its apostates.

'China,' writes Zhang Zhongxiao on 25 May 1951, 'is now in the throes of a great turmoil and feudalistic forces, maniac-like, are engaged in slaughtering people. The extent of this turmoil reaches far and wide.'

In September, Russian writer Ilya Ehrenburg and Chilean poet Pablo Neruda visit China to award a Stalin Peace Prize to Madame Sun Yat-sen, and Ehrenburg notices that there are sessions everywhere devoted to 'criticism and self-criticism' over the most private of matters. How did this unmarried woman end up pregnant? Why does this worker always show up late for work? In the National Federation of Literature and Art Circles, Ding Ling runs several such sessions. A true believer, she takes her own self fiercely to task, dubbing herself 'a pusillanimous individualist'.

This is not a strategy for survival, and when Stalin dies, a painful cultural reappraisal leaves her between a rock and a hard place. A lot of leftist writers have learned to hate the click of her literary jackboot; meanwhile the Soviet writers she's been emulating so assiduously are, very publicly, throwing off the yoke of 'socialist realism'.

Mao's having none of it, and has Zhou Yang launch a thorough campaign against anti-Party views.

Now, Zhou Yang has a number of old scores to settle, and a lot of personal history in Shanghai that he can now rewrite to his own advantage.

His spat with Lu Xun still hangs over him like a cloud; that will have to be rewritten. A scapegoat will be required – but who to sacrifice? Ding Ling would be an obvious target, but she is still in Mao's good books. Instead, in the spring of 1955 Zhou Yang cooks up a campaign against Hu Feng, Ding Ling's friend of more than twenty years; who published her magazine *Big Dipper*, and was arrested for his trouble; who delivered letters to her mother, and drove the cab that spirited her out of Nanjing; the man to whom she had entrusted the telegram containing Mao's poem 'The Immortal from Linjiang'.

The charge sheet against Hu Feng is almost absurdly long: he stands accused of being anti-Marxist, antisocialist, anti-Party, antipeople and antirealist. He is supposed to have argued that all organisations for literature and art should be disbanded, and that the Party should relinquish its leadership.

It is Ding Ling's greatest test of Party loyalty yet, and she outdoes herself:

Having read the materials brought to light by Shu Wu in the 13 [May] issue of the *People's Daily*, and Hu Feng's reply, there is no way I could go on with my daily routine. It is truly enough to send cold shivers down the spine. Where is the enemy? The enemy is right in front of our eyes, right in our own ranks, to our left and right, right next to us. An exposed weapon is easy to parry, a concealed one most difficult to evade! All the while Hu Feng, wearing the garb of a revolutionary, petit-bourgeois intellectual, under a cloak of Marxism-Leninism, has mingled with us and called us 'friend', when in reality he has been hiding the most dark, hostile thoughts against us, despising us, regretting that he cannot trample over our feelings and continue with his careerist plot to organize things.

On 16 May, while Hu Feng is eating dinner, the doorbell rings. Marshals from the Public Security Bureau have arrived with an arrest warrant.

The trouble with witch hunts is that they are a machinery without brakes. Hu Feng becomes such a notorious figure, a campaign is started to find his accomplices. Soon, one in twenty of the Party and the government are found to be counter-revolutionaries, and by August, the Movement for the Suppression of Counterrevolutionaries at the Writers' Union has begun to review the case of Ding Ling.

At a meeting of the Central Propaganda Bureau, it is declared – without any new evidence – that the reason Ding Ling travelled to Yan'an in 1937 was because the Kuomintang sent her. At the twelfth session of the Party Committee, the writer and up-and-coming bureaucrat Lin Mohan delivers the committee's findings.

Since entering the Party, Ding Ling has faced three crucial tests, and has failed two of them. Whether or not she passes the third depends on her.

The first test was during her 'captivity' in Nanjing. Clearly, her sojourn with the Kuomintang was anything but imprisonment. Not only had she shown no antipathy toward the apostate Feng Da, she had a child by him! And she brought him flowers every day when he was sick!

The second test was in Yan'an. Publishing Wang Shiwei's 'Wild Lily' and her own 'Thoughts on March 8' could not have played better into the hands of the Kuomintang, who copied these materials for their own propaganda effort.

Ding Ling has yet to fail the third test, but things aren't looking good. Can she resist the temptations of fame and power? It certainly doesn't look as if she can. Almost all of the positions of leadership in the field of literature have been handed over to her: vice chair of the Writers' Association, leadership of its Party Committee, chief editor of the *Literary Gazette* and *People's Literature*, head of the Central Literary Research Institute, head of the Literature and Art Section of the Central Propaganda Bureau . . .

Ding Ling is, when you come down to it, just like her heroine Miss Sophie: a totally self-centred individual!

Lin whips up a storm. Among the slogans being chanted in the hall: 'Down with the anti-Party element Ding Ling!'

Ding Ling is pushed onto the stage and instead of speaking she bows her head, sobbing. The meeting breaks up in uproar.

On 16 September, nearly fifteen hundred people turn up to the Capital Theatre for the final struggle session against Ding Ling and her 'co-conspirators' – including her old friend Feng Xuefeng, whom she's consistently shunned and insulted ever since he stood up publicly for Wang Shiwei. Some are dragged up on stage but are forbidden to speak. Others aren't even allowed to hear their sentences read out.

Zhou Yang delivers the *coup de grâce* in a speech of exquisite cruelty:

Several comrades have mentioned 'Miss Sophie's Diary'. If you want to understand Ding Ling's character and her way of thinking, read this famous work that she wrote thirty years ago, and it will help you. The heroine of the story is an individualist, a nihilist. She tells lies, deceives, toys with men, enjoys seeing other people in pain and even regards her own life as a plaything. Although this character seems like a rebel against traditional Confucian ethics, in reality she is an embodiment of the decadent tendencies of a declining class. Of course, an author may depict all manner of social types, the question is what attitude one adopts toward them. Obviously, Ding Ling harbours enormous sympathy for a character that should have been rejected.

'Sophie is Ding Ling!' comes a voice from the crowd.

Then, 'Ding Ling is Sophie!'

Soon, they're all at it. 'Sophie is an evil woman!' 'Ding Ling is an evil woman, too!'

Ding Ling, labelled a 'level six rightist', loses all her appointments and even her Party membership. If she wants, she can remain in the capital, working away at a reduced salary.

But this is not what she wants.

From Manchuria, her husband Chen Ming (they met in the Front Service Corps, back in 1937) has been sending her clippings from *China Pictorial*. From its photographs she has assembled a vision of a new future. An ancient forest whose trees block out the day. Deer moving like shadows through the green gloom. Clear streams, fresh grass, fresh flowers.

Already labelled a rightist, Chen writes to her from Farm 853 about his work, drilling wells, melting ice into cooking water, building barracks. 'The vast wilderness and the undulating mountains of Beidahuang were captivating to them,' Ding writes. 'He and his friends were actually waging a war to transform heaven and earth.'

Only those who give up the self completely and devote themselves heart and soul to working for the people can understand true happiness.

'Come,' says Chen, 'I think the best thing is to be here with me. There are lots of people here. All of them are concerned about you. They say they'll build a small thatched hut just for you.'

Epilogue

His name is Walter Lippmann, and he is born in September 1889 in a 'gilded Jewish ghetto' (that's his biographer Ronald Steel talking) on New York's Upper East Side. From infancy, he is ridiculously well-connected. As a boy he shakes hands with President McKinley, he's formally presented to Admiral Dewey, and he charms the pants off Theodore Roosevelt. Later he studies at Harvard with George Santayana, takes tea with William James, chisels for Lincoln Steffens, argues socialism with Bernard Shaw and H. G. Wells.

On 29 July 1914, Lippmann, who's been drifting about Ostend and Bruges and Ghent, writes in his diary, 'War in Europe impending. Panic in Brussels. Run on banks. Collapse of credit.' On the train from Ostend, Lippmann finds it decidedly impolitic to speak German. He arrives in London the next morning, shaken and exhausted.

He's at the House of Commons when Britain declares war.

In the second week of December 1917, the US president Woodrow Wilson hires the twenty-seven-year-old – already the founding editor of *The New Republic* – to help begin drafting a European peace settlement. But Lippmann is far from happy with the results.

'It seems to me,' he writes to his old friend Newton Baker, 'to stand the world on its head to assume that a timid legal document can master and control the appetites and the national wills before which this Treaty puts such immense prizes.'

Lippmann takes his politics seriously. Among several impressive hobby horses: the economic origins of power politics; the emotional foundations of patriotism; the methods of diplomacy; the obstacles in the way of international organisation.

By 1922 he has begun to realise that politics is like Gertrude Stein's Oakland: there is no 'there' there.

Public Opinion. It is his first major work in a career that will span sixty years. In it, Lippmann argues that citizens in a modern mass democracy make decisions purely on the basis of media-generated stereotypes. They have no choice in this. It's not a matter of intelligence. It's a matter of scale. Modern states are altogether too vast and complex for the citizen to even begin to comprehend the ramifications of even the most major decisions. They cannot work from facts; they can only work from values.

This is why governments need public relations experts: experts to control and adjust the flow of information so that the pictures in citizens' heads line up with realities that only a few full-time experts can possibly be expected to wrap their heads around.

Three short years later, and Lippmann's thinking has grown yet more disconcerting. Much of his book *The Phantom Public* is devoted to often very funny demonstrations of why political circumstances are too unstable to be 'taught', and why even political ethics don't really offer a stable basis for 'informed opinion'. Informed from what point of view? There are so many viewpoints, *all* legitimate, *all* morally justified!

So government, Lippmann concludes, is run neither by the people (who can't possibly be expected to understand everything), nor by experts (whose expertise only covers some particular subject). Government is run by a constantly churning gaggle of *insiders* – people whose first-hand knowledge in a particular affair lets them direct expertise where it's required.

By this point, we have pretty much reconstituted a vision of government – massively centralised, running on influence and reputation – which would have been familiar to the court of Louis XIV. We may even have begun to seriously question whether democracy is desirable, never mind possible.

Even as *Public Opinion* lands in US bookshops, in the hills above Lake Garda in northern Italy, the Marquesa Luisa Casati is playing piano in the music room of the Vittoriale, Gabriele D'Annunzio's ridiculously overstuffed mausoleum of a home (reliquaries, swords, bronzes, ecclesiastical furniture). On the window seat, listening to her, are her younger sister Jolanda (a cellist) and D'Annunzio himself, half blind and syphilitic, in slippers and pyjamas.

Though it has a history – Franz Liszt once stayed here – D'Annunzio's last home looked quite ordinary when his secretary Antongini first spotted it: an eighteenth-century farmhouse, secluded on a steep hillside outside the town of Gardone Riviera.

Now you can barely get inside because of the marble column blocking the front hall. (Biographer Lucy Hughes-Hallett nails the scene perfectly when she points out that everything in the Vittoriale is placed on something else: 'A rosary is draped over a statuette which stands on a piece of embroidered velvet, which covers a majolica box which is set upon a carved table which stands on an oriental rug.')

The whole house is, as always, as hot as a greenhouse and stuffy besides, and the windows are wide open.

What are the chances that D'Annunzio, his blood fizzing with cocaine and laudanum and heaven knows what else, makes what we may delicately call 'a pass' at young Jolanda? In any event, he is now falling head-first out of the window and onto the gravel, ten feet below.

For three days he lies in a coma. When he wakes, he describes his fall as his 'archangelic flight' (and on the third day, did he not rise again?)

The fascists insist on sending D'Annunzio gifts. The motorboat in which he carried out the raid on the harbour of Buccari. A seaplane. The casings of several unexploded shells. The prow of a battleship, the *Puglia*, which casts a near-permanent shadow over the rose garden. A spy – but, it turns out, a decent one: a police officer called Giovanni Rizzo who reassures Mussolini about his charge and manages to bury local police reports about the old man's driving.

Mussolini is right to be worried, and wise to receive D'Annunzio's messages patiently, and grant him every reasonable favour. Following the Fiume adventure D'Annunzio, who was not punished for his sedition, or even charged, has a greater popular following in Italy than the government does. Several factions are trying to recruit him. His own legionnaires won't leave him alone. Mussolini would like to turn him into a sort of human mascot, but the best he gets is D'Annunzio's signature on a joint message sent to the king, declaring their 'mutual regard'.

D'Annunzio believes his movement has been 'squandered and falsified' by the fascists, and is wary of the uses to which his increasingly infrequent appearances are being put. Around the time of his defenestration he writes a note to himself, '*Tempus tacendi*' – time to be silent.

And why should he speak? What else has he left to prove? This is the poet who created a new dramatic form, made of poetry and charisma and hysteria, and recruited an entire nation to its realisation!

True, he never had the talent or temperament to make much from it other than a series of theatrical productions, but Mussolini and the fascists have found a way to keep D'Annunzio's show running, night after night and year after year, and after them will come Joseph Goebbels and his peers in Germany's National Socialist Party, who will apply the latest science and technology to the enterprise. In so doing, they will rid Europe for ever of the absurd notion that political ideas spread through books and high culture and homework.

On 1 March 1938, aged seventy-four and working at his desk, D'Annunzio dies of a brain haemorrhage. The telephonist who transmits the news to Mussolini's headquarters hears someone cry, 'At last!'

Maurice Barrès dies, aged sixty-one, in Neuilly-sur-Seine on 4 December 1923. The conservative National Bloc government organises a state funeral for him on a positively Pharaonic scale; Paris hasn't seen the like since Victor Hugo passed.

And that's it for Barrès. Only the reputation remains: the long shadow of the 'castrated eagle', and the ponderous late literary leavings of a man who famously never lost control of a yacht, or fucked a woman in a punt, or touched Ida Rubinstein's knees.

Except that there's this odd late work – and no one really knows what to make of it – called *Un jardin sur l'Oronte* (*A Garden on the Orontes*). Even its Edwardian-style wrapper is unlike the Barrès we know; more the sort of plot gewgaw Wilde might employ, or Max Beerbohm. It tells how, one night in June 1914, an Irish archaeologist button-holed Barrès in a café in Hama by the Orontes River, and there translated for him an ancient tale of thwarted love between 'a Christian and a Sarrasin' . . .

The novel caused a minor scandal when it was published in 1922. The Catholic press was outraged. Undeterred (or encouraged; is that possible? Was he *chasing* scandal, suddenly?) Barrès began work with composer Alfred Bachelet on an operatic version. He said he had in mind a work of Wagnerian scale: a *Gesamtkunstwerk*, enthralling every sense.

It seems, for nine long years, as though Barrès's shade will just have to content itself with an ostentatious funeral. Then, on 7 November 1932, what do you think appears on the stage of the Paris Opéra, with music by Alfred Bachelet, and libretto by Franc-Nohain?

Now Paris is really confused. True to the original novel, *Un jardin sur l'Oronte* is all about the clash of East and West, the irreconcilability of people, about land and identity and nation and all those gloomy, chewy Barrèsian themes. Bachelet has made the most of this, interweaving cod-medieval polyphony and sinuous 'oriental' vocal runs to heighten the theme of racial conflict. To this solid enough conception, he has then added every possible frill and furbelow: recitatives, airs, chants, 'proverbes', processionals . . .

The result is not so much a clash of cultures; more their postmodern melding into something very like 'world music'.

Now that a leftist government has just taken power in France, the right-wing press are hardly going to rubbish their saintly Maurice Barrès, are they? So here we have the bizarre spectacle of Paris's most conservative voices singing the praises of what, when you come down to it, is a splendid mutt of an opera: an inadvertent melting pot of colours and cultures.

What the lugubrious shade of Maurice Barrès thinks now about his late-flowering *Gesamtkunstwerk* is anyone's guess.

But one would like to think he remembers his friend's *Le Martyre de saint Sébastien* with its 'Again! Again! Again! Again!'; that he realises what his id has really been up to, and what it has been chasing. And in that case – who knows? – maybe he will even be able to laugh.

When a writer tries to be politically useful, what happens to their work?

It becomes a hat.

André Gide:

> Barrès's mind recalls a machine for making hats of which I remember seeing an extraordinary advertisement some ten years ago: a drawing represented in summary fashion the machine and the hats it produced. Everything fed into the machine came out in the form of a hat – any material whatsoever would serve. At last, among the admiring spectators, a very young child, who was leaning too close, got caught in the mechanism; the machine swallowed him up. The parents were depicted and their gestures of despair; but their child, the delicate creature, emerged a moment later, at the other end of the machine, to the delight of all eyes, to the joy of his parents, in the form of a perfect little hat: 'A hat, ladies and gentlemen, which it is my pleasure to doff to you,' concluded the inventor. The child was at last useful for something.

Sometimes – and this is even more strange – society insists that the production of hats is a vital industry.

André Malraux and his wife Clara disembark in Leningrad with the Ehrenburgs on 14 June 1934. Ilya Ehrenburg has persuaded Malraux to attend the First Soviet Writers' Congress.

Malraux, at this point a convinced Stalinist, sends admiring reports back home about 'the conditions of socialist work'. He seems not to notice the surveillance around him, perhaps because it's other writers who are doing the spying.

Though as a delegate he has special hotels and shops to frequent, he can see that the city has shortages. 'At the zoo, the chimpanzee keeper, when asked "Does the monkey eat bread?" replies bitterly: "Yes, but only the bread that's made for foreigners: not ours."'

Still, the scale of the problem escapes Malraux: how the people are suffering worse deprivation now than some countries suffered during the First World War.

The conference expects that Malraux will use his speech to cement his reputation as a firm Western ally of communism (or 'useful idiot': an expression Lenin is supposed to have coined, but probably didn't).

Come his time to speak, however, Malraux has sat through not just Gorky's maunderings (God as the summing up of the products of labour, and all the rest), but also Andrei Zhdanov, pronouncing on the official style of Soviet culture, which depicts 'reality in its revolutionary development'.

He's listened to Anatoly Lunacharsky explaining how the bourgeois realist 'does not understand that truth does not sit in one place ... truth is the day after tomorrow'.

And:

'The Socialist Realist does not accept reality as it is. He accepts it as it will be.'

And:

'The Communist dream is not a flight from the earthly but a flight into the future.'

By the time Lunacharsky has finished pretzelling the notion of truth, lying seems the only possible way to go.

It is a measure of Malraux's failure to understand the

society around him that he's happy to show his temper at all this folderol. He launches blithely into a speech that, had he been a local, would have got him summarily killed.

Art is not a submission, he says: it is a conquest.

'If writers are the engineers of the soul,' he says, 'do not forget that the highest function of an engineer is to invent.'

By early 1936, Maxim Gorky's constitution, weakened by a lifelong battle with TB, has begun to fail. An acquaintance running into him on a Moscow street is shaken: the great man is reduced to a skeleton.

Why didn't he stay in Sevastopol? Why return to all that noise and confusion? Gorky doesn't even like Moscow.

By 1 June come the first reports that he is ill.

From 6 to 17 June, all the papers delivered to Gorky arrive by special delivery, minus the bulletins about his health. Meanwhile, the rest of the world is being prepared for his death. (Despite persistent rumours to the contrary, it's unlikely that Gorky was assassinated. He was very obviously dying for quite a while.)

Stalin's pact with Adolf Hitler is about to go public. Gorky has caught wind of this. The last thing Stalin needs right now is a dying man's celebrity curse. Best, then, to seal this walking corpse off from the world. Gorky's magazines are immediately shut down. All those connected with their production and publication, down to the typesetters, are arrested. While Gorky lies on his deathbed, his friend Genrikh Yagoda and assistants ransack his study and destroy his papers.

Within hours of his death, doctors have sawn open Gorky's skull, scooped out his brain, and slopped it into a bucket of saline. An orderly rushes it round to the Neurological Institute in Moscow, where arrangements are already in hand for its long-term preservation and study.

Had Gorky died a few years earlier, mourners and the curious might have been able to visit it – one of more than a dozen brains in carefully labelled vitrines, lined up along the wall of what, in this old merchant's palace, was once a ballroom. All the greats resided here for a time. Vladimir Mayakovksy, decorticated at speed before the relatives caught wind of what was going on. Even Lenin, his vitrine turned at an angle to hide the stroke damage that finally killed him. They say there were also a few vitrines standing empty, awaiting their glorious dead. But no photograph survives, and by the time Gorky's grey matter reaches the institute, the room is closed to the public, its treasures removed to the laboratory in Room 19.

Originally conceived as a 'Pantheon of Brains' (a title it can never quite shake off), the Institute does solid scientific work. Along with significant public figures, it also studies 'brains from the various nations of the Soviet Union', morbid cases, and the brains of displaced people. (Still, it's the list of celebrities that catches the eye today: imagine Josef Stalin sharing shelf-space with Andrei Sakharov!)

While Russia was in the throes of its revolution, Gorky had talked endlessly about culture: culture nurtured, culture extended, culture promoted, culture preserved. This is why the West fell in love with him: they thought the culture Gorky was talking about was their own.

It sounded like theirs. He talked about rational government. He conjured up visions of a Baconian 'city of science, a series of temples where each scholar is a priest who is free to serve his god'.

Thinking that the English philosopher Francis Bacon belonged to them, it never occurred to Western observers to suppose that a second, quite different Atlantis might spring from his 'soil of exact observation, directed by the iron logic of mathematics': a place Saint-Simon and Auguste Comte might have dreamed into existence, and which Yevgeny Zamyatin, writing *We* in 1920, surely visited in his dreams. A nightmare realm where only the rational rule.

Francis Bacon's city of science, we may remember, boasted 'all sorts of beasts and birds, which we use ... for dissections and trials; that thereby we may take light what may be wrought upon the body of man.'

In times of crisis, any state is capable of recruiting eloquent voices to its cause. London's writers during the Blitz generated almost no good fiction about their plight (James Hanley's *No Directions* is a shining exception). They did, though, produce surprisingly accurate propaganda and often genuinely entertaining public information films, and all at an industrial pace. We saw the best minds of our generation, dragging themselves through White City towards the BBC. Quite right, too. There was a war on.

The trouble only begins when no victory condition can be found. For then the war, and all its patriotic hacking, must trundle on for ever.

No one asked George Bernard Shaw to be a Stalinist; or Edward Upward; or André Malraux. Mussolini did not seduce Ezra Pound. Oswald Mosley didn't bundle Henry Williamson into the British Union of Fascists.

But a writer's life is a lonely life, and writers do love to feel useful.

Writers often forget that literature is good at fomenting dissent, bad at rallying the troops.

They forget that words are a solvent, not a glue.

*

For nine years, Ding Ling and her husband Chen Ming spend their days in the Great Northern Wasteland (among forests, snowbanks, birds, squirrels and clear streams) building their promised land. Patrons and supporters send them supplies of special food, medicines and paper. Ding Ling is free to write if she wants to, and the sequel to *Sanggan River* is already under way.

But then, Ding Ling also has her chickens to look after. When she arrived she needed a proper job to earn some money, and because her back was bad, she was assigned a little light labour, gathering eggs. At first she barely knew what she was doing (and fancy that: that the simple act of collecting eggs turns out to be a skill!) Within a few months she was raising fowl and tending sick birds, nursing them back to health on top of a brick stove in her hut in Tang Yuan. She loves her chickens. And why should a writer not raise chickens? 'There is nothing to complain about working in a chicken run,' she says. 'Why should a writer be distinguished from the commoners?'

A thought report from 1960 describes her spiritual evolution:

> The only correct path is to thoroughly reform myself by learning from workers and peasants ... In the past two years I have lived and worked with them and have come to appreciate their nobility. That labour is a duty and that performing it is a glory. This is what I should learn from them. Engaging with them in this physical labour, I have moved from reluctance to enthusiasm and happiness.

Now, words are cheap, and can be forced. But we also have witnesses: Ding Ling the gregarious worker, the good friend, the jolly neighbour, in constant communication with friends and family, and so well liked in the village of Baoquanling, so highly respected, the local Party Committee votes to raise her salary and demands that her rightist label be removed.

Ding Ling can return to the thick of it any time she wants. She has received a *government invitation*.

Perhaps it's fear that keeps her in the back of beyond. But it may also be that she is happy here – happier than she has ever been before.

It is possible.

Sequels do not write themselves. *In the Bitter Winter*, about the villagers' attempts to wrestle their newly won land into production, languishes, while Ding Ling explores the best methods for raising healthy fowl. Using the cardboard from old toothpaste containers, she builds a model of an ideal chicken complex.

Elsewhere in the country, Mao's 'Great Leap Forward' industrialisation campaign has triggered a nationwide famine that kills one in twenty of the rural population.

In this 'wasteland', though, there is always enough to eat.

It takes Ding Ling until 1966 to finish *In the Bitter Winter* – at which point Mao, whose fear of old age has grown pathological, launches the youth of his country against government and Party. Mao's political regeneration is paid for with a tide of screaming anarchy. Red Guard thugs invest Baoquanling and order Ding Ling and her husband out of their guest house and into a cow-pen. The manuscript for *In the Bitter Winter* is lost. Ding Ling is kicked and beaten to the point where she can't get out of bed.

'Don't blame them,' she tells her husband, 'they are victims, too. One day they will understand.' They can break her body, but her spirit is indomitable. Of course it is: the Party's finest work went into it.

At sixty-two she is paraded through the streets in blackface and wearing a tall paper hat. Her husband, watching from a window, feels as though he has been stabbed in the heart. But Ding Ling? She's ironclad.

On the evening of 20 May 1975, a seventy-year-old woman is let out of a Chinese prison. She has no idea where she is. For the last five years, her cell and the courtyard where she exercised have been her whole world.

They tell her they are driving her to Changzhi, a town in south-eastern Shanxi. It takes until the afternoon of the next day to get there, by which time she dimly understands that she has spent the last five years in Qincheng, a prison dedicated to the incarceration of political offenders.

She spends the night in Changzhi. In the morning the journey continues to Zhangtou, a village in the Taihang Mountains. There, in a farmhouse in the hills, she is finally reunited with her husband.

For five years Ding Ling and Chen Ming have heard nothing from each other. Imprisonment itself, in 1970, was probably a mercy; the Cultural Revolution had spun wildly out of control, and had the pair not been jailed, they would surely have been murdered. But no one, now or later, can explain to them why they were kept apart. One can only assume institutional malice – the same malice that for five years has kept them incarcerated, one directly above the other, on different floors of the same prison.

In 1976 the 'Gang of Four', the leadership group responsible for the worst excesses of the Cultural Revolution, is arrested. Chinese culture begins to thaw. Young female writers like Yu Luojin and Dai Houying get up the courage to express views different from those of Mao Zedong.

And Ding Ling, the woman they revere? Celebrity survivor of the Cultural Revolution? Publicly, she slaps them down.

It gets quite awkward, in the end: the way Ding spends her last years swanning around the literary establishment, enforcing a political orthodoxy no one else values or even remembers. In interviews she waxes lyrical about Mao and other great comrades she has known, but she evades every difficult question, and professes herself stumped when people try and draw her out about women's issues.

The Party remade her in its image. How can she repudiate it now? They tore her apart and rebuilt her. Why, now, would she tear herself apart just to please some first-time novelist? Some bourgeois journalist? Some Yank academic?

'Old Shameful.'

At her last – she dies in 1986 – China's engineer of human souls acquires a new nickname.

Acknowledgements

This book benefited hugely from the forensic efforts of my agent Peter Tallack and my editor Holly Harley. David Bamford discovered many an error and infelicity in the original manuscript. Any that remain are mine.

I did not spend a year swanning from one life-changing intellectual encounter to another. (Who are these people with their interminable thank-yous to their Parnassian friends?) I read until my eyes bled. Anton Pjetri and his team at The Teapot in Forest Hill fed and watered and mopped me until I was done.

Marthe Buaillon was there at the birth of this book, and gave me a very large table to scribble on. The Maurice Barrès chapters are for her. The China chapters are for my brother Richard Ings, who first introduced me to the work of Ding Ling. Cheryl Lamb pulled ideas from the aether before I even knew I needed them; she also read every page I wrote, and threw the duff ones back at me. At a very late stage, Geoffrey Bagels Princess of Darkness and Mr Dusty Bum assisted with the pagination.

Setting the tone throughout was this saving advice from Walter Lippmann, which remains pinned above my desk:

That is what kills political writing, this absurd pretence that you are delivering a great utterance. You never do.

You are just a puzzled man making notes about what you think. You are not building the Pantheon, then why act like a graven image? You are drawing sketches in the sand which the sea will wash away.

SOURCES AND
FURTHER READING

Most quotations are referenced in the text. These notes offer
further guidance. Readers after more precise citations can
drop me a line at http://www.simonings.com.

For an insight into the vexed psychology of intellectu-
als, see Alan Kahan's *Mind vs. Money: The War Between
Intellectuals and Capitalism* (Transaction Publishers, 2010),
Daniel Kapust's *Flattery and the History of Political Thought*
(Cambridge University Press, 2018) and Mark Lilla's *The
Reckless Mind: Intellectuals in Politics* (NYRB, 2001).
Renee Winegarten's *Writers and Revolution: The Fatal Lure
of Action* (Franklin Watts, 1974) covers the political entan-
glements of writers from Lord Byron to Jean-Paul Sartre.
*Intellectuals in Politics: From the Dreyfus Affair to Salman
Rushdie*, edited by Jeremy Jennings and Anthony Kemp-
Welch (Routledge, 1997) poses worthwhile questions.

Studies of fellow-travelling in the twentieth century
include David Caute's *The Fellow-Travellers: A Postscript to
the Enlightenment* (Weidenfeld & Nicolson, 1973; revised
1988 through Yale University Press). A natural pairing is
Richard Griffiths's *Fellow Travellers of the Right: British
Enthusiasts for Nazi Germany, 1933–1939* (Faber, 1983).
Charles Kurzman identifies formative intellectual rightists in

Democracy Denied, 1905–1915: Intellectuals and the Fate of Democracy (Harvard University Press, 2008).

MAURICE BARRÈS

Not only is there no English-language biography of Maurice Barrès, precious little of his work has made it into English, either. Curtis's excellent critical study has Barrès down as an 'antirepublican' which, though just, wouldn't have pleased the old man at all.

Chapter One
For the Paris Exposition, see Jullian. For Morès, see Curtis. For the banquet at the Trocadéro, see Brown. 'I had been at the baptism . . .', see Doty. For Barrès's early years, see Weber. For Barrès the egoist, see Huneker. For Barrès the symbolist, see Carroll.

Chapter Two
Doty provides rich resources for this chapter; Millaud's parliamentary parody comes from him. For Georges Boulanger, Harding is hugely entertaining. Barrows, Nye and Le Bon (of course) explore the psychology of crowds. For Paul Déroulède, see Byrd. For Barrès's campaigning, see Sternhell. 'It would be a cowardly act . . .', see Brown. For Boulanger's final hours, see *Le Petit Journal.*

Chapter Three
Cheydleur and Fishbane trace Barrès's evolution from symbolist to nationalist. 'The crowd has always needed a battle cry . . .', see Barrès, 1890. Carroll, Sternhell and Winock discuss Barrès's antisemitism. For Barrès as proto-fascist, see

Soucy. For the Dreyfus affair, see Forth and Leroy. For the debacle in Champenoux, see Doty.

GABRIELE D'ANNUNZIO

For biographers, D'Annunzio has been the gift that keeps on giving. Hughes-Hallett's opus is invaluable; likewise Antongini's memoir. Jullian and Rhodes are treasure-troves. For Mussolini, Bosworth and Farrell were my first ports-of-call. Susan Bassnett's translation of D'Annunzio's novel *Il Fuoco* was published by Marsilio Publishers in 1991. *Pleasure*, an English translation of *Il Piacere* by Lara Gochin Raffaelli was published by Penguin in 2013.

Chapter Four
For D'Annunzio in France, see Gullace. For Ida Rubinstein, see Brody. For Italian nation-building, see Rhodes. For D'Annunzio's 'hedge speech' and his ideas about national genius, see Re. For Italy's colonial impulse, see Gregor. D'Annunzio's verses on the Turkish war were eventually collected as *Merope: Canzoni della gesta d'oltremare* (1915). For his *Canti*, see Härmänmaa. For his relations with Giuseppe Garibaldi, see Woodhouse. 'O blessed be those who have more . . .', see Ledeen.

Chapter Five
For Mussolini in Trentino, see Stefano Biguzzi's essay in Di Scala & Gentile. For Mussolini's boyhood, see Philip Cannistraro's contribution to the same volume. For Mussolini's crowd psychology, see Gregor. For the Arditi, see Ledeen. 'Italy's hour has not yet rung . . .', see Mallett.

Chapter Six
For *La Nave*, see Chandler. Macdonald's hostile eyewitness account of D'Annunzio's Fiume adventure is arresting. See also Ledeen, Janša and Reill. For D'Annunzio's correspondence with Mussolini, see Peterson. For Mussolini and the *squadri*, see Falasca-Zamponi.

MAXIM GORKY

Many works by Gorky are available in English translation. 1967 was the year for Gorky biographies: Dan Levin and Bertram Wolfe are both excellent. Then we had to wait thirty-two years for Tova Yedlin's political biography in 1999 (also excellent). I drew much from memoirs by Bunin, Khodasevich and Zamyatin.

Chapter Seven
For Gorky's US visit, see Poole and McDowell. The Andreyeva affair generated many column inches; the *New York Tribune*'s record is especially good; see also McDowell. 'I did not mean to do Mr Roblee or any one an injustice ...', see 'Gorky Driven with Actress'. 'Black blood-soaked wings of death ...', see 'Gorkey [sic] Appeals to American People'. For Russian travel writing, see Fedorova. 'I had never met Lenin until that year ...' may confuse, since Gorky later 'remembers' earlier meetings in line with Stalinist mythology. For the Fifth Congress, see Rappaport.

Chapter Eight
For Gorky's travels on foot, see Zamyatin. For his early celebrity, see Loe. For his attitude to intellectuals, see Tertz. For his early political involvements, see Kaun and Kondoyanidi.

For god-building, see Williams. 'I'm lost in a sort of fog . . .', see Barratt. For Letopis, see Hickey. For Gorky's bleak view of the October Revolution, see Kondoyanidi. For literary life immediately after 1917, see Scherr.

Chapter Nine

'Concentration camps for the intelligentsia', see Hickey (the expression is Viktor Schlovsky's). For H. G. Wells, see Parrinder and Wells. For the famine relief effort, see Finkel. For angry letters to Gorky, see Shentalinsky & Conquest. For Gorky and Stalin, see Spiridonova. For the Pressa exhibition, see David-Fox and Wolfe.

Chapter Ten

For Gorky's 'Around the Union' visits, see David-Fox. For Ugresha, see Howell & Krementsov. 'The events in London . . .', see Booth. For Gorky's praise of the Gulag, see Weiner. 'The USSR is going to be . . .', see Clark & Dobrenko. For the White Sea–Baltic Canal, see Booth. For Gorky's *History*, see Ruder. For working conditions, see Draskoczy. John Maynard Keynes nailed Wells's later prose style as 'a man struggling with a gramophone'. 'The selfish creation of superfluous people . . .', see Scott. 'Everything's going so smoothly . . .', see Clark. For the First Soviet Writers' Congress, see Rosenthal. For socialist realism, see Tertz. 'Who has shouted loudest . . .', see Conner. For Rolland's visit, see Yedlin.

DING LING

Ding Ling's short stories can be found in English translation with relative ease. Her novel *The Sun Shines over Sanggan River* is more elusive. Before Charles Alber's two-volume biography (2002/2004), Feuerwerker was our best source of information.

Chapter Eleven
For the League of Left-Wing Writers, see Hsia and Wong. For intellectual life before the revolution, see Kurzman. For the 'May Fourth' movement, see Mitter and Schwartz & Furth. 'I longed to write a story ...', see Ip. For Chinese genre fiction, see Hung and Pan. 'Revolution by wizard ...', see Holock & Holock. For Hu Yepin the writer, see Hsia. For his arrest, see Wong. For Ding Ling's travelling theatre, see Judd. For life in the Jiangxi Soviet, see Halliday and Opper. For life in Yan'an, see Esherick and Wang Ning.

Chapter Twelve
For literary production in Yan'an, see Holock & Holock and Laughlin. For Zhou Yang in Yan'an, see Apter & Saich and Birch. For Xiao Jun, see Rubin. For Wang Shiwei, see Cheek. For the struggle sessions against him, see Goldman. For rectification, see Lifton and Lovell.

Chapter Thirteen
For the last day of the Yan'an Forum on Literature and Art, see Hsia. For readings of *Sanggan River*, see Hodges and Wang Dewei.

EPILOGUE

For Walter Lippmann, see Eulau and Steel. For the Bachelet/Franc-Nohain opera, see Fulcher. Gide's hatter's tale comes from his *Pretexts*. I've used Justin O'Brien's 2017 Routledge translation. For Malraux, see Todd. For Gorky's city of science, see Josephson.

BIBLIOGRAPHY

Maurice Barrès

Barrès, Maurice, Philippe Barrès, and François Broche. *Mes cahiers*. Sainte-Marguerite-sur-Mer: Éditions des Équateurs, 2010.

Barrès, Maurice. 'La Formula antijuive', *Le Figaro*, 22 February 1890.

Barrès, Maurice. 'Socialisme et Nationalisme', *La Patrie*, 27 February 1903.

Barrès, Maurice. *Le voyage de Sparte*. Patrimoine des héritages. Paris: Dualpha éditions, (1905), 2020.

Barrès, Maurice. *Les déracinés*. Paris: Eug. Fasquelle, 1897.

Barrès, Maurice. *Scenes et doctrines du nationalisme*. Paris: Emile-Paul. 1900.

Barrès, Maurice. *Sous l'oeil des barbares*. Paris: Charpentier, 1902.

Barrows, Susanna. *Distorting Mirrors: Visions of the Crowd in Late Nineteenth-Century France*. New Haven, CT: Yale University Press, 1981.

Brown, Frederick. *For the Soul of France: Culture Wars in the Age of Dreyfus*. New York, NY: Alfred A. Knopf, 2010.

Byrd, Edward Leavell. 'Paul Déroulède, Revanchist'. Texas Tech University, 1969.

Carroll, David. *French Literary Fascism: Nationalism,*

Anti-Semitism, and the Ideology of Culture. Princeton, NJ: Princeton University Press, 1995.

Cheydleur, Frederic D. 'XXVI. Maurice Barrès as a Romanticist'. *PMLA/Publications of the Modern Language Association of America* 41, no. 2 (June 1926): 462–87.

Cornell, Kenneth. *The Symbolist Movement*. New Haven, CT; Paris: Yale University Press; Presses universitaires de France, 1951.

Curtis, Michael. *Three Against the Third Republic: Sorel, Barrès and Maurras*. London: Routledge, 2017.

Doty, Charles Stewart. 'Maurice Barrès and the Fate of Boulangism: The Political Career of Maurice Barrès (1888–1906)'. Ohio State University, 1964.

Drake, David. *French Intellectuals and Politics from the Dreyfus Affair to the Occupation*. Basingstoke: Palgrave Macmillan, 2005.

Fishbane, Jonathan. 'From Decadence to Nationalism in the Early Writings of Maurice Barrès'. *Nineteenth-Century French Studies* 13, no. 4 (1985): 266–78.

Forth, Christopher E. 'Intellectuals, Crowds and the Body Politics of the Dreyfus Affair'. *Historical Reflections/Réflexions Historiques* 24, no. 1, (1998): 63–91.

Harding, James. *The Astonishing Adventure of General Boulanger*. New York: Charles Scribner's Sons, 1971.

Huneker, James. *Egoists: A Book of Supermen*. New York: Charles Scribner's Sons, 1909.

Jullian, Philippe. *The Triumph of Art Nouveau: Paris Exhibition, 1900*. Paris: Larousse, 1974.

Le Bon, Gustave. *The Crowd: A Study of the Popular Mind*. Mineola, NY: Dover Publications, 2001.

Le Petit Journal. 'Suicide of General Boulanger 1891'. *Le Petit Journal*, 1 October 1891.

Lemaître, Jules. 'Donec eris felix', *Le Figaro*, 12 October 1889.

Leroy, Géraldi. *Les Ecrivains et l'affaire Dreyfus*. Collection Université d'Orléans. Paris: Presses universitaires de France, 1983.

Millaud, Albert. 'Le Premier discours de M. Barrès à la Chambre', *Le Figaro*, 5 November 1889.

Nye, Robert A. *The Origins of Crowd Psychology: Gustave Le Bon and the Crisis of Mass Democracy in the Third Republic*. New York: AstroLogos Books, 1975.

Soucy, Robert. 'Barrès and Fascism'. *French Historical Studies* 5, no. 1 (1967): 67–97.

Sternhell, Zeev. 'National Socialism and Antisemitism: The Case of Maurice Barrès'. *Journal of Contemporary History* 8, no. 4 (1973): 47–66.

Sternhell, Zeev. 'Paul Déroulède and the Origins of Modern French Nationalism'. *Journal of Contemporary History* 6, no. 4 (1971): 46–70.

Weber, Eugen. 'Inheritance and Dilettantism: The Politics of Maurice Barrès', *Historical Reflections/Réflexions Historiques* 2 (1 July 1975): 109–31.

Winock, Michel. *Nationalism, Anti-Semitism, and Fascism in France*. Stanford, CA: Stanford University Press, 1998.

Gabriele D'Annunzio

Antongini, Tommaso. *D'Annunzio*. London: Heinemann, 1978.

Benda, Julien, and Roger Kimball. *The Treason of the Intellectuals*. New York, NY: Routledge, (1927) 2017.

Bosworth, R. J. B. *Mussolini*. London: Bloomsbury, 2002.

Bosworth, R. J. B. *Mussolini's Italy: Life under the Fascist Dictatorship, 1915–1945*. New York, NY: Penguin, 2014.

Brody, Elaine. 'The Legacy of Ida Rubinstein: Mata Hari of the

Ballets Russes'. *Journal of Musicology* 4, no. 4 (1 October 1986): 491–506.

Chandler, David (ed.). *Essays on the Montemezzi-D'Annunzio Nave.* Translated by Monica Cuneo. Norwich: Durrant Publishing, 2012.

D'Annunzio, Gabriele, and Stephen Sartarelli. *Notturno.* Margellos World Republic of Letters. New Haven, CT: Yale University Press, 2012.

D'Annunzio, Gabriele. *Le canzoni delle gesta d'oltremare.* Milan: Corriere della Sera, 1911.

D'Annunzio, Gabriele. *Il Fuoco* (1900). For an English translation, D'Annunzio, Gabriele, and Susan Bassnett. *The Flame.* New York; St Paul, MN: Marsilio Publishers, 1999.

D'Annunzio, Gabriele. *Il Piacere* (1889). For an English translation, D'Annunzio, Gabriele, and Lara Gochin Raffaelli. *Pleasure.* New York, NY: Penguin, 2013.

Di Scala, Spencer M., and Emilio Gentile, eds. *Mussolini 1883–1915.* New York, NY: Palgrave Macmillan, 2016.

Falasca-Zamponi, Simonetta. *Fascist Spectacle: The Aesthetics of Power in Mussolini's Italy.* Berkeley, CA: University of California Press, 1997.

Farrell, Nicholas. *Mussolini: A New Life.* London: Weidenfeld & Nicolson, 2003.

Gentile, Emilio. *The Struggle for Modernity: Nationalism, Futurism, and Fascism.* Westport, CT: Praeger, 2003.

Gregor, A. James. *Young Mussolini and the Intellectual Origins of Fascism.* First edition. Berkeley, CA: University of California Press, 1979.

Gullace, Giovanni. *Gabriele d'Annunzio in France: A Study in Cultural Relations.* Syracuse: Syracuse University Press, 1966.

Härmänmaa, Marja. 'Gabriele D'Annunzio and War Rhetoric in the *Canti della guerra latina*'. *Annali d'italianistica* 33 (2015): 31–52.

Hughes-Hallett, Lucy. *The Pike: Gabriele D'Annunzio: Poet, Seducer and Preacher of War*. London: Fourth Estate, 2013.

Janša, Janez. 'Free Love and Artificial Paradises', in Comisso, Giovanni. 'Il porto dell'amore'. Fiume, 5 April 2019.

Jullian, Philippe. *D'Annunzio*. Translated by Stephen Hardman. London: Pall Mall, 1972.

Knight, Patricia. *Mussolini and Fascism*. Routledge, 2013.

Ledeen, Michael Arthur. *The First Duce: D'Annunzio at Fiume*. Baltimore, MD; London: Johns Hopkins University Press, 1977.

Macdonald, J. N. *A Political Escapade*. London: John Murray, 1900.

Mallett, Robert. *Mussolini in Ethiopia, 1919–1935: The Origins of Fascist Italy's African War*. Cambridge: Cambridge University Press, 2018.

Mussolini, Benito. *The Cardinal's Mistress*. London: Cassell, 1929.

O'Brien, Paul. *Mussolini in the First World War: The Journalist, the Soldier, the Fascist*. London: Bloomsbury, 2014.

Pergher, Roberta. *Mussolini's Nation-Empire: Sovereignty and Settlement in Italy's Borderlands, 1922–1943*. Cambridge: Cambridge University Press, 2017.

Peterson, T. E. 'Schismogenesis and National Character: The D'Annunzio–Mussolini Correspondence'. *Italica: Bulletin of the American Association of Teachers of Italian*, 81 (2004): 44–64.

Re, Lucia. 'D'Annunzio's Bitter Passion and Mediterranean Tragedy'. In Carravetta, Peter, *Discourse Boundary Creation*, 131–47. New York, NY: Bordighera Press, 2013.

Reill, Dominique. 'How to Survive in a Holocaust City: D'Annunzio and Fiume'. *Atti Del Convegno Fiume 1919–2019. Un Centenario Europeo Tra Identità, Memorie e Prospettive Di Ricerca. Vittoriale Degli Italiani*, 1 January 2020.

Rhodes, Anthony. *The Poet as Superman: A Life of Gabriele D'Annunzio*. London: Weidenfeld & Nicolson, 1959.

Rimoch, David. 'The Affair or the State: Intellectuals, the Press, and the Dreyfus Affair', University of Pennsylvania, 2008.

Starkie, Walter. *The Waveless Plain*. First American edition. Boston, MA: E. P. Dutton & Co., 1938.

Woodhouse, J. R. 'Caveat Lector: D'Annunzio's Autobiographical Prestidigitation'. *The Modern Language Review* 91, no. 3 (July 1996): 610.

Maxim Gorky

'Gorkey Appeals to American People'. *The Pensacola Journal* (Pensacola, FL), 29 July, 1906, s1, p.1.

'Gorky Driven With Actress From Hotel'. *The Evening World* (New York, NY), 14 April, 1906, Final Results Edition, p. 1.

'Gorky Honored Guest'. *New York Tribune* (New York, NY), 12 April, 1906, p. 4.

'Maxim Gorky Arrives'. *New York Tribune* (New York, NY), 11 April, 1906, p. 1.

Barratt, Andrew. 'Maksim Gorky and the Russian Revolution: The Crisis of 1910'. *New Zealand Slavonic Journal*, no. 2 (1978): 59–74.

Booth, Lisa L. *Intellectuals, the Soviet Regime, and the Gulag: The Construction and Deconstruction of an Ideal*. Gainesville, FL: University of Florida, 2006.

Bunin, Ivan Alekseevich, Maksim Gorky, and Aleksandr Ivanovich Kuprin. *Reminiscences of Anton Chekhov*. Translated by Samuel Solomonovitch Koteliansky and Leonard Woolf. New York, NY: B.W. Huebsch, 1921.

Clark, Katerina, E. A. Dobrenko, A. N. Artizov, and Oleg V.

Naumov. *Soviet Culture and Power: A History in Documents, 1917–1953*. New Haven, CT: Yale University Press, 2007.

Conner, Tom, ed. *André Gide's Politics: Rebellion and Ambivalence*. New York, NY: Palgrave Macmillan US, 2000.

David-Fox, Michael. *Showcasing the Great Experiment: Cultural Diplomacy and Western Visitors to the Soviet Union, 1921–1941*. Oxford; New York, NY: Oxford University Press, 2011.

Draskoczy, Julie. 'The "Put" of Perekovka": Transforming Lives at Stalin's White Sea–Baltic Canal'. *The Russian Review* 71, no. 1 (January 2012): 30–48.

Draskoczy, Julie. *Belomor: Criminality and Creativity in Stalin's Gulag*. Myths and Taboos in Russian Culture. Brighton, MA: Academic Studies Press, 2014.

Fedorova, Milla. *Yankees in Petrograd, Bolsheviks in New York: America and Americans in Russian Literary Perception*. DeKalb, IL: NIU Press, 2013.

Finkel, Stuart. *On the Ideological Front: The Russian Intelligentsia and the Making of the Soviet Public Sphere*. New Haven, CT: Yale University Press, 2007.

Gorky, Maxim. *The Collected Short Stories of Maxim Gorky*. Secaucus, NJ: Kensington Publishing Corp., 1998.

Gorky, Maxim, translated by Hugh Aplin. *The Mother: New Translation (Alma Classics)*. London: Alma Classics, 2020.

Gorky, Maxim, and R. Wilks. *My Childhood*. London; New York, NY: Penguin Classics, 1990.

H. G. Scott, ed., *Problems of Soviet Literature: Reports and Speeches at the First Soviet Writers' Congress*. Moscow: Cooperative Publishing Society of Foreign Workers in the U.S.S.R, 1935.

Hickey, Martha. 'Maksim Gor'kii in the House of Arts (Gor'kii and the Petrograd Literary Intelligentsia)'. *SPSR The Soviet and Post-Soviet Review* 22, no. 1 (1995): 40–64.

Howell, Yvonne, and N. L. Krementsov, eds. *The Art and Science of Making the New Man in Early 20th-Century Russia.* London; New York, NY: Bloomsbury Academic, 2021.

Kahan, Alan S. *Mind vs. Money: The War between Intellectuals and Capitalism.* New Brunswick, NJ: Transaction Publishers, 2010.

Kaun, Alexander. 'Maxim Gorky and the Bolsheviks'. *The Slavonic and East European Review* 9, no. 26 (1930): 432–48.

Khodasevich, V. F, trans. Sarah Vitali. *Necropolis.* New York, NY: Columbia University Press, 2019.

Koestler, Arthur. *The Yogi and the Commissar,* London: Cape, 1945.

Kondoyanidi, Anita A. 'The Prophet Disillusioned: Maxim Gorky and the Russian Revolutions'. Georgetown University, 2019.

Lenin, Vladimir Ilyich. *Collected Works of V. I. Lenin.* New York, NY: International Publishers, 1927.

Levin, Dan. *Stormy Petrel: The Life and Work of Maxim Gorky.* London: Frederick Muller, 1967.

Loe, Mary Louise. 'Maksim Gor'kii and the Sreda Circle: 1899–1905'. *Slavic Review* 44, no. 1 (1985): 49–66.

McDowell, Judith H. '"As Exciting as Being in Hell": Maxim Gorky in the United States', *The Kentucky Review* 4, no. 3 (1983).

Parrinder, Patrick, and John S. Partington. *The Reception of H. G. Wells in Europe.* New York, NY: Thoemmes Continuum, 2005.

Poole, Ernest. 'Maxim Gorki in New York'. *Slavonic and East European Review.* American Series 3, no. 1 (May 1944): 77.

Rappaport, Helen. *Conspirator: Lenin in Exile.* New York, NY: Basic Books, 2010.

Rosenthal, Bernice Glatzer. *New Myth, New World: From Nietzsche to Stalinism.* University Park, PA: Pennsylvania State University Press, 2002.

Ruder, Cynthia A. 'Modernist in Form, Socialist in Content: The History of the Construction of the Stalin White Sea–Baltic Canal'. *Russian Literature* 44, no. 4 (November 1998): 469–84.

Ruder, Cynthia Ann. *Making History for Stalin: The Story of the Belomor Canal*. Gainesville, FL: University Press of Florida, 1998.

Scherr, Barry. 'Notes on Literary Life in Petrograd, 1918–1922: A Tale of Three Houses'. *Slavic Review* 36, no. 2 (June 1977): 256–67.

Scott, H. G., ed. *Problems of Soviet Literature: Reports and Speeches at the First Soviet Writers' Congress*. Moscow: Cooperative Publishing Society of Foreign Workers in the U.S.S.R., 1935.

Shentalinsky, Vitaly, and Robert Conquest. *The KGB's Literary Archive*. Translated by John Crowfoot. New edition. London: The Harvill Press, 1997.

Spiridonova, Lidiia. 'Gorky and Stalin (According to New Materials from A. M. Gorky's Archive)'. *Russian Review* 54, no. 3 (July 1995): 413.

Tertz, Abram. *On Socialist Realism*. Translated by George Dennis. New York, NY: Pantheon Books, 1960.

Trotsky, Leon. *Stalin: An Appraisal of the Man and His Influence*. Translated and edited by Alan Woods. London: Wellred Books, 2016.

Weiner, Douglas R. 'Man of plastic: Gor'kii's visions of humans in nature'. *Soviet Post-Soviet Rev.* 22, no. 1 (1995).

Wells, H. G. *Russia in the Shadows*. London: Hodder and Stoughton Ltd., 1920.

Williams, Robert C. 'Collective Immortality: The Syndicalist Origins of Proletarian Culture, 1905–1910'. *Slavic Review* 39, no. 3 (1980): 389–402.

Wolfe, Bertram D. *The Bridge and the Abyss: The Troubled*

Friendship of Maxim Gorky and V. I. Lenin. Westport, CT: Greenwood Press, 1967.

Wolfe, Ross. 'El Lissitzky's Soviet Pavilion at the Pressa Exhibition in Cologne, 1928'. *The Charnel-House* (blog), 1 March 2014. https://thecharnelhouse.org/2014/03/01/el-lissitzkys-soviet-pavilion-at-the-pressa-exhibition-in-cologne-1928/.

Yedlin, Tovah. *Maxim Gorky: A Political Biography.* Westport, CT: Praeger, 1999.

Zamyatin, Yevgeny Ivanovich, and Mirra Ginsburg. *A Soviet Heretic: Essays.* Evanston, IL: Northwestern University Press, (1970) 1992.

Ding Ling

Alber, Charles J. *Embracing the Lie: Ding Ling and the Politics of Literature in the People's Republic of China.* Westport, CT: Praeger, 2004.

Alber, Charles J. *Enduring the Revolution: Ding Ling and the Politics of Literature in Guomindang China.* Westport, CT: Greenwood Publishing Group, 2002.

Apter, David E., and Tony Saich. *Revolutionary Discourse in Mao's Republic.* Cambridge, MA: Harvard University Press, 1994.

Birch, Cyril. 'Fiction of the Yenan Period'. *The China Quarterly* 4 (December 1960): 1–11.

Chang, Jung, and Jon Halliday. *Mao: The Unknown Story.* London: Vintage, 2007.

Cheek, Timothy. 'The Fading of Wild Lilies: Wang Shiwei and Mao Zedong's Yan'an Talks in the First CPC Rectification Movement'. *The Australian Journal of Chinese Affairs* 11 (January 1984): 25–58.

Ding Ling, Tani E. Barlow, and Gary J. Bjorge. *I Myself Am a Woman: Selected Writings of Ding Ling*. Boston, MA: Beacon Press, 1989.

Ding Ling, *The Sun Shines over the Sanggan River*. Translated by Xianyi Yang and Gladys Yang. Beijing, China: Foreign Languages Press, 1984.

Esherick, Joseph W. *Accidental Holy Land: The Communist Revolution in Northwest China*. Oakland, CA: University of California Press, 2022.

Feuerwerker, Ye-tsi Mei. *Ding Ling's Fiction: Ideology and Narrative in Modern Chinese Literature*. Cambridge, MA; London: Harvard University Press, 1982.

Goldman, Merle. 'Writers' Criticism of the Party in 1942'. *The China Quarterly* 17 (March 1964): 205–28.

Hodges, Eric. *Messianism in Ding Ling and Zhou Libo's Novels: A Study of* The Sun Shines over the Sanggan River *and* The Hurricane *and Their Literary and Philosophical Milieu*. Saarbrücken: Lap Lambert Academic Publishing, 2012.

Holock, Donald, and Shu-ying Tsau Holock. '"Not Marxism in Words": Chinese Proletarian Fiction and Socialist Realism'. *Journal of South Asian Literature* 27, no. 2, (1992): 1–28.

Hsia, Tsi-an. *The Gate of Darkness: Studies on the Leftist Literary Movement in China*. Seattle, WA: University of Washington Press, 1968.

Hung, Chang-tai. *War and Popular Culture*. Berkeley, CA: University of California Press, 1994.

Ip, Hung-yok. *Intellectuals in Revolutionary China, 1921–1949*. Oxford; New York, NY: Routledge Curzon, 2005.

Judd, Ellen R. 'Prelude to the "Yan'an Talks": Problems in Transforming a Literary Intelligentsia'. *Modern China* 11, no. 3 (1985): 377–408.

Kurzman, Charles. *Democracy Denied, 1905–1915: Intellectuals and the Fate of Democracy*. Cambridge, MA: Harvard University Press, 2008.

Laughlin, Charles A. 'The Battlefield of Cultural Production: Chinese Literary Mobilization during the War Years'. *Journal of Modern Literature in Chinese* 2, no. 1 (1998): 22.

Lifton, Robert J. 'Thought Reform of Chinese Intellectuals: A Psychiatric Evaluation'. *Journal of Social Issues* 13, no. 3 (July 1957): 5–20.

Lovell, Julia. *Maoism: A Global History*. London: The Bodley Head, 2019.

Mitter, Rana. *A Bitter Revolution: China's Struggle with the Modern World*. Oxford; New York, NY: Oxford University Press, 2010.

Opper, Marc. 'The Chinese Soviet Republic, 1931–1934'. *People's Wars in China, Malaya, and Vietnam*. Ann Arbor, MI: University of Michigan Press, 2019.

Pan, Lynn. *When True Love Came to China*. Hong Kong: HKU Press, 2015.

Rubin, Kyna. 'Writers' Discontent and Party Response in Yan'an Before "Wild Lily": The Manchurian Writers and Zhou Yang'. *Modern Chinese Literature* 1, no. 1 (1984): 79–102.

Schwartz, Benjamin I., and Charlotte Furth. *Reflections on the May Fourth Movement: A Symposium*. Cambridge, MA: East Asian Research Center, Harvard University, 1973.

Stein, Gunther. *The Challenge of Red China*. New York, London: Whittlesey House, McGraw-Hill, 1945.

Wang, Ban. 'Passion and Politics in Revolution'. In *The Oxford Handbook of Modern Chinese Literatures*. Edited by Carlos Rojas and Andrea Bachner. Oxford: Oxford University Press, 2016.

Wang, David Der-wei. *The Monster That Is History: History, Violence, and Fictional Writing in Twentieth-Century China*. Berkeley, CA: University of California Press, 2004.

Wang, Ning. *Banished to the Great Northern Wilderness:*

Political Exile and Re-Education in Mao's China. Ithaca, NY: Cornell University Press, 2017.

Warner, Lia. 'Ding Ling's Feminism: The Contradictions of Female Subjectivity in China'. *Confluence* (blog), 2019. https://confluence.gallatin.nyu.edu/context/interdisciplinary-seminar/ding-lings-feminism.

Wong, Wang-chi. '"The Left League Decade"– Left-Wing Literary Movement in Shanghai, 1927–1936'. SOAS, University of London, 1986.

Zedong, Mao. *Mao's Road to Power: Revolutionary Writings 1912–1949. Volume VIII, From Rectification to Coalition Government 1942–July 1945*. Edited by Stuart R. Schram, Timothy Cheek, and Nancy Jane Hodes. New York: Routledge, 2015.

Epilogue

Eulau, Heinz. 'Wilsonian Idealist: Walter Lippmann Goes to War'. *The Antioch Review* 14, no. 1 (1954): 87.

Fulcher, Jane Fair. *The Composer as Intellectual: Music and Ideology in France, 1914–1940*. New York, NY; Oxford: Oxford University Press, 2008.

Gide, André, and Justin O'Brien. *Pretexts: Reflections on Literature and Morality*. London: Routledge, 2017.

Josephson, Paul R. 'Maksim Gor'kii, Science and the Russian Revolution'. *Soviet Post-Soviet Rev.* 22, no. 1 (1995): 15–39.

Lippmann, Walter. *The Phantom Public*. New York, NY: Macmillan, 1927.

Lippmann, Walter. *Public Opinion*. Sioux Falls, SD: Greenbook Publications, 2010.

Steel, Ronald. *Walter Lippmann and the American Century*. New Brunswick, NJ: Transaction, 1999.

Tertz, Abram. *On Socialist Realism*. Translated by George Dennis. New York, NY: Pantheon Books, 1960.
Todd, Olivier. *Malraux: A Life*. New York, NY: Knopf, 2005.

INDEX

Liszt, Franz 309
Literary Resistance Association 287
Long March 261, 265, 268, 275, 276
Longoni, Attilio 120
Lu Xun 235, 258, 259, 260, 261, 280,
    290, 298, 303
Lu Xun Arts Academy 274
Lugovskoi, Vladimir 222–3
Lunacharksy, Anatoly 164, 170, 171,
    172, 173, 174, 175, 196–7, 233,
    314
Luo Feng 281
Luxemburg, Rosa 159, 174
Lvov, Georgy 181

MacBeth, George 122
Maisky, Ivan 228
Makarenko, Anton 210–11, 213
Mallarmé, Stéphane 11
Malraux, André 230, 231, 232,
    313–15, 317
Malsagov, S.A. 215
Mao Dun 298
Mao Zedong 243, 244, 261, 265,
    266, 267–9, 272–3, 277, 281–2,
    288, 299
    and Ding Ling 265, 266–7, 289,
        294, 295, 297–8, 301
    Great Leap Forward 319
    'The Immortal from Linjiang'
        266–7, 303
    on the job of the writer 292, 293,
        295
    Long March 261, 265, 268
    rectification campaign 282–3, 286
    'Yan'an talks' 274
Marinetti, Filippo 13, 81, 102, 103,
    119–20, 125, 234
Martin, John 143, 153, 156
Martov, Julius 160, 182, 184
Marx, Karl xii, 94, 170
mass politics 28, 48, 95, 308
Maurras, Charles 6, 7, 46, 91
Mayakovsky, Vladimir 316
Mazzini, Giuseppe 83
Meyer, Arthur 34, 35
Michels, Roberto 89
Milton, John 288
Mirsky, Dmitri 187
Moréas, Jean 11
Moreau, Lucien 7
Morès, Marquis de 6
Moyer, Charles 147
Mu Mutian 260

Mussolini, Benito 81, 82, 83–9,
    90–104, 123, 129–30, 133–4,
    317
    crowd psychology 95
    and D'Annunzio 114, 115, 117–18,
        119, 120, 126, 136–7, 310, 311
    Duce 134, 137
    editor of *Avanti!* 86, 92–3, 94, 97,
        98
    editor of *Il Popolo d'Italia* 98, 99,
        101, 112, 115, 117–18, 132
    expelled from Italian Socialist Party
        98
    Fasci Di Combattimento 102,
        103–4, 120
    fascism 132, 135–6
    fiction writing 85
    and First World War 96, 97–8,
        100
    irredentism 103, 120
    leadership of Italian Socialist Party
        90, 92, 97
    nationalist socialism 101
    on the power of myth 133–4
    propagandist 93–4
    on socialism 86–7, 88, 93–4, 95,
        96

Nanjing, liberation of (1949) 300
Nansen, Fridtjof 198
Napoleonic wars 71
Narodny, Ivan 142, 143, 145
nationalism 40–1, 71, 86, 90
nationalist socialism 5, 99, 101
Nazism xiii, 311
Neruda, Pablo 302
Nicholas II, Tsar 152, 158, 169, 176,
    179
Nietzsche, Friedrich xiii, 66, 205
nihilism 179, 183, 201, 242, 247
Nitti, Francesco Saverio 110, 114,
    118, 125, 129, 130
North Korea 302
Northwest Front Service Corps
    270–1, 274
Novikov-Priboy, Alexey 233

Oldenburg, Sergey 192
oligarchy 88, 89
Olivetti, Angelo 91, 95, 97
Orlando, Vittorio Emanuele 109,
    112
Ortega y Gasset, José 72
Orwell, George 284